HILARY ABNER HERBERT

MEMOIRS OF THE
AMERICAN PHILOSOPHICAL SOCIETY
Held at Philadelphia
For Promoting Useful Knowledge
Volume 110

Fig. 1. HILARY ABNER HERBERT (1834-1919).
Courtesy of Library of Congress.

HILARY ABNER HERBERT:
A Southerner Returns to the Union

HUGH B. HAMMETT

THE AMERICAN PHILOSOPHICAL SOCIETY
Independence Square · Philadelphia
1976

Library of Congress Catalog Card Number 75-19516
International Standard Book Number 0-87169-110-8
US ISSN 0065-9738

for *Jenny*

Contents

Illustrations

Tables

Preface

HILARY ABNER HERBERT served as a congressman from Alabama from 1877 to 1893 and was secretary of the navy in the second Cleveland administration. Although Herbert has been in large part overlooked by historians, he was easily one of the most important southerners of his day. He was the editor of and chief contributor to the book *Why the Solid South?*, the leading literary apology for the Bourbon "redemption" that ushered in the New South at the close of the Reconstruction period. At the same time, however, Herbert was a man primarily of Old South mentality. His views on the "Negro problem," for example, were more in line with the paternalistic, indulgent attitudes of his father than with the strident, violent racism of the Progressive Era in Dixie. He was consistently conservative in his political philosophy, believing that the best government was limited, economical, and efficient.

Although he never denied his regional faith, Herbert became an ardent nationalist in the years after the Civil War. During three of his terms in Congress, he served as chairman of the powerful Committee on Naval Affairs of the House of Representatives and became the acknowledged master of naval legislation among the Democrats in Congress. No man was more intimately connected with the rise of the "New American Navy" during these years. As a result of his expertise in naval matters, in 1893 Grover Cleveland appointed him secretary of the navy. Herbert's work on behalf of a strong, revitalized fleet was a significant contribution to the forces in the Progressive years that thrust the United States forward as a world power. His efforts brought great credit to himself and his region in a time when few southerners were able to find outlets for service on the national level. A biography of Hilary Abner Herbert should add to our knowledge in several areas: the development of Reconstruction historiography; the return of southerners to national life after 1877; the development of southern racial attitudes; and the growth of the New American Navy and its role in our nation's rise to world power.

No book manuscript could ever be completed without those thoughtful, unselfish people who are willing to share their skills and knowledge. Ithaca College generously provided the services of Mrs. Dottie Owens, a fine manuscript typist. Professor Willie Lee Rose of Johns Hopkins University read much of the text and made numerous incisive suggestions. My friend and former teacher Edward Younger of the University of Virginia offered encouragement and the benefit of his wise counsel and experience, and the book is better because of his sturdy blue pencil. My wife Jenny bravely bore the intrusion of Hilary Herbert into our lives. A disgustingly liberated woman, she never even learned to type; but she did pay the bills during part of the time I needed to do research. Finally, I would be remiss if, in this first book, I did not recall with gratitude the lasting impression made upon me by my first history teachers: Delbert Harold Gilpatrick, Newton Bond Jones, and the late Winston Chandler Babb, all of Furman University.

H.B.H.

Rochester Institute of Technology

I. The Bending Twig

A Charlestonian was walking out on the Battery
bright and early one morning with his friend,
expatiating upon the former grandeur of their
present environment, when the northerner rap-
turously called attention to the glances of the
rising sun. "You ought to have seen that sun
rise, sir, before the war," was the reply.

—Hilary Abner Herbert in
"Reminiscences"

SPRING usually comes early to the South Carolina up-
country. Beginning in early March, the soft rains start to prod
and pamper the earth into life again. The occasional cold
snaps, the last lashes of a beaten winter, have little effect on
the inevitable regeneration whereby the countryside becomes
a lush green once more.

The spring of 1834 found signs of life evident in the drowsy
little village of Laurensville, South Carolina, which nestled
complacently among the gently rolling hills that lie between
the Reedy and Enoree rivers. Gentlemen out surveying their
fields found it necessary by midmorning to remove their coats
and carry them across their arms. In the evening the Negroes
occasionally sat outside their cabins; if the weather was chilly,
they sometimes huddled around small fires.

The two-story, white frame house that belonged to Thomas
Edward Herbert, the headmaster of the Laurensville Female
Academy, bubbled with a kind of gentle excitement. Mammy
Sally, the cook, took special pains in the preparation of the
meals. Her husband, old Uncle Peter, smiled wryly but as usual
made little comment. On March 12, Thomas Herbert's wife,
Dorothy, had given birth to a son. Christened Hilary Abner
Herbert, the boy was the only son of the family to live through
childhood.

Thomas Herbert was proud to have a son to carry on his
name. As with many families of the Old South, genealogy had
always been a matter of pride among the Herberts. The schoolmaster could trace his line without a break as far back as 1667

1

when John Herbert I was granted an estate of 1227 acres in
Virginia. The Herberts had come to the Palmetto State through
Thomas Herbert's grandfather, Lieutenant Thomas Herbert,
who had settled in "Old Dutch Fork" of the Newberry District
of South Carolina prior to 1772.[1] Young Hilary never took any
interest in the family genealogy, however, and at one point he
sorely aggravated his sensitive father by remarking, "Well Pa,
I suppose the Herberts must be great people as I have never
heard of one of them being in either the penitentiary or the
poor house."[2]

Thomas Herbert himself had been born in the Newberry
District in 1804. The son of George Herbert, a farmer and sur-
veyor who had been a member of the South Carolina legislature, the boy gained an early appreciation for such education
and culture as one might obtain in the still-primitive Piedmont.
His education, primarily at the hands of a Scottish tutor, was
informal but thorough.[3]

As a young man, Thomas Herbert had charge of several "old
field schools" in the Newberry District.[4] After marriage in

---

1 Dora Calhoun Royall, "Descendants of Lt. Thomas Herbert of Virginia and
South Carolina," *The Researcher: A Magazine of History and Genealogical Ex-
change* 2 (October, 1927): pp. 52-53; Charles F. McIntosh, "Four Generations of
Herberts of Lower Norfolk Co., Va.," *The Researcher* 1 (July, 1927): pp. 249-252.

2 Quoted in Hilary Abner Herbert to Robert McKee, July 30, 1897, Robert
McKee Papers, Alabama Department of Archives and History.

3 Hilary Abner Herbert, "Grandfather's Talks about his Life under Two Flags,"
unpublished MSS memoir, 1903, Vol. 1, Hilary Abner Herbert Papers, University
of North Carolina Library (hereafter referred to as Herbert, "Reminiscences").
A word about the "Reminiscences" is necessary. This memoir is an invaluable
document of almost 400 pages. It was dictated by Herbert in the summer of
1903 at Hendersonville, North Carolina, as a record for his descendants of his
impressions of a long and eventful life. Only a few typescript copies of the
"Reminiscences" were made. Two have come to rest in libraries, one in Montgomery in the Alabama Archives and the other at the University of North
Carolina Library at Chapel Hill. Other copies may remain with the family or
possibly have been lost. Because Herbert wrote the memoir as a personal family
document and not for public consumption, the "Reminiscences" have a tone
of honesty and objectivity about them that is often lacking in published memoirs.
Except on occasion in the matter of small, easily forgotten details, I have found
the document to be unusually reliable. When at all possible, I have verified
cited material in other places. In some instances, however, especially in the
narrative concerning Herbert's early life, I have judiciously relied on the
"Reminiscences" as a single source since no alternative resource material exists.

4 The "old field schools" were loosely organized and often temporary institutions set up to meet the elementary and secondary needs of a community at a
given time. They were organized alongside the more durable "academies," the

1831, he moved to Laurensville and became the principal of the female academy there. The people of the town always thought of Herbert as a "quiet, unassuming man, inclined to be stout, well-informed and devoted to his profession."[5]

Although Thomas Herbert was noted for his congeniality, he could—in the typical southern tradition—become angrily aroused over the breach of principle or honor. Accordingly, when the principle of state rights was questioned in 1832, Herbert took his place in the camp of the ardent nullifiers. Two years before his son's birth, the mild-mannered schoolmaster had taken up a rifle to drill with the Laurensville militia unit that was pledged to stand by South Carolina. Herbert's actions during the nullification controversy left little doubt as to what his position would be when the secession crisis arose almost thirty years later. It is difficult to see how in subsequent years young Hilary Herbert could have avoided absorbing some of his father's passionate feeling about state rights. Yet, the nullification issue died away rapidly; in his early years the boy never heard any talk in his father's house that presumed a future civil war or its consequences.[6]

One of Thomas Herbert's greatest assets was his wife Dorothy. Dorothy Teague Herbert was the daughter of Abner and Isabella Young, a prosperous planter couple who had migrated to South Carolina from Virginia. Dorothy Young was born in Shady Grove in the Laurens District of South Carolina in 1807. An intelligent and talented girl, in 1825 she entered the famous Salem Female Academy in North Carolina.

In 1826 Dorothy Young's sister, Isabella, joined her at the Salem academy. Three years later the two sisters returned to Laurensville where they implemented their advanced ideas concerning higher education for women and established "The Misses Young's School for Young Ladies." The enterprise had been underway for only a short time when Isabelle married and moved to Columbia. Soon afterwards, in June, 1831, Doro-

---

distinct type of secondary schools that appeared in America's early national period. See Edgar W. Knight, *The Academy Movement in the South* (Chapel Hill, University of North Carolina, 1919), pp. 1-6.

[5] *The Advertiser*, Laurens, South Carolina, February 28, 1893, clipping in Vol. 7, Herbert Papers. Hereafter all newspaper citations referring to any volume in the Herbert Papers are clippings included in the voluminous Herbert scrapbooks.

[6] Herbert, "Reminiscences," p. 26.

thy married a teacher from the Newberry District, Thomas
Edward Herbert. Thomas Herbert shared his wife's views on
education. Following their marriage, "The Misses Young's
School for Young Ladies" became the Laurensville Female
Academy. Thomas Herbert was the principal of the school;
his wife served as his assistant.

Dorothy Herbert was responsible for much of the success of
the new academy. The people of Laurensville thought of her
as a woman of "active, strong intellect and executive ability."
The girls in the school were quite fond of her; she was not only
a teacher but also a "veritable mother" to the twelve or fifteen
students in the academy.[7] Hilary Herbert always remembered
his mother, who died when he was eighteen years old, as a
woman of "wonderful energy, . . . perhaps more intellectual
than my father." A devout Episcopalian, Dorothy Herbert
thoroughly indoctrinated her son with the teachings of Chris-
tianity. Although Herbert did not formally acknowledge any
adherence to religious faith until he was twenty-nine years old,
he always considered his faith to be the "precious inheritance"
that his mother had left him.[8]

Hilary Herbert's boyhood was among the happiest times of
his life. In later years when he spoke of "the good old ante-
bellum days," he was not simply giving rein to the blind senti-
mentality that so many southerners of his generation developed
about life in the Old South. The ante-bellum days, as he knew
them, *were* good. His home was noted for its attention to education and culture. Although his father never accumulated
great wealth, the family by no means lacked the necessities of
life.

The Herbert home in Laurensville was a white, two-story
frame house, set back on a small rise and surrounded by a grove
of large oaks. Fifty feet to the rear of the house was the kitchen,
a large building with a fireplace in the middle which opened
to provide heat to the two rooms on either side. Presiding over
the kitchen was the magisterial cook, Mammy Sally, a devoted

---

7 *The Advertiser*, Laurens, South Carolina, February 28, 1893, Vol. 7, Herbert
Papers. See also an extract copied from the *Alumnae Record* of Salem College,
Salem, North Carolina, April, 1919, but dated March, 1931, in the correspondence
of the Herbert Papers; Louise McCullough Richardson, "The Development of
Education in Laurens County" (M.A. thesis, University of South Carolina, 1928),
pp. 19-21.

8 Herbert, "Reminiscences," p. 11.

slave who had nursed Thomas Herbert himself as a baby, and whose status in the family gave her the authority to impose her will on all the "chilluns," both white and black. The water the family used for all purposes came from a spring about 300 yards away. In the creek below the spring, the washwoman Nancy cleaned the family linen. Thomas Herbert owned a number of other slaves, most of whom worked on his plantation of 320 acres which was about three and a half miles from the house.[9] Evidently, Thomas Herbert was more interested in education and the operation of the academy than in planting. His son's comprehensive memoirs contain scarcely a mention of the agricultural operations of the plantation.

In this comfortable setting, Hilary Herbert spent the first twelve years of his life. Young Hilary impressed his neighbors as an active, bright boy.[10] In the summer he often fished and swam with school companions. In the winter he spent many hours hunting with Mark and Duck, two of the slave boys who belonged to his father. Recalling his days in Laurensville, Herbert wrote, "Enterprising boy that I was I knew every family and person, and I might say every hunting dog and fighting cock in the village."[11] According to one later newspaper account, the handsome little boy was "exceedingly fond of dogs and girls." The people of Laurens noticed the attention that was lavished on him:

> The young ladies at his mother's boarding house were constantly making much of him, and he did not fail to reciprocate their attentions even though he had not then entered his teens.[12]

In a family that so valued education it would have been unusual had Herbert not begun his schooling at an early age. Until he was eight years old, his mother taught him at home. Then he began his formal education at the "old field school" in Laurensville taught by David J. Williams. As in many schools in the South at the time, there was a strict "code of honor" to which the boys adhered. No boy could allow his word to be questioned; none could ever refuse a dare. When

---

[9] *Ibid.*, pp. 18, 27-30.
[10] *The Advertiser*, Laurens, South Carolina, February 28, 1893, Vol. 7, Herbert Papers.
[11] Herbert, "Reminiscences," pp. 25-26.
[12] *The Advertiser*, Laurens, South Carolina, February 28, 1893, Vol. 7, Herbert Papers.

Herbert entered school he was expected, as a part of the established ritual, to fight a boy of his own size on the first day.
Having no knowledge of such hoary traditions, Dorothy Herbert had elicited from her son a pledge that he would not fight
at school. For three days Herbert obeyed his mother's instructions and found himself disgraced in the eyes of his classmates.
Thomas Herbert, having been apprised of the unfortunate situation, told his son to defend his honor. It took several fights
before Herbert had redeemed his name and established himself in good standing in the miniature academic community.[13]

It is not surprising that the schoolboys of Laurensville had
their own "code of honor." They were, in effect, only imitating
on a smaller scale the principles to which their fathers adhered
in daily practice. The "code" was a decided reality in South
Carolina at this time. Even as late as 1858, a South Carolinian
published at Charleston a manual describing the correct procedures that a gentleman was obliged to follow in defending his
integrity with a pistol in polite but deadly serious combat. The
reputations of women were carefully guarded, and it was almost
impossible to settle a dispute regarding a woman without the
threat of bloodshed. Although he jealously guarded his own
reputation, Thomas Herbert took the enlightened view that
the periodic duels in Laurensville were senseless. He was a
leader among those in the community who tried to aid in the
amicable settlement of arguments, and because of his efforts
some of the citizens accorded him the nickname "Peace-
maker."[14]

Of special significance in the attitudes that Hilary Herbert
developed as a boy was the relationship between his family and
their slaves. Before Thomas Herbert came to Laurensville in
1831, he owned eight slaves. By 1840 the number had doubled.
After the family moved to Alabama in 1846, the schoolmaster-
planter owned between twenty and thirty slaves.[15]

---

13 Herbert, "Reminiscences," pp. 13-15.

14 *Ibid.*, pp. 15-16. See also John Lyde Wilson, *The Code of Honor; or Rules
for the Government of Principles and Seconds in Duelling* (Charleston, James
Phynney, 1858).

15 Fifth Census of the United States (1830), South Carolina, III, Newberry
District; Sixth Census of the United States (1840), South Carolina, IV, Laurensville District; Herbert, "Reminiscences," p. 8. The Butler County, Alabama,
census returns for 1850 and 1860 do not list the number of blacks each slave-
holder owned. For studies of the slave regimes in the two states in which Herbert

It is unfortunate that no records written by any of the Herbert slaves are known to exist. Indeed, one cannot even be sure that any of them could read and write (since it was unlawful to teach a slave such arts); but it is also hard to imagine that, living with a family which was daily involved in education, a number of the house servants at least might not have become literate. Because his is the only existing record, one must rely on Hilary Herbert's own accounts concerning the family slaves —not so much for what he says about slave life but for the subtle characterization which the narrative reveals about himself.

Like most slaveowners the Herberts were in constant contact with their blacks. As C. Vann Woodward has contended, the segregation of the races such as came to exist in the post-bellum South would have been "an inconvenience and an obstruction to the functioning of the [slave] system."[16] Unlike the situation at this writing, in ante-bellum Laurens blacks and whites worshiped together in every church, the only distinctions being made in seating arrangements and in some congregations in the order of taking communion.[17]

In his youth two of Hilary Herbert's trusted companions were Mark and Duck, slave boys belonging to his father. The boys were not only playmates but were also sometimes combatants. Herbert recalled the latter relationship:

> It is amusing to remember the invariable prelude: A negro boy of nine or ten saying, "Marse Hilary, will you give me a white man's chance?" and the unfailing "Yes." I always lived up to my contract, though sometimes the consequences were damaging.[18]

In relating the incident Herbert, of course, intended the story to be humorous. Apparently it never struck him as tragic that his nine-year-old playmates were aware, even at that tender age, that "a white man's chance" and the one given a black man were two different matters entirely.

---

spent his boyhood, see H. M. Henry, *The Police Control of the Slave in South Carolina* (Emory, Virginia, n. p., 1914) and James Benson Sellers, *Slavery in Alabama* (University, Alabama, University of Alabama Press, 1950).

16 C. Vann Woodward, *The Strange Career of Jim Crow* (2d rev. ed., New York, Oxford University Press, 1966; originally published 1955), p. 12.

17 Herbert, "Reminiscences," p. 34.

18 *Ibid.*, pp. 14-15.

That is not to say, however, that the Herberts were completely oblivious to the moral implications of holding other
human beings as chattels. Graphically demonstrating the cruel
dilemma in which southerners of sensitive and humane feeling
found themselves in the Old South, the Herberts referred to
their Negroes as "servants" rather than as "slaves." Of course,
Hilary Herbert knew that the blacks owned by his father were
slaves. Nevertheless, he did not hear the word "slave" used in
the presence of a Negro until he was almost fifteen years old;
then he took offense at the young man who used the term. At
the time Herbert considered the callous young speaker "a prig
and an upstart, putting on lordly airs." Recalling the incident,
Herbert wrote:

> The expression [slave] was not in use among my people. It
> was inconsistent with the kindly relations between master and
> servant which had always obtained wherever I had moved. . . .
> We were friends. Every slave my father owned was his friend.[19]

In their own unique way, therefore, the Herberts contributed
to the mythmaking, the unreality, which became so characteristic of southerners at this time. No matter how considerate or
kind the family might have been toward its blacks, the fact
remains, of course, that the "servants" were slaves—regardless
of what polite label was used to refer to them.

According to Hilary Herbert, the family slaves received com-
mendable treatment; the blacks on their land were always well
fed and clothed. Thomas Herbert seldom physically punished
his slaves. His son could recall only two incidents when a slave
had been whipped. Moreover, the schoolmaster respected slave
marriages. One of young Hilary's earliest and most vivid memories was of the wedding festivities at the marriage of Ben, the
carriage driver, to the washwoman Nancy. When the family
moved to Alabama in 1846, Herbert's father sold at a loss two
of the blacks who had married off the plantation so that they
could remain with their mates.[20]

There is no reason to doubt Hilary Herbert's word that the
slaves belonging to his father were treated reasonably well.
Dorothy and Thomas Herbert probably did accord their Negroes better treatment than the average slaveowner in South

---

19 *Ibid.,* pp. 18-19.
20 *Ibid.,* pp. 20, 22-23, 30.

Carolina or Alabama. The two were sensitive and charitable people. As a young woman, Dorothy Herbert had been an avowed emancipationist. Unfortunately, after the rise of the abolitionist movement in the North and the terrifying Nat Turner rebellion in Virginia in 1831, she never again felt at liberty to express her convictions openly. It is also possible that the slaves received more lenient treatment because Thomas Herbert's comparatively small farming operations did not require the constant driving that was often necessary to make a large plantation pay. Many of the blacks performed duties around the house and the academy and would have been considered domestic servants.

It is not especially surprising then that young Hilary Herbert saw no great evil in the institution of slavery. The cruelty and callousness with which many slaves were abused throughout the South was simply not a part of his personal experience. It was only after the Civil War, in fact, that he came to feel that it was wrong for one human being to exercise "arbitrary power over another."[21]

In that he tended to universalize the experience of the family slaves as *he* interpreted it, Herbert had a part in the creation of that curious southern legend of the happy slave. Herbert's descriptions of slave life throughout the South were obviously generalized, romanticized pictures of life on his father's plantation. He wrote:

In every old slave-holding family was the old "mammy" on the retired list, when she would still have been on the active, if free. But she had nursed "master" or "mistress" when a baby, and now she was permitted to smoke her pipe in ease and peace while she scolded and petted the children, both white and black. The counterparts of the "mammy" among domestic servants were on the plantation. While
      The young folks rolled on the old cabin floor,
      All merry, all happy and gay,
the superannuated field hands, with never a thought of possible want on tomorrow, looked after them and smoked and chatted the time away. It is certainly not the purpose of the writer to set up any lament over the abolition of slavery. He

---

21 Hilary Abner Herbert, *The Abolition Crusade and Its Consequences: Four Periods of American History* (New York, Charles Scribner's Sons, 1912), p. 11; *ibid.*, p. 22.

rejoices, as all intelligent men now do, that it is gone forever;
yet, it is a fact that no human institution was ever so much mis-
represented and misunderstood as African slavery in the
southern states of America.[22]

Herbert did admit that there were "exceptional cases" in
which slaves were brutally misused; for the most part he argued
that blacks had been protected not only by the "ordinary in-
stincts of humanity" but also by the self-interest of the planter
in keeping his expensive property in sound condition. Moreover, Herbert maintained, the primitive Negro had received
great benefit from the privilege of intermingling with white
southerners. In learning the ways of the white man, the Negro
had attained in America a "higher civilization than anywhere
else in the world."[23]

In spite of Herbert's repeated reassurances about the happy
slave, in retrospect he always seemed to have lingering doubts.
One telling incident is his recollection of Uncle Peter, a
grizzled old black who in young Hilary's view incorporated all
the terrors and mysteries of the Dark Continent from which
he came. Herbert wrote:

> Another peculiarity of Uncle Peter was that he *would* eat
> snakes, a habit which of course he had brought with him from
> Africa. The snake was a link between him and his past. . . .
> Aunt Sally, however, would have nothing to do with such a
> heathenish practice.
>
> Barring snakes Uncle Peter was a good Christian. He and
> Aunt Sally were devoted Methodists. . . .
>
> I have often thought, in looking back to that part of my life,
> that I ought to have gotten Uncle Peter before he died to tell
> me all about Africa. . . . Whether he wanted to go back to the
> jungles among which he was born I never did know.
>
> I wonder if . . . [he] ever contrasted his surroundings in
> Laurens with his conditions in Africa. . . . Did the old fellow

---

22 Hilary A. Herbert, "Alabama in Federal Politics," *Memorial Record of
Alabama* 2 (Madison, Wisconsin, Brant & Fuller, 1893): p. 42.

23 Herbert, "Reminiscences," pp. 22-23; Herbert, "Additions to 1903 Memoirs,"
1917, Vol. 6, Herbert Papers. It is only in the past few decades of this century
that American historians have recognized how primitive were the notions of the
men of Herbert's time concerning the great cultures of sub-Saharan Africa. For
example, see the pathbreaking study by Melville J. Herskovits, *The Myth of the
Negro Past* (New York, Harper & Brothers, 1941).

ever really sigh to give up God and the land of the white man
and worship fetishes again in the darkness of Africa? If we
only knew, it might throw some light on . . . the slavery
question.[24]

Whatever inner doubts he might have had, throughout his
life Herbert insisted on the picture of the happy slave. He
argued with great vigor that "generally the treatment of slaves
was so humane that they were devotedly attached to their
masters. . . . All efforts to excite insurrection were futile."[25]
As the student of southern history will recognize, Herbert's
views were not dissimilar to those of the eminent historian
Ulrich B. Phillips, whose ideas dominated American historical
thinking about slavery for many years. Phillips, for example,
spoke of the blacks as "in an essentially slow process of transi-
tion from barbarism to civilization" and added that "on the
whole the plantations were the best schools yet invented for
the mass training of that sort of inert and backward people
which the bulk of American negroes represented."[26]

It is evident, however, that the Herbert slaves themselves
were not cognizant of the benefits that "Marse Hilary" felt
they were receiving. Jenkins, the slave youth who was supposed
to accompany Herbert as a body servant during his Civil War
career, expressed his ingratitude by running off to the Yankees
at the first opportunity. Nor could Herbert understand why,
when emancipated, all of the "servants" wanted to leave. Even
the seventy-five-year-old Mammy Sally, who had her own room

---

[24] Herbert, "Reminiscences," pp. 31-35.
[25] *Ibid.*, p. 59.
[26] Ulrich B. Phillips, *American Negro Slavery* (New York and London, D.
Appleton-Century Co., 1936; originally published 1918), pp. 342-343. For an
opposite view, depicting the harshness of the slave regime, see Kenneth M.
Stampp, *The Peculiar Institution: Slavery in the Ante-Bellum South* (New York,
Alfred A. Knopf, Inc., 1956). Readers wishing to pursue the question of the
nature of American slavery should see two recent studies that appeared just
prior to the printing of this manuscript. A controversial quantitative study by
Robert William Fogel and Stanley L. Engerman, *Time on the Cross: Volume
One, The Economics of American Negro Slavery; Volume Two, Evidence and
Methods* (Boston, Little, Brown, 1974) would seem to suggest that the adequate
care and material conditions afforded the Herbert slaves were typical of many
southern plantations. Eugene D. Genovese's *Roll, Jordan, Roll: The World the
Slaves Made* (New York, Pantheon, 1974) explores many of slavery's subtler
relationships; this comprehensive study has already received several scholarly
awards and has been hailed by many critics as the most mature study of slavery
yet to appear.

and had been "practically free for years," insisted on moving
out. Herbert often thought of her:

> Her elation when emancipated was intense. Much to my an-
> noyance, she insisted upon leaving, in spite of my promise to
> take care of her as before, and with her son Wade, a young man
> about twenty, she set up housekeeping for herself. Wade was
> not able to care for her as I would have done. But perhaps,
> after all, the old woman's conduct was not strange. All she had
> previously lacked of being free was absolute independence. To
> enjoy that she insisted on setting up her own household. I
> thought she would repent and come back, but she never did.[27]

The Herbert plantation did, however, produce one true
"Sambo," such as Stanley Elkins has described in his stimulating monograph concerning the effect of the peculiar institution on blacks. Old Ben, who had been Thomas Herbert's
carriage driver, never left the family, even when freedom came.
The old man lived to be ninety years of age; Herbert provided
him with occasional work and then with a pension for the last
years of his life. At the time of Ben's death in 1902, the *Greenville Advocate* reported:

> He was an heirloom of the Herberts for generations. He de-
> plored negro emancipation as bad for his race and especially
> bad for himself. He was faithful and affectionate as a slave and
> continued so to his last moments.[28]

Undoubtedly, the experience with old Ben only reinforced
Herbert's beliefs concerning the basic goodness of the slave
regime.

It was in his early years that Herbert's impressions were
formed concerning slavery and the place of the black man in
the South. As much as any man could be, Herbert was a product of and a participant in the myth of the Old South. Certainly, many of his assumptions about the by-gone golden days
of the ante-bellum South rested in the indisputable facts of his
own experience. Tragically, he was never able to grasp that his
romantic assumptions about the nature of the slave regime in

---

27 Herbert, "Reminiscences," p. 8, 116-123.
28 *Greenville Advocate*, September 26, 1902, clipping in Vol. 7, Herbert Papers.
See also Stanley M. Elkins, *Slavery: A Problem in American Institutional and
Intellectual Life* (Chicago, University of Chicago Press, 1959).

ante-bellum Dixie were never shared by the blacks who had been its victims.

Throughout his life Herbert exhibited the same indulgence and paternalistic concern for the Negro which he was learning from his parents at this time. In later years he would think back to these days and draw on his reservoir of experience; in so doing he remained always a paternalist *par excellence*.

II. Son of the South

Born and reared a Southerner, with ancestors for
generations back, all Southerners and slavehold-
ers, I adopted early in life, indeed might almost
say inherited, the strictest views of Southern
rights. . . .

—Hilary Abner Herbert in
"Reminiscences"

ONE of the characteristics of American society from the
first of the nineteenth century until the Civil War was a steady
migration of people from the older states to new lands in the
West. In early December, 1846, Hilary Herbert's family joined
the trek toward the frontier.[1] It is not recorded why Thomas
Herbert decided to leave South Carolina. Worn out land, the
social and economic unrest that characterized the time, and
the hope of new lands and a more democratic life in the West
all probably played a part in his determination to move to
Alabama.

The journey ended about forty miles south of Montgomery,
in Greenville, the principal town of Butler County. Undoubtedly Thomas Herbert chose the town because two brothers, Hilary and George Ballard Herbert, had already settled
there in 1819 and were leading citizens. Dorothy Herbert
approved the location. Beset by a constant fear of slave rebellion, she preferred living in a county that was not in the
Black Belt area of the state with its large Negro population.
During the Nat Turner hysteria a number of years earlier, two
blacks in the Laurens district of South Carolina had been convicted of conspiracy to launch their own revolt; since that time
Dorothy Herbert had never been able to conquer her fears of
the possibility of a slave uprising.[2]

Shortly after their arrival the Herberts established the Green-

---

1 Herbert, "Reminiscences," p. 37.
2 Dora Calhoun Royall, "Sketch of Col. Hilary Abner Herbert," *The Researcher,* 2 (October, 1927): pp. 45-47; Herbert, *Abolition Crusade,* p. 11; Henry,
Police Control of the Slave in South Carolina, p. 153.

ville Female Academy. The school flourished until Dorothy Herbert's death in 1852 but then passed into other hands and eventually became the South Alabama Institute. Thomas Herbert continued to manage his plantation and also served for a time as receiver at the county land office.[3]

Hilary Herbert's school days in Greenville were much the same as those in Laurensville until, at age nineteen, he was ready to go to college. In October, 1853, Herbert arrived in Tuscaloosa and was registered in the sophomore class at the University of Alabama. A gregarious young man, he immediately began the task of winning friends, and shortly after his arrival at the university he joined Delta Kappa Epsilon, the strongest fraternity on the campus.[4]

The 125 young men enrolled at the university began their school day promptly at six o'clock in the morning with a chapel service over which members of the faculty or President Basil Manly, a Baptist preacher, presided. From daybreak until the students were in bed at night, their daily routine was strictly regulated; the young men were told when to eat, when to study, and when to go to sleep. It required, of course, considerable energy on the part of the faculty to see that the students obeyed all the rules of the college. One of the most distasteful duties that befell the professors was that of patrolling the campus and the dormitories in search of lawbreakers. It was on these patrols that the hapless teachers sometimes found themselves in the gravest dangers: they were met in the dark by hails of stones and sticks, they were drenched with buckets of water poured from upstairs windows, and they were occasionally assaulted by drunken students.[5] If the professors found their duties of police inspection distasteful, the students reacted even more violently. As a result of one unfortunate incident in the

---

3 Eighth Census of the United States (1860), Butler County, Alabama; John B. Little, *The History of Butler County from 1815 to 1885* (Cincinnati, Elm Street Printing Company, 1885), pp. 90-91; *Greenville Advocate,* September 5, 1883.

4 Thomas W. Palmer, ed., *A Register of the Officers and Students of the University of Alabama, 1831-1901* (Tuscaloosa, University of Alabama, 1901), p. 110; Aldice G. Warren, ed., *Catalogue of the Delta Kappa Epsilon Fraternity* (New York, John C. Winston Company, 1910), p. 368; Herbert, "Reminiscences," p. 92.

5 George Little, *Memoirs of George Little* (Tuscaloosa, Weatherford Printing Company, 1924), pp. 10-16. Little was a junior at the University of Alabama the year that Herbert attended; his memoirs record aspects of campus life in considerable detail. See also Ellis Merton Coulter, *College Life in the Old South* (New York, Macmillan Company, 1928), pp. 82-91.

spring of 1854, the sophomore class, led by Hilary Herbert, revolted.

The students had devised their own system for coping with the periodic dormitory visitations. When the teacher assigned to inspect began his rounds in the buildings, the first student to see him would cry at the top of his voice, "Wolf! Wolf!" Then throughout the dormitories, all noise, drinking, card games, and other prohibited activities would cease. The professor would find every student bent over his desk, studying intently.

The faculty retaliated by announcing that any young man caught giving the warning would be suspended. It was over this new rule that one James Doby stumbled, earning for himself suspension but also gaining immortality in the annals of the university. One evening in March as Professor George Benagh was inspecting in the dormitories, Doby gave the cry of "Wolf!" Called before the faculty, Doby was uncooperative in confessing either guilt or innocence of the alleged crime. Thereupon, the faculty promptly suspended him.

Doby was, as Hilary Herbert later described him, "a poor devil," then almost twenty-seven years old. He was paying for his education entirely on his own and had neither friends nor influence in the state. Herbert and his fellow sophomores believed that the faculty had chosen to make an example of Doby because he had no influential supporters. Additionally, the young man had implied to his classmates that he had denied the charge against him, and the boys felt that the teachers had impugned Doby's honor by refusing to accept his word.

The sophomores immediately rushed to Doby's defense. Meeting in solemn convocation, the class elected Hilary Herbert to be the chairman of the rebellion. After numerous intemperate speeches, Herbert was instructed by unanimous vote to deliver a petition to the faculty decreeing that the sophomores would boycott all classes and school functions until Doby had been reinstated. The professors then suspended all thirty-three sophomores, and President Manly gave them twenty-four hours to leave the university.[6]

---

6 Herbert, "Reminiscences," p. 83; James B. Sellers, *History of the University of Alabama* (Tuscaloosa, University of Alabama Press, 1953) 1: pp. 220-222; Minnie Clare Boyd, *Alabama in the Fifties: A Social Study* (New York, Columbia University Press, 1931), p. 154; Little, *Memoirs,* p. 17.

The incident aroused much indignation across Alabama. Newspapers accused the well-meaning teachers of spying and of invading the privacy of honorable young men. Many parents visited the university. No one was more incensed than Thomas Herbert, who agreed with his son that the terms on which the faculty offered to reinstate the suspended students were dishonorable. The elder Herbert was, in his son's words, "a veritable Hotspur" where a matter of principle was concerned; his resentment came out in an acrimonious exchange with President Manly. As a result of the unhappy affair, Thomas Herbert decided that his son should not have been at the University of Alabama in the first place. He immediately began making plans for Hilary to attend the more prestigious University of Virginia in the fall.[7]

The students at the University of Virginia were not known for their docile nature, and on occasion Charlottesville had been rocked by student revolt. Thus, the faculty at the university was not enthusiastic about admitting a student whose record indicated a rebellious temperament. Nevertheless, on October 26, 1854, the professors agreed to allow Hilary Herbert to attend lectures without matriculating until information could be obtained from the University of Alabama on the circumstances of his separation. President Manly, miffed because the boy refused to return to Tuscaloosa, "with a malignity unbecoming his sacred profession," tried to prevent Herbert's acceptance at Virginia.[8] Within a month, however, the chairman of the faculty, Professor Socrates Maupin, had satisfied himself that the young man had departed honorably from the University of Alabama and, therefore, Maupin led the faculty to adopt the following resolution:

> It appearing from satisfactory sources of information that Mr. Herbert left the University of Alabama on the 16th of March last under suspension for an indefinite period—that the Faculty of said University subsequently proposed conditions in writing upon subscribing which Mr. Herbert would be admitted

---

7 Herbert, "Reminiscences," p. 83; Little, *Memoirs*, p. 17. Hilary Herbert never harbored any bad feelings against the University of Alabama. In 1876, in fact, he became a member of its Board of Trustees. See Sellers, *University of Alabama* 1: p. 319.

8 Herbert to Washington P. Smith, February 2, 1868, Washington M. Smith Papers, Duke University.

as a student—that Mr. H was willing and is still willing to
subscribe these conditions in substance, but not in terms, as
he considered the terms would place him in a degraded attitude—It appearing further from his monthly circulars and other
testimony that Mr. Herbert maintained the highest standard
of deportment and scholarship, up to the time of his suspension—and that the offence for which he was suspended, was
the effect of momentary excitement operating on him in common with many other students, but not implying that moral
delinquency which ought to exclude him altogether from other
institutions.

Therefore—Resolved, that Mr. Herbert be allowed to ma-
triculate as a student of this institution.

Shortly afterwards, Herbert was officially entered as a student
at the University of Virginia.[9]

He immediately began his studies with energy and enthusiasm. In his first year he studied in three schools: Ancient Languages, Modern Languages, and Moral Philosophy. In his
second year he also entered the School of Law. Herbert was
evidently a good student. He satisfactorily completed his examinations in English; he distinguished himself in Latin and
French.[10] He was never once mentioned in the long columns
of the Faculty Minutes in which were listed the names of students who were recalcitrant in their attention to studies or in
the payment of fees.

Herbert's stay at the university was a significant time in his
development; in the shadow of the Rotunda, he began to
formulate political views that would remain with him for the
rest of his life. Undoubtedly, James P. Holcombe, a professor
of law, had much to do with Herbert's formulation of a political philosophy. Holcombe was, according to the leading biographer of the university, "the most ardent and eloquent advocate
of Secession in the Faculty and the University of Virginia."[11]
Herbert greatly admired the fiery Holcombe and listened in-

9 "Minutes of the Faculty, 1848-56," 7: pp. 369, 373-374, Manuscript Division,
University of Virginia Library; "Matriculation Books, 1826-1879," November 23,
1854, Office of the Registrar, University of Virginia.

10 "Minutes of the Faculty," 7: pp. 402-403, 416-417; Catalogue of the Uni-
versity of Virginia: Session of 1854-55 (Richmond, H. K. Ellyson, 1855) p. 12;
Catalogue of the University of Virginia: Session of 1855-56 (Richmond, H. K.
Ellyson, 1856), p. 9.

11 Philip A. Bruce, History of the University of Virginia, 1819-1919 (New York,
Macmillan Company, 1921), 3: pp. 71-72.

tently as his teacher elaborated the rights that the states should enjoy within the Federal Union. Herbert later recalled:

> I . . . never took any stand in politics until in 1856 Professor Holcombe at the University of Virgina had expounded to our class the theories on which the two schools of our politicians founded their policies. Thenceforward I was a Democrat and believed in the right of secession, like my father.

Even after the Civil War, Herbert never abandoned the belief that the South had exercised a legitimate constitutional right in implementing the doctrine of secession; nor was he ever shaken from his firm conviction in the sanctity of state rights.[12]

Herbert's two years at the University of Virginia passed rapidly. An enthusiastic participant in many student activities, he was active in the prestigious Jefferson Society, a debating club that had been organized in 1825. Herbert was awarded a signal honor when he was elected by the society to read the Declaration of Independence at the annual celebration of Jefferson's birthday. Unfortunately, the young man was unable to claim the honor that had been bestowed upon him. In February, 1856, he became so severely ill with a stomach ailment that he decided to go home to recover. The faculty of the school thought his decision wise; although they were not reputed to be overly generous with money, the teachers voted to return to Herbert a portion of his rent and one-third of his professors' fees.[13]

By the autumn of 1856, Herbert had fully recovered his health. Instead of returning to the University of Virginia, however, he began reading law in his hometown of Greenville under the direction of Judge John K. Henry. Studying with a fellow student Edward A. Perry, a bright young man who was eventually to become the governor of Florida, Herbert made rapid progress. Judge Henry arranged for the two to take their law examinations after only five months of study. To their delight and surprise, they passed the examinations with little difficulty and were admitted to practice before the bar of the Alabama Supreme Court. In March, 1857, Herbert and his brother-in-law Samuel Adams opened a law office in Greenville. The partnership was a notable success, and the older Adams

---

12 Herbert, "Additions to 1903 Memoirs," 1917, Vol. 6, Herbert Papers.
13 Herbert, "Reminiscences," p. 92; "Minutes of the Faculty," 7: p. 464.

was elected to the Alabama General Assembly that same year. Herbert had not yet evidenced any political ambitions at this time and was content to mind the practice while Adams attended sessions of the legislature at Montgomery.[14]

It is not difficult to see how the twenty-three-year-old lawyer presented an appealing picture to the citizens of Greenville. A handsome young man of medium height and build, with a fair complexion and deep blue eyes, Herbert showed an enthusiastic interest in the eligible young ladies in the town, and the young ladies, of course—as much as was proper in that day— reciprocated. The product of a society that stressed honor and character as one of the primary criteria by which a man was measured, Herbert was committed to the steadfast maintenance of both. He was an energetic and affable man with a remarkable aptitude for telling a good story, and he made friends easily with his quick mind, keen wit, and urbane manner. Aware of his solid family heritage, yet not presumptuous about it, the young lawyer was always able to draw on the reservoir of sensitivity and quiet dignity which had marked the attitudes of his parents. Herbert's attitudes about what was honorable were similar to those of many southerners of the time. His outlook evidenced that intense individuality which Wilbur J. Cash had found so characteristic of the southern mind in the antebellum days. As expressed in the "gentlemen's code," this quality often took the form of a gentle graciousness which, nevertheless, could also become a liability—as when it caused the individual to place major emphasis on form and appearance rather than substance. For example, it was this extreme dedication to individuality and to outward forms of honor that caused Herbert to act rashly as in the unfortunate "Doby Rebellion" when he refused to return to school over an incident that was trivial and uncertain. Nevertheless, Herbert's good qualities of character and personality far outweighed any minor faults which he might have had.[15]

The years in which Hilary Herbert was working to establish himself in the legal profession in Butler County were years of enormous significance for the nation. The rancorous section-

---

14 Herbert, "Reminiscences," p. 95; Little, *History of Butler County,* pp. 158-159, 180.

15 See Wilbur J. Cash, *The Mind of the South* (New York, Alfred A. Knopf, 1941), pp. 31-34.

alism that had steadily pushed the North and South apart was becoming increasingly evident. Not even the sleepy little town of Greenville, Alabama, could be oblivious to the monumental issues of the day. There could be no doubt as to where Herbert would stand on matters that divided the North and the South. He was a secessionist and the son of a secessionist.[16]

There were many men in Alabama who were not eager for the dissolution of the Union; nor were the majority of the citizens of Butler County convinced of the merits of secession. Early in 1860, however, Hilary Herbert aligned himself with the Southern Rights group led by the fiery William L. Yancey. Yancey was a magnificent speaker and rabble-rouser, and the young Greenville lawyer was charmed on each occasion that he heard Yancey speak. Even after the war, Herbert continued to insist that Yancey was "distinctly the greatest orator I ever heard."[17]

Political events moved rapidly in Alabama in 1860. About the middle of May, a meeting was held in Greenville so that Thomas Jefferson Burnett, the district representative who had attended the National Democratic Convention at Charleston, could report on that meeting. Loud applause from many in the audience greeted Burnett's vivid descriptions of the withdrawal of the Alabama delegation from the convention when the body refused to endorse a pro-slavery platform. At the conclusion of the report, Hilary Herbert took the platform to give his views on the matter. Herbert accused the Democratic party of subverting the rights of southerners and heartily commended the Alabamians for their conduct at the convention. He ended his statements by inviting "all true men of the South to unite with us and make common cause for our country in maintaining the rights of the South."[18]

In June, Herbert attended the state Democratic convention and was selected as an alternate elector in behalf of the presidential ticket composed of John C. Breckinridge and Joseph C. Lane, the Southern Rights candidates who had been chosen by the Charleston seceders in a meeting in Richmond that same

16 Herbert, "Reminiscences," p. 1.

17 *Ibid.*, pp. 98-99. See also Lewy Dorman, *Party Politics in Alabama from 1850 through 1860* (Wetumpka, Alabama, Wetumpka Printing Company, 1935), pp. 176-177.

18 *Southern Messenger,* Greenville, Alabama, May 16, 1860.

month. Evidently many citizens in Greenville harbored the outlandish notion that Breckinridge and Lane had a good chance of winning the national election. *The South Alabamian,* the Greenville newspaper that supported the Southern Rights group, predicted that the ticket would carry not only the lower South but also New Jersey, Pennsylvania, Delaware, Maryland, Tennessee, Kentucky, Virginia, California, and Oregon. Herbert shared the delusion that his party might win. As late as October, he sent *The South Alabamian* a letter that he had received from an acquaintance in the North who foresaw encouraging prospects for the ticket in Virginia, Maryland, Delaware, New Jersey, and Pennsylvania.[19]

Herbert determined to work energetically on behalf of the Southern Rights cause. His plans to canvass the county were spoiled, however, when he traveled on business to Mississippi in August and was detained there when he contracted a fever. Undaunted in his zeal by the illness, he wrote a long letter to the citizens of Butler County warning them that the South faced a "most portentous struggle." He argued that relations between the South and North had for years been assuming a "sectional character." Northern public opinion had been stirred up by fanatical demagogues who were determined to undermine all that was dear to the South. Calling up vivid images of the enemy, Herbert could only conclude:

> Nothing can save us in the Union from the terrors of mobocracy except a firm and determined purpose to stand by the reserved rights of the states made under the Constitution. We have made compromise after compromise with the spirit of Abolitionism, but as if this were a meat upon which the monster fed, he has only grown more terrible in his proportions and more rapacious in his demands.

The young lawyer scored the Republican party for its efforts to limit slavery in the territories, declaring that

> every citizen of the United States has an equal right to go into the territories of the United States with whatever property is recognized under the Constitution and that neither Congress nor a territorial legislature has any right to *intervene* and destroy his rights.

---

19 *The South Alabamian,* Greenville, Alabama, June 16, 1860; July 7, 1860; October 20, 1860.

While the moderate Constitutional Unionists of Greenville admonished the citizens of Butler County to support "the Constitution of the Country, the Union of States, and the enforcement of the laws," Hilary Herbert was calling for allegiance to "Truth, Justice, and the Constitution."[20]

The election of Abraham Lincoln in November, 1860, was decisive in Alabama's decision for disunion. Although the Republican party platform opposed only the extension of slavery into the territories, many Alabamians had come to view the "Black Republicans" as dedicated to total abolition. Butler County had given the Constitutional Unionists the majority of its votes in the November election.[21] With the triumph of the Republicans, however, the citizens of Butler abandoned their hopes for a moderate solution to the difficulties that separated South and North. Hilary Herbert suddenly found himself a part of the overwhelming majority, a majority bent on following the fateful course of secession.

---

[20] *Ibid.*, August 11, 1860.

[21] Walter L. Fleming, *Civil War and Reconstruction in Alabama* (New York, Columbia University Press, 1905), p. 20; Clarence P. Denman, *The Secession Movement in Alabama* (Montgomery, Alabama State Department of Archives and History, 1933), p. 87. In the presidential election, the Constitutional Unionist candidates, Bell and Everett, won 41,000 votes in Alabama. The Breckinridge-Lane ticket polled only 7,000 votes more.

III. For God, Constitution, Caucasians, and General Lee

> That great war was not, as it has been seditiously
> taught in so many school books a "slaveholders'
> rebellion." While on the one side it was a war for
> the preservation of the Union, on the other it was
> a war by slaveholders and non-slaveholders,
> standing together for the right of self-govern-
> ment handed down to them from the fathers,
> and for the supremacy for the white race or-
> dained by Almighty God.
>
> —Hilary Abner Herbert,
> speech in Laurens,
> South Carolina, 1912

I

ABOUT the time of the fall election of 1860, a local militia
was formed in Greenville. Hilary Herbert enlisted immediately
and was elected to be the second lieutenant of the Greenville
Guards. The Guards were a smartly dressed outfit; for their
lack of military knowledge, they compensated in dress. Their
uniforms were gray with brilliant red trimmings.

In January, 1861, Herbert and his comrades had their first
real taste of military life. The Guards were among the units
ordered by Governor Andrew B. Moore of Alabama to assist
Florida troops in the capture of the Navy Yard and the forts
at the mouth of the Pensacola Bay. During their stay of about
a month and a half, the men saw no fighting—except among
themselves. The Federals, aware of their impending fate, had
quietly abandoned the Navy Yard and other installations and
had moved their entire garrison out to Fort Pickens on Santa
Rosa Island, thus granting the Confederates a minor victory
by default. With no military action to occupy their minds,
the men soon became acutely aware of the cramping restraints
of military life. They voiced the usual soldiers' complaints
about the food and rations. Moreover, there was considerable
grumbling about the "fine airs" of the officers, who attempted

24

to assert their authority over their undisciplined companions from home. By the time the once-proud Guards had returned to Greenville, they were in spiritual tatters, and the company had almost completely broken up as a result of the feuding.

Alabama had, of course, already seceded from the Union when the Greenville Guards returned home. While the secession convention had met, other volunteer groups all across the state were learning military drills. The news of the convention's action elicited a wild outburst of celebration throughout most of Alabama. Montgomery had been chosen as the first capital of the Confederacy, and on February 18, 1861, Jefferson Davis had been inaugurated its first president.

On his return home from Pensacola, Hilary Herbert went to Andalusia in Covington County to attend the spring term of court. When he arrived back in Greenville at the completion of his duties at the court session, he learned that all of the officers and a number of the enlisted men of the Greenville Guards had resigned. The men who remained prevailed on Herbert, as the only remaining officer, to take charge and reorganize the unit. He reluctantly agreed, and although he had never conducted a military drill, he became the captain of the Guards.[1]

Great excitement erupted in Greenville when Fort Sumter fell in April of 1861. The news of the fort's capitulation reached the town late Saturday evening, April 13. The enthusiastic citizens were determined to illuminate the town, and virtually every window of each home was filled with light from flickering lanterns and candles. At the Court House the Greenville Guards marched to fife and drum. The gathered throng was entertained by many patriotic speeches, one of them given by the new commander of the Guards, Hilary Herbert.[2]

In May, 1861, Hilary Herbert received orders to take his unit to Richmond, where it was destined to become a part of General Robert E. Lee's Army of Northern Virginia. The ladies of Greenville were not content to let their sons go to war dressed like ordinary soldiers. They made for each soldier a brightly colored Turkish headgear, adorned with a havelock

1 Herbert, "Reminiscences," pp. 94-104; Joseph Wheeler, "Military History of the State," *Memorial Record of Alabama* (Madison, Wisconsin, Brant & Fuller, 1893) 1: p. 106; *Greenville Advocate,* February 27, 1889.

2 *Southern Messenger,* Greenville, Alabama, April 17, 1861.

and with long tassels. Although the hats were highly decorative, the men found that they were of no use once they got out of Greenville. The ladies also presented the company a flag, with Herbert's own sister Aurelia making the presentation speech.[3]

In spite of the moving quality of the occasion, Hilary Herbert was hardly at a loss for words. He spoke in response to the gifts that the men had received. Reminding the citizens of Greenville that the struggle which was beginning was long in the making, he said:

> In vain for thirty years did the sentinels whom we had placed upon the watch tower point our Northern brethren to the great principles upon which our government was founded and warn them that we were ready like our ancestors of the Revolution to pledge "our lives, our fortunes, and our sacred honor" in their defense.

The warnings, however, had gone unheeded. Northern fanatics, determined that there would be an "irrepressible conflict," mocked all the South's efforts at conciliation and launched "an unholy crusade against the Constitutional equality of the states." Time for conciliation had now run out. Herbert asserted:

> The government of our forefathers has been overthrown. The people of the North lost sight of the grand fundamental idea upon which it was founded. . . . In their lust for power and plunder they denied to sovereign states the right to "regulate their own affairs in their own way." They excluded these from the public property purchased by the common blood and treasure.

The North had made the Federal Union into a "Consolidated Despotism." The national government, according to Herbert, had now been dedicated to the purpose of "enthroning the hairy-headed monster Abolitionism to reign over us who had been taught to lisp the language of liberty—even at our mother's breasts." The South, he contended, now had no choice but secession, for the only alternatives were "degradation in the Union or independence out of it." The young orator challenged his audience to forsake party politics and stand squarely behind their great cause. In a burst of enthusiasm he even

---

[3] Herbert, "Reminiscences," pp. 16, 103-104.

promised his hearers that the women and children of the county would "never see the smoke of the campfires of the enemy"—an assurance he, unfortunately, was unable to keep.[4]

In June of 1861 his company of Guards arrived in Richmond, and Herbert took his place as one of the ten company commanders of the Eighth Alabama Infantry Regiment. It was not until 1862, however, that the unit saw any real action. The men of Herbert's company were fortunate to have a relatively mild autumn and winter in which to become adjusted to military regimen. Few of them had received any prior training, and most were unacquainted with any kind of strictly regulated life.

Exposure to wet weather, poor cooking, and irregular hours took their toll among the men. Diarrhea, measles, whooping cough, and colds were the most persistent medical complaints. Homesickness was also a difficult problem; the clay hills of Alabama had never looked as good in reality as they did in the memories of the homesick soldiers. In spite of a past record of frequent illness as a youth, Herbert's own health was quite good for the first winter and, indeed, throughout the war. Excepting the time he was wounded, he missed only a day and a half of duty because of sickness during his entire military career.[5]

Captain Herbert had no illusions about his military ability. Admitting his "deplorable ignorance," he set out to master thoroughly Hardee's *Tactics,* a copy of which had been given to every commissioned and non-commissioned officer in the regiment. After many hours of memorization and practice, he set up a school for tactics in his company. Later when he took command of the regiment, he extended the school to all of the

---

[4] Pitt S. Milner to Herbert, March 14, 1911, Herbert Papers. Milner's father, John A. Milner, was in the audience and made a copy of Herbert's speech. Fifty years later, Pitt Milner discovered the address in his father's papers and mailed Herbert a copy of the speech that had been so long forgotten.

[5] Hilary Abner Herbert, "Short History of the 8th Alabama Regiment," unpublished MSS, Vol. 2, p. 1, Herbert Papers (hereafter referred to as Herbert, "Short History"); Herbert, "Reminiscences," pp. 110-116; *The War of the Rebellion: A Compilation of the Official Records of the Union and Confederate Armies* (Washington, Government Printing Office, 1880-1901) 1: pp. 326-328 (hereafter the collection is referred to as *OR;* all references are in series I unless otherwise noted). For a detailed account of Herbert's military career see Hugh B. Hammett, "Hilary Abner Herbert: The Early Years, 1834-1865" (M.A. Thesis, University of Virginia, 1967); this paper was distributed in December, 1967, by the Butler County, Alabama, Historical Society to its membership.

companies. Herbert was especially pleased in the winter of
1863-1864 when an inspector from General Lee's staff remarked
that the men of the Eighth Alabama looked as good in drill as
any unit under West Point officers.[6]

In the spring of 1862, the Eighth Alabama participated in
the Confederate defense at Yorktown against General McClel-
lan and then in the withdrawal up the peninsula to Williamsburg. At Williamsburg on May 5, the Alabamians received
their first real taste of battle and suffered their first significant
losses. For Herbert this initial trial was made somewhat easier,
owing to his promotion to the rank of major on the evening
of the battle.[7]

On the first day of June, 1862, the Eighth Alabama joined in
General Joseph E. Johnston's attack against the Union forces
at Seven Pines near the Chickahominy River. Caught in the
midst of a Yankee ambush, Major Herbert was toppled from
his horse by a bullet which struck him in the back. When he
recovered his senses, Herbert found to his dismay that he had
been taken prisoner by his adversaries. Fortunately, the missile
which struck him left only a flesh wound, although the ball
had missed his spine only by inches. The men of Herbert's
regiment supposed that the major had been killed and sent
word to Thomas Herbert that his son had died gallantly at
Seven Pines. George Noland Lewis, an acquaintance from
home, added authenticity to the tale when he wrote to his
sister in Greenville that an officer of a North Carolina regiment had recovered the slain major's watch but had been
unable to get his sword.[8]

Within a few days after his capture Herbert, quite alive and
well, was sent to Fort Delaware, an island prison located in
the Delaware River, in which more than 2,000 Confederate
prisoners of war were detained. Surprisingly, life in prison was
quite comfortable for Herbert and the officers who were his
fellow captives. Indeed, the incarceration allowed him a good
rest and well-deserved vacation from his duties. The ingenious
officers finagled a generous food allotment from the old colonel

---

6 Herbert, "Reminiscences," p. 114.

7 *Ibid.*, pp. 123-128; Herbert, "Short History," pp. 3-8.

8 *Ibid.*; George Noland Lewis to Sarah E. Lewis, n.d., George Noland Lewis
Letters, in the possession of Mrs. Myra Crenshaw, Butler County [Alabama] Historical Society.

who ran the prison and were able to purchase supplies for
sumptuous meals, cooked by two enlisted prisoners whom they
employed. Herbert later wrote of his two and a half months
in prison:

> I shall never forget that delightful fare at Fort Delaware, and
> I cannot to this day remember any time during my life when I
> ever enjoyed eating more decidedly. The contrast between the
> fare I had in the army before and after Fort Delaware, causes
> that table in the casemate to stand out in my memory like an
> oasis in the desert.[9]

Early in August, 1862, as a part of a general cartel for prisoner exchange Hilary Herbert was among a group of officers
returned to southern hands. Rejoining the Eighth Alabama
near Richmond, he found that, owing to casualties and resigna-
tions, he was the ranking officer and thus in command of the
regiment. It did not take him long to discover that the unit
was in shambles. The Eighth Alabama had not only suffered
heavy losses in battle but also was plagued with wholesale
desertions. Throughout the war it was not unusual for men
in the Confederate army to go home or to transfer to other
commands without formal arrangements. Many of the men in
the Eighth Alabama, unhappy with a former commander, had
simply moved to other regiments.

Herbert concluded that firm measures were needed to deal
with the problem. He sent out word that all deserters had two
weeks to return to their proper place; any men who stayed
away and were later apprehended would be court-martialed
and shot. Although most of the men returned, two deserters
were caught several months afterwards and by court-martial
were sentenced to be executed. Now temporarily imbued with
the military mentality. Herbert felt that he had to stand by
his word in order to preserve discipline. He therefore refused
to endorse the prisoners' applications for pardon. Nevertheless,
President Jefferson Davis pardoned both men, and in later years
Herbert was relieved and thankful that Davis had intervened
and the unfortunate episode had ended bloodlessly.[10]

Herbert remained in command of the regiment until late
September, 1862; that same autumn he was promoted to lieu-

---

9 Herbert, "Reminiscences," pp. 131-135.
10 *Ibid.*, pp. 137-138.

tenant colonel. In late August his regiment had participated in the battle of Manassas. Herbert, somewhat the romantic, later wrote of the "grandeur of the spectacle" of Manassas:

> Our army in one grand onward victorious sweep was every-where driving the enemy as far as the eye could reach, and the enthusiasm of our boys was intense. At one point to which we had hurried, Hood's Texas Brigade, after a hot fight, had re-pulsed a gallant assault by the New York Zouaves, and when we reached the scene of their fight the victorious Texans had gone forward, leaving the green sward strewn thickly with dead and wounded lying all about in great baggy, red breeches. Looking exultingly over the field some one in the regiment shouted aloud, "Look, boys, what a bed of roses! Didn't our fellows pluck 'em."[11]

Nevertheless, Herbert's euphoria over the Manassas victory was rudely demolished. Within a few days he was involved in the bloodiest fighting of the entire war, and from that time on, the Confederate cause was on the rapid, downhill course that led to defeat.

After an escape from near disaster at Harper's Ferry, Her-bert's regiment joined the forces that General Lee had drawn together near Sharpsburg, Maryland, on the hills west of An-tietam Creek. By this time the Alabamians, like many of their fellow soldiers, had come almost to immortalize General Lee. Herbert's most vivid memory of Lee, whom he later described as that "audacious genius," came from the battle of Antietam:

> As we went in that morning we passed General Lee, who stood upon a rock. I have always thought him the handsomest man I ever saw; he was certainly the most superb figure my eyes have ever looked upon during a long lifetime that morning as he stood upon that rock, the sun shining upon his gray hair and whiskers, the light of battle in his eyes, his hat off acknowl-edging the "rebel yell" we gave him as we passed.[12]

Lee was not only respected by his own troops but also was admired by the men of the other side. An episode the following winter provided Herbert with one of his favorite stories:

> In the winter of 1863-64, the writer, then an officer in Lee's army, met between the picket lines near Orange Court House,

---

11 *Ibid.*, pp. 125, 139-140; Herbert, "Short History," pp. 15-16, 25.
12 Herbert, "Reminiscences," pp. 144-145, 152-153.

Virginia, a lieutenant of a New York regiment. During our conversation the lieutenant said, "Well, we are on the road to Richmond again." "Yes," was the reply; "but you will never get there." "Oh, yes, we will after a while," said the lieutenant, "and if you will swap generals with us, we'll be there in three weeks."[13]

The bloody battle of Antietam was the last major engagement for Herbert's men in 1863. The regiment spent the following winter near Fredericksburg, Virginia. The enemy across the Rappahannock River was in plain sight of the regiment during the entire winter. A Federal battery of two guns was no more than three-quarters of a mile away and could have dropped shells into the camp at will. The pickets of the opposing armies walked up and down the banks of the narrow river and could have shot each other at any time. Herbert admitted that the situation was unusual but explained why it was so:

> But we were now real soldiers on both sides and well knew that mere picket shooting helped neither side and was only murder; so by a sort of tacit consent we dropped everything of the kind. Pickets talked and bantered each other across the river. . . .

To Herbert it was evident that the Army of Northern Virginia and the Army of the Potomac had developed a mutual respect.[14]

Herbert always loved music in the camp. Often at night the men of the opposing armies would sing. A band on the Union side of the river would play "Yankee Doodle" and be answered by "Maryland, My Maryland" from the Rebel camp. "The Star Spangled Banner" was countered with "Dixie." Then at the conclusion of the concerts, the defiance would cease, and the Federals on the one side and the Confederates on the other would join in singing "Home Sweet Home." In such situations as that on the Rappahannock, Herbert saw in retrospect the "faint beginnings of the reunion between the North and South."[15]

---

13 Hilary A. Herbert, "Losses in the Battles of the Civil War and What They Mean," *The Photographic History of the Civil War* (New York, Review of Reviews, 1911) 10: p. 132.
14 Herbert, "Reminiscences," pp. 154-155.
15 Herbert, "Additions to 1903 Memoirs," 1917, Vol. 6, Herbert Papers.

Fighting broke out again along the Rappahannock in April of 1863. When Colonel Young L. Royston, who had only recently reassumed command of the Eighth Alabama, was wounded at the battle of Salem Church, Herbert once more took command of the regiment. General Wilcox, commander of their brigade, took pains in his report of the battle to commend both Herbert and Royston as "intelligent, energetic, and gallant" in the conduct of their men.[16]

In June the regiment joined in General Lee's ill-fated invasion of the North which climaxed in the famous battle of Gettysburg. Herbert's regiment participated in some of the bloodiest fighting; over half of the 420 men who entered the fray were counted as casualties when the battle had ended. Again, Lieutenant Colonel Herbert was singled out by General Wilcox as "deserving of especial praise."[17]

Lee's escape to the South early in July, 1863, ended for that year most of the fighting between the two sides in the East. Herbert remained in command of his regiment when it went into winter quarters near Orange Court House, Virginia. The people of Orange were very hospitable. A number of attractive girls resided in the town, and the lieutenant colonel found himself quite the ladies' man and society beau. He took a special interest in pretty Miss Nina Cove. In a moment of literary ardor, he penned, along with other appropriate lines, in her album:

> So on the tablet of your heart,
>   If 'tis not written over,
> Reserve a place when we shall part,
>   For your devoted lover.[18]

The war stirred within Herbert religious feelings that he had never known before. He gradually came to the conviction that "it was by reason of His intercession that God had sheltered me under His Hand in the day of battle." Thus, during the winter Herbert gave expression to his feelings and went to the minister of the Episcopal Church at Orange and requested confirmation in that faith. Apparently, Herbert's conviction was not simply a thing of the moment to be forgotten when

---

16 *OR*, XXV, Pt. 1, 860; Herbert, "Short History," pp. 28-30.
17 *OR*, XXVII, Pt. 2, 620; Herbert, "Short History," pp. 32-42.
18 Herbert, "Reminiscences," p. 201.

wartime passions had cooled. Throughout his life he maintained his religious affiliation.[19]

The spirits of the men of the Eighth Alabama remained high even though rations were slim and very irregular. Often they had no meat at all. In spite of the hard circumstances, the unit was among the first in the Confederate army to volunteer to extend its enlistment for the duration of the war. Herbert was always proud of his men for the patriotic action that they took at Orange. General Lee was proud too; in February, 1864, he cited the regiment's action as a "noble example" to the rest of the army.[20] During the winter Herbert wrote his accurate and uncommonly detached "Short History of the 8th Alabama Regiment" at the request of Colonel Fowler, who was attached to the staff of the governor of Alabama.

Although fighting erupted again in May, 1864, Herbert's participation in the struggle came to an abrupt end. On May 6 at the battle of the Wilderness, he was severely wounded in the left arm. At a field hospital the surgeon found that the bullet had so badly shattered the limb that he could only remove four or five inches of the bone and sew up the wound. For several days Herbert ran a dangerously high fever and remained in critical condition. It required almost six weeks of recuperation before he could be sent home to Alabama.[21] His left arm, hanging uselessly at his side, always served as a visible reminder of his participation in the great struggle and of the personal price he had paid on behalf of the southern cause.

At home Herbert found a grim situation; by 1864 hard times had come to the Confederacy. Coffee and tea were impossible to obtain. Flour and salt were scarce. Every blanket in Herbert's home, except that on the bed of his invalid father, had been sent to the battlefield. Even the carpets had been cut up and sent as blankets. The family was in mourning over the loss of a cousin and of George Cook, a brother-in-law. The only able-bodied men who remained in the family were Herbert and his former law partner, Samuel Adams, now a brother-in-law; shortly after Herbert returned home, Adams, who was colonel of the Thirty-Third Alabama Regiment, was killed near Atlanta.

---

19 *Ibid.*, p. 11.
20 *OR* 33: pp. 1144-1145; Herbert, "Short History," p. 44.
21 Herbert, "Reminiscences," pp. 201-216.

Realizing that he would never use his left arm again, in September, 1864, Herbert wrote to his brigade and requested retirement from the Eighth Alabama. He also recommended the immediate promotion of the officers in line, so that the necessary ranks would be filled. Shortly afterwards, Herbert received a letter from his regiment saying that his former commanding officer Colonel Royston had also petitioned for retirement. The officers in line for promotion had met and had refused any advance in rank until Herbert had been promoted. Accordingly, Royston's request was accepted first. Herbert was then advanced to the rank of colonel, after which his retirement papers were processed. The action of the officers of his former command was to Herbert a "compliment that gave me as much solid satisfaction, I think, as any other incident in my life."[22]

Herbert had every reason to be proud of this episode and, indeed, of his entire military career. As a commander he evidently was able to win the respect, loyalty, and confidence of his men. In May, 1862, he had been gratified at the unusual action of his men who protested his promotion to major because they did not want to lose him as their company commander.[23] William Bird, who served as a captain in the Eighth Alabama when it was in Herbert's charge, later described the abilities of his commanding officer:

> While always a disciplinarian, Colonel Herbert was as he had been in civil life, conservative and always prudent in action as well as in speech. It was not in his nature to be a martinet. He only wanted his men to do their duty. There was never any danger or hardship too great for him to share with them; in fact, he led them in what most tried their mettle and endurance, and when he was off duty he was literally one of the boys, as genially democratic in his manners as the most easygoing soul among them.[24]

Unfortunately for romantic effect, the war ended for Hilary Herbert in a whimpering sort of way. It was not until he re-

---

22 *Ibid.*, pp. 218-220; Little, *History of Butler County*, p. 55. See also Albeit B. Moore, *History of Alabama and Her People* (Chicago, American Historical Society, 1927) I: p. 556.

23 Herbert, "Reminiscences," pp. 125, 211. The attitude of the men of Company F toward Herbert is substantiated in a letter to him from John A. Browne on April 14, 1896. Herbert copied a part of the letter in his memoirs.

24 *Nashville American,* Nashville, Tennessee, undated clipping, Vol. 9, Herbert Papers.

turned home from the Wilderness that he finally admitted to himself that the South was losing the war. Then in less than a year General Lee had requested the terms of surrender at Appomattox. Herbert did not even receive word of the capitulation from a faithful comrade who knew of the joy and the sorrow of those who had worn the gray. Rather, the news came to him from the lips of a polite, but unfeeling, Yankee officer. It all ended in a flat, undramatic way. The pieces of life that remained had to be picked up and arranged in some order.

In a real sense, however, the war did not end in 1865. For Herbert and for thousands of other bewhiskered veterans like him, the saga was relived a million times. In song, in story, in recollection, the Blue and the Gray took the field again and again; the same battles were fought over and over. For a great many of the veterans, North and South, the war was the central event of their lives; when it was over, little else ever mattered again.

Although Herbert was to go on to greater accomplishment and significant achievement on the national scene, the Civil War remained for him an abiding concern. It is probably safe to say that Herbert would have evaluated his wartime experience as more significant in his development than any other episode in his life. Nearly half of his reminiscences, a document of almost 400 pages, is concerned with the war or its causes and results. The greatest part of his correspondence and his published writings, other than that concerning naval and congressional matters, is on that same theme. Additionally, it is quite evident that during his wartime experience, Herbert began to emerge as a leader, as a distinctly uncommon man.

II

In later years Herbert never tired of writing and speaking about the war. In some ways, however, it is apparent that he learned very little from the experience. Although he always insisted that he had accepted fully the results of the war, he never gave up his intellectual and emotional commitment to the old, legalistic state rights argument that the firebrands of the Old South had so successfully exploited. The South, he maintained, had been entirely within its constitutional rights in choosing the course of secession; the secession doctrines of 1860 were directly descended from the Virginia and Kentucky Resolves of Madison and Jefferson, two of the Founding Fathers. To Herbert, the men of the ante-bellum South had not been radicals or revolutionaries when they left the Union; rather, they were genuine conservatives, fighting to uphold time-honored constitutional principles.[25] Indeed, Herbert felt that, when the war was over, the nation was literally living "under a new constitution."[26]

Herbert's assessment of the causes of the Civil War is an excellent representation of the defensive posture of southern thinking concerning this issue in the post-bellum years.[27] Reversing the commonly held northern contention that the war had been a slaveowners' conspiracy, Herbert maintained that the conflict was the result of a gigantic conspiracy by unscrupulous abolitionist agitators to destroy the South. He emphatically rejected the idea that the South had fought merely to preserve the defunct institution of slavery; four-fifths of the Confederate soldiers had never owned a single slave. Nevertheless, in spite of his denials, Herbert was never able to get away from the idea that slavery *did have* something to do with the coming of the war—if only because it was the southern institution which bore the brunt of the abolitionist assault. Moreover, Herbert recognized that slavery had been more than just a labor system; it was, he admitted, "entertwined with the very fabric of both economic and social life" of the region.[28]

In reading Herbert's profuse apologies, one can hardly avoid the impression that he was concerned not so much with the defense of the peculiar institution itself as with the specter of what the South would have been like *without* slavery. The slavery controversy stirred the South's deepest racial fears. Herbert asked:

> When the Negroes should be set free, numerous as they were, what would be done with them? The social, industrial, and

---

25 Herbert, *Abolition Crusade*, pp. 16-17; Herbert, "Additions to 1903 Memoirs," 1917, Vol. 6, Herbert Papers.

26 Herbert, *Abolition Crusade*, p. 209.

27 For a perceptive general analysis of southern opinion, see Thomas J. Pressly, *Americans Interpret Their Civil War* (New York, Free Press, 1965; originally published 1954), 81-126.

28 Herbert, "Additions to 1903 Memoirs," 1917, Vol. 6, Herbert Papers. See also Herbert, "Losses and Battles of the Civil War," p. 134.

political relations between whites and blacks would require readjustment.

He confessed that the South was "more or less in constant dread for its women and children."[29] The abolition crusade, then, had been in Herbert's view an attack on whiteness, an attempt to undermine the southern caste system. Southerners, who gloried in their racial superiority, could never accept the doctrine that black men were their equals. Even the most lowly non-slaveholder, Herbert pointed out, could feel important in the ante-bellum South because the Negro was always there for comparison. Southern whites were enraged at the abolitionist contention that the Negro was only "a white man in ebony."[30] In large part then, in Herbert's view, southerners were reacting with rightful indignation against abolitionist propaganda which besmirched the image of whites and glorified that of the blacks. He observed:

> The privilege of belonging to the superior race and of being free was a bond that tied all Southern whites together, and it was infinitely strengthened by a crusade that seemed from a Southern stand-point, to have for its purpose the levelling of all distinctions between the white man and the slave hard by.[31]

It was only after his retirement from public life that Herbert took the opportunity to set the historical record, as he saw it, straight. In 1912 in his book *The Abolition Crusade and Its Consequences,* he published his most ferocious attack on the northerners whose extremism he blamed for the war. *The Abolition Crusade* was in a sense, then, a revisionist work; its purpose was admittedly biased—to explain the coming of the war "from a Southern viewpoint." The author expressed his hope that his book would serve as a corrective to the northern versions of war guilt that had dominated in practically all school textbooks.[32]

Herbert's thesis was that there was a direct cause and effect relationship between the rise of the abolition crusade and the growth of southern sectionalism. Nowhere was this central

---

29 Herbert, "Reminiscences," pp. 40, 61.
30 Herbert, "Additions to 1903 Memoirs."
31 Herbert, *Abolition Crusade,* p. 159.
32 *Ibid.,* pp. 9-11.

theme more directly or simply stated than in the introduction
of his book:

> What a creature of circumstances man is! The writer's beliefs
> about a great moral question [slavery], his home, his school-
> mates, and the companions of his youth, were all determined
> by a movement begun in Boston, Massachusetts, before he was
> born in the far South![33]

To Herbert, the most galling aspect of the abolitionist approach had been its tone of extreme self-righteousness. He contended, "I might say, the fundamental idea of the abolitionist
crusades was 'I am holier than thou.' This assumption of course
Southern people bitterly resented." Additionally, Herbert felt
that southerners themselves would have found a way to end
slavery had they only been left alone. Citing the experience of
his own mother, he argued that the abolition agitation had
nipped in the bud a growing sentiment in the South for eman-
cipation. The arch villain of all of those who participated in the
growing conflict was William Lloyd Garrison "in whose eyes
every slave-holder was a fiend."[34]

In Herbert's view the abolitionists had not only painted a
false picture of the peculiar institution but also had perpetrated a distorted image of the social structure of the South.
Herbert flatly rejected the generally accepted view of southern
society as a three-tiered structure with the plantation owners
on top, slaves at the bottom, and only "poor white trash" in
between. The average nonslaveholding, white agriculturist was,
Herbert observed, an attractive personality: honest, independent, thrifty, and often educated. This class of yeoman farmers
was not despised by the lordly slaveowners; indeed there was
little friction between them. The two groups were often political allies, and both shared widely in the process of state government. Southern society, Herbert argued, was far more complex and varied than the abolitionists had assumed.[35]

The modern scholar will likely have little use for Herbert's
book on the coming of the war. The volume evidently had a
rather limited circulation; and, unlike Herbert's other book,
Why the Solid South? is rarely found in bibliographical lists.

---

33 *Ibid.*, p. 11.
34 Herbert, "Reminiscences," p. 57; *ibid.*, pp. 49-59, 130-131.
35 Herbert, *Abolition Crusade,* pp. 154-157.

Although the American public generally accepted in later years
the revisionist or southern point of view concerning Reconstruction, there has never been much disposition to absolve
the South, as Herbert did, from a major share of the blame for
the coming of the Civil War. For the most part, then, Herbert's
book remains a curiosity piece. In that he inconsistently argued
that the war was not over slavery and, yet, at the same time was
unable to talk about the growing tension without constant reference to the peculiar institution, Herbert was unconsciously
not far from the position generally held by scholars today—
that slavery was indeed the chief cause of the conflict.

Interestingly enough, had Herbert based his description of
the class structure of the ante-bellum South on documentary
evidence rather than on purely personal observation and had
his ideas been more widely disseminated, he might have made
a real contribution to modern historiography. His recognition
of the important place of the yeoman farmer in the southern
social structure came several decades in advance of the monumental work of the "Owsley school" on that same topic.

Although historians will, of course, reject Herbert's conspiracy theory concerning the abolitionists, the most fair-
minded will readily admit that the role of the extremist, the
agitator, the demonstrator in moving historical events in our
nation has never been adequately assessed.[36] In the case of the
abolitionist agitators, however, most modern historians, with
racial assumptions unlike those of Hilary Herbert, will probably view them with admiration rather than with reproach.

Although in later years Herbert rekindled again and again his
fiery views concerning the war's origins, he adopted an increasingly mellow attitude toward the Civil War itself. In his mind's
eye, he apparently forgot about the blood and the dying. He
would never have understood the cynical "lost generation"
which came to maturity in the aftermath of World War I or the
disillusioned "peaceniks" who inhabited American college cam-
puses in the 1960's. In retrospect Herbert, ever the incurable
romantic, saw the war as a noble adventure. He assured one
group of fellow veterans that "we . . . contemplate with a

---

36 See the stimulating piece by Howard Zinn, "Abolitionists, Freedom-Riders
and the Tactics of Agitation," in Martin Duberman, ed., *The Anti-Slavery Vanguard: New Essays on the Abolitionists* (Princeton, N.J., Princeton University
Press, 1965), pp. 417-451.

patriotic pride that knows no bounds the splendid exhibitions
of American manhood that lit up every battlefield of the civil
war with a halo of glory."[37]

Increasingly, Herbert also came to feel that the war had been
necessary, if not inevitable. The passions and hatred of men
both North and South had become so deeply ingrained that it
was "difficult to see how anything else but actual war could
have rooted them out."[38] The war, then, was a necessary
learning process. Herbert believed that "the war solved questions that could be solved in no other way" and that it was a
"difficult step forward in the progress of the human race."[39]
Many years later he undoubtedly summed up the feelings of
many aging veterans when he said:

> Our civil war was a great school. Those who survived it were,
> most of them physically hardened and toughened, mentally
> they were broadened and morally very many were much im-
> proved.[40]

In the years following Reconstruction, Herbert became
especially concerned with bringing about reconciliation between South and North and with carrying his section down the
road to reunion to a place where southerners were once again
in harmony with the national purpose. It was then that he even
began to see the war itself as an instrument of reconciliation.
For one thing the war did not look quite so horrible to him
when compared to Reconstruction, which immediately followed
and which Herbert believed was the most tragic and disgrace-
ful period in American history. The Reconstruction period,
Herbert contended, had been "more disastrous to the South
than had been even the civil war."[41] Herbert explained:

> Time has only hallowed the memory of the glorious man-
> hood displayed in those days by the men of both armies. The
> soldiers, had their sentiments prevailed, would soon have bound
> up the wounds of war, as they did those received in battle.
> But politicians, for a time, interfered.[42]

---

[37] Herbert, Chattanooga speech, September 18, 1895, in correspondence, Herbert Papers.
[38] Herbert, "Additions to 1903 Memoirs," 1917, Vol. 6, Herbert Papers.
[39] Herbert, Chattanooga speech.
[40] Herbert, "Reminiscences," p. 117.
[41] *Ibid.*, p. 79.
[42] Herbert, "Losses in the Battles of the Civil War," p. 136.

Most importantly, however, it was during the war itself that reconciliation had begun. Herbert could even argue, "The civil war was worth all it cost; it taught the people of the north and south to respect each other." The war had abolished sectionalism once and for all.[43] Herbert asked:

> How, it may be asked, could there come out of the dead carcass of so much slaughter the sweet honey of reunion? The answer is not far to seek. True courage, willingness to die for one's convictions, the noblest of human virtues is akin the world over, and, as every true soldier saw it once, it could not be that all the heroism and manhood displayed on the one side were the promptings of a wicked desire to destroy free institutions, or, on the other, the lust for power. . . .
>
> Respect, confidence, admiration took the place of hatred and distrust, and out of the grave in which sectionalism was buried rose the triumphant spirit of Americanism.

In Herbert's mind, the war had given birth to a new nation, stronger and more secure than ever before.[44]

Undoubtedly, Herbert's views were fairly representative of those of many of the veterans of both sections who looked back on the conflict in later years. Modern man with his automatic revulsion at the thought of war is hard-pressed to understand how the men of a generation only recently passed could so glorify and immortalize such a brutal, bizarre episode. Today the war is considered a national tragedy. The fact remains, however, that many of the men who saw it firsthand believed that it was a time of national glory and honor. For the South, at least, the war was the fulfillment of a long process. The legend of the Old South was not damaged by the struggle; the war, in fact, became an integral part of that delightful but dangerous fantasy. The *Ivanhoe* delusion was carried at last to its logical conclusion. Southern men, like medieval knights, kissed their lovely ladies good-bye, mounted their dashing steeds, and charged off to fight and die for home and honor.

Hilary Herbert was a participant in that myth. It is not surprising, then, that for the remainder of his life he preferred to be called "Colonel Herbert." The war was always that one

---

[43] *The Plain Dealer,* Cleveland, Ohio, undated clipping in Vol. 12, Herbert Papers.

[44] *Washington Post,* May 26, 1899.

central event to which he felt he could relate with both insight and emotion. It is clear that the war experience had a maturing effect on him. He was called to lay on the line his abilities of leadership; his mettle was tried in the crucible of combat and found to be free from serious imperfections. The men who served with him sensed and acknowledged the uncommon quality of his character. It is impossible, of course, for the historian to portray in a series of words the metamorphosis that the war wrought in Herbert. It is undeniable, however, that his participation in the drama gave a certain tone, a certain direction, to his life. Call it what one will. The war came, and Hilary Herbert was never the same again.

With the ending of the conflict, the great tasks remained ahead for Hilary Herbert. The immediate problem of scratching out an existence and reassembling the shattered pieces of life left him little time for romanticizing or musing over the meaning of the war. The story of his later years is, when reduced to its simplest terms, a case study of how a successful southerner could step out of the ashes of the war and become a successful American.

IV. Redeeming Alabama

Its terrible losses and stinging defeat had naturally caused throughout the south much bitterness toward the North. This is well illustrated
by the anecdote of the Virginian whose wife told
him, one bright morning, that every negro had
left the place; that he must cut the wood, and
she must get the breakfast. It is not recorded
that the wife indulged in any expletives; but the
husband, with the first stroke of the axe, damned
"old Abe Lincoln for freeing the negroes"; with
the next he went further back, and double-
damned George Washington for setting up the
United States government; and with the third,
going back to the first cause of all his woes, he
double-double-damned Christopher Columbus
for discovering America!

—Hilary Abner Herbert
in "Conditions of the Reconstruction Problem,"
Atlantic Monthly

I

W ITH the end of the Civil War, Hilary Herbert's family
was destitute. The slaves had all been freed. His father, now
debilitated by the ravages of stroke and advancing age, had
accumulated around $5,000 in debts. Although Herbert's sister
Dora retained some land left to her by her late husband, it was
of little value. In fact, the only "good money" which the family possessed was forty-five cents in silver.

Herbert's family was utterly dependent on him. Borrowing
ten dollars from a friend to help with expenses, he immediately
reopened his law office and soon found himself hard at work on
many cases of litigation resulting from the war's disruption.[1]
Turning his thoughts from the conflict in which he had taken
part, he first began the personal reconstruction of his practice,
home, and life.

---

[1] Herbert, "Reminiscences," pp. 235-237.

Like Herbert himself, the people of the small Alabama town of Greenville experienced diverse feelings at the end of the war. Those whose relatives had returned safely from the campaigns were pleased and happy; a great many, however, had lost members of their family. For the Herberts as well as many other families, the cup from which they drank contained a strange mixture of both bitterness and joy.

These years which came to be known in the history books as Reconstruction were a difficult time for Herbert personally. Apparently, he was scarred more by the struggle of this time than he had been by the war itself. In later years he could never talk about this period without some display of emotion and venom, and he always contended that Reconstruction was the "most shameful period in American History."[2] In a later book he graphically portrayed the suffering of the people around him as he remembered it:

> The wretchedness of these people in the spring of 1865 was indescribable. The labor system on which they depended for most of their money-producing crops was destroyed. Including the disabled, twenty per cent of the whites, who would now have been breadwinners, were gone. The credit system had been universal, and credit was gone. Banks were bankrupt. Confederate currency and bonds were worthless. Provisions were scarce and money even scarcer. Many landholders had not even plough stock with which to make a crop.[3]

From reading Herbert's later descriptions of the tragedies of Reconstruction, one might easily get the idea that the nine years before Alabama's "redemption" were a hellish, personal nightmare for him. Actually, such a description would seem to exaggerate. Owing to a growing law practice in these years, Herbert was undoubtedly better off financially than many others throughout the South. These were years, however, in which he had to make many adjustments and assume heavy responsibilities. Most traumatic, perhaps, was his rapid psychological alternation between boundless happiness and overwhelming despondency. On the one hand he experienced the joy and elation of the birth of his first two children; and on the other he had to cope with the family losses from the war, the death of

---

2 Herbert, "Additions to 1903 Memoirs," 1917, Vol. 6, Herbert Papers.
3 Herbert, *Abolition.Crusade,* p. 214.

his father in 1868, and a growing personal alarm concerning the political situation in the state.

Herbert was fortunate in immediately being able to reassume the practice of his profession with the ending of the war. At first he formed a partnership with an old friend, David Powell; but later Powell was replaced by David Buell, who subsequently became Herbert's brother-in-law. The practice was successful in terms of volume of business if not in cash receipts. Although he was able to provide the necessities of life for his family, Herbert was able to accumulate very little cash reserve, owning to indebtedness and heavy family obligations. His financial situation continued to be a source of genuine concern to him. In the harsh fall of 1868 he lamented:

> Money is now uncommonly scarce. Everybody seems to be dreading hard times & hoarding accordingly. We had no Court here this Fall for want of a Sheriff. We are all making next to nothing at law. . . . I do not know when business will improve or where lawyers are to make money in the future. I am getting desperately tired of this feeling of insecurity and uncertainty as to the future.[4]

It was, perhaps, because Herbert assumed the added responsibility of beginning a family of his own that he longed for greater material security. Shortly after the war's close, he met the lovely Ella B. Smith of Selma. Recalling his first impressions, Herbert later recorded that she was "my ideal woman . . . a fine figure, a low sweet voice, a merry singing laugh, an attractive manner, and eyes with more of heart and soul in them than I had ever seen before, or have ever since seen."[5] After an arduous and stormy period of courtship, Herbert succeeded in winning Ella's hand, and the two were married on April 23, 1867, amidst such friends of the bride as John Tyler Morgan and Edmund Winston Pettus, both of whom eventually became United States senators, and General Joseph E. Johnston.[6]

The marriage was an immediate source of joy to all concerned. Although Ella was widely reputed to be a woman of

---

[4] Herbert to Washington M. Smith, October 4, 1868, Washington M. Smith Papers. See also Herbert, "Reminiscences," pp. 155, 242.

[5] Herbert, "Reminiscences," p. 239.

[6] Herbert to Ella B. Smith, February 24, 1867, Washington M. Smith Papers; *ibid.*

great beauty, she had always been quite fragile and delicate
and was also prone to be sickly. Nevertheless, she attacked her
new household duties with vigor, and Herbert assured her parents that he was "delighted at it beyond measure."[7] Happily,
Ella's father, a planter and the former president of the Bank of
Selma, was pleased with his daughter's mate. Little more than a
month after the union, Colonel Washington M. Smith confided
to his son:

> I think Col. Herbert is a hightoned gentleman and a man
> of fine intellect, and I believe that Ella has made a good choice—
> he improves upon acquaintance. He is certainly very devoted
> to her. I was in his law office, and I learn that he is at the head
> of the Greenville bar. He tells me that his practice is large.
> . . . I am satisfied that Ella would not probably have done
> better.[8]

Once he entered politics, Herbert always considered his wife
to be one of his greatest political assets. Ella's grace and wit,
especially when directed toward putting strangers and new ac-
quaintances at ease, were a constant source of pride to her husband. As he assured Ella's mother, "She has more remarkably
than any other person I have ever seen the power of adapting
herself to the circumstances and people by whom she is surrounded."[9] Evidently, Ella was the object of Herbert's complete devotion and adoration. In writing only to her would he
sign his letters by his affectionate nickname "Bruin."[10]

The union of the young couple was blessed by the arrival
of three children in these years, each of whom immediately
became another object of Herbert's unending affection. Leila
was born within a year after the wedding date; Ella Aurelia
(named after her mother and Herbert's sister Aurelia) was
born the following year, 1869; and a son, Hilary Abner Herbert, Jr., arrived in 1877. Undoubtedly the presence of the
children brightened these years considerably for Herbert, and

---

7 Herbert to Washington M. Smith, May 7, 1867, Washington M. Smith Papers.
8 Washington M. Smith to Washington P. Smith, May 31, 1867, Washington M.
Smith Papers; John Hardy, *Selma: Her Institutions, and Her Men* (Selma,
Alabama, Times Book and Job Office, 1879). p. 152.
9 Herbert to Susan Parker Smith, May 16, 1867, Washington M. Smith Papers;
Herbert, "Reminiscences," pp. 240-241.
10 Herbert to Ella Herbert, March 4, 1872, Washington M. Smith Papers;
Herbert, "Reminiscences," p. 240.

on at least one occasion he wrote to his brother-in-law Oscar about the good life, assuring him that "we are living in Clover."[11]

Nevertheless, the joy of family life could not blot out from Herbert's mind the most deep-seated fears and dismay concerning the direction of political events in Alabama. Increasingly, his alarm intensified over the course of action the federal government had adopted in dealing with the returning southern states. It was the problem of racial relationships which most agitated Herbert, however; and he later confessed that he always believed that Reconstruction had been nothing less than "a bitter political struggle to decide whether the negro or the white man was to rule the South."[12] For Herbert, the "Negro problem" was *the problem* of Reconstruction; he later conjectured, "In truth, the civilization of the South was being changed from white to negroid."[13] He frankly admitted that white southerners were utterly repelled by the idea of Negro equality and, thus, it should not have been surprising that they were "naturally prejudiced against meeting their inferior, the negro, as an equal at the ballot box."[14]

It was not until the spring of 1867, with the congressional passage of the Reconstruction Acts, that Herbert was stirred to direct participation in politics. Although several prominent state leaders were calling for acquiescence, a group of citizens under the leadership of James Holt Clanton, a former Whig, determined to try to influence the course of events in Alabama rather than leave the field to the radicals alone. Around the middle of May, Clanton wrote to Hilary Herbert, asking the young lawyer to lead the resistance to congressional Reconstruction in Butler County. Herbert had no hesitation about joining the effort; he later recorded, "From that day until we redeemed the State in 1874, I was an active and zealous worker."[15]

---

11 Herbert to Oscar E. Smith, July 12, 1868, Washington M. Smith Papers. See also Paul B. Barringer, Gaines M. Garnett, and Rosewell Page, eds., *University of Virginia: Its History, Influence, Equipment, and Characteristics* (New York, Lewis Publishing Company, 1904) 1: p. 410.

12 Herbert, "Additions to 1903 Memoirs," 1917, Vol. 6, Herbert Papers.

13 Herbert, *Abolition Crusade*, p. 226.

14 Herbert, "The Conditions of the Reconstruction Problem," *Atlantic Monthly* 87 (February, 1901): pp. 148-149.

15 Hilary Abner Herbert, "How We Redeemed Alabama," *Century Magazine*

In early September the new Democratic and Conservative party, as the resistance organization was called, met in Montgomery. Apparently, many delegates were motivated by the same racial prejudices which had driven Herbert into the group. Herbert recalled that black rule was the chief topic discussed and that many of the participants sincerely believed that a "death-struggle" between whites and blacks was imminent. Additionally, the group was haunted by the past; for "looming up in the gloom appeared the ghosts of the San Domingo massacre in 1814 and of the Nat Turner insurrection in Virginia in 1831. . . ."[16]

Herbert found the initial efforts to organize the people into an effective opposition to be tremendously discouraging. Most of the citizens with whom he talked were tired of war and struggle; they were demoralized and exasperated and did not want to take the chance of further antagonizing the Congress. As Herbert explained, "The farmers were tired of voting; voting had brought on the war; Congress could do as it pleased anyhow. . . ." During the first part of 1868 Herbert and Thomas Jefferson Burnett, also of Greenville, canvassed the counties of Butler, Crenshaw, and Covington, speaking on behalf of their party. In spite of his fervent and emotional appeals, Herbert was hard put in these early days to lure a decent audience; and on numerous occasions he addressed groups of scarcely a half-dozen persons. As the national election of 1868 neared, he made a number of speeches on behalf of the national Democratic ticket of Seymour and Blair and even traveled to several northern Alabama counties for that purpose.[17]

Herbert did not try to hide his discouragement and dismay from his family during the early days of the struggle in Alabama against the Republicans. On a number of occasions he considered leaving the state. He first thought of moving to St. Louis, Missouri, along with Ella's family and their friend John Tyler Morgan, who had formulated the scheme; but afterwards he began to dream of the fabled wealth and oppor-

85 (April, 1913): pp. 854-855. See also Fleming, *Civil War and Reconstruction in Alabama*, pp. 508-512 and Allen J. Going, *Bourbon Democracy in Alabama, 1874-1890* (University, Alabama, University of Alabama Press, 1951), p. 14.

16 Herbert, "How We Redeemed Alabama," p. 855.

17 *Ibid.*, pp. 856-857. See also Herbert to Oscar E. Smith, September 16, 1868, Washington M. Smith Papers; Herbert, "Additions to 1903 Memoirs."

tunity that California might offer.[18] He wrote to Ella, giving
an especially pessimistic assessment of conditions in Alabama:

> Since you left I have thought much of the condition of our
> unhappy country and the more I see of it the darker seems its
> future. Our people are broken-spirited and bankrupt and we
> have no prospect that our state Gov't will be stable or just, or
> that agriculture will be remunerative. Politically and primarily,
> it seems to me that the condition of the country is hopeless. The
> political reaction now taking place at the North comes too
> late to effect a satisfactory solution of the issues which distract
> the South & the control we once had over the cotton market
> of the world has passed away from us forever.[19]

On another occasion Herbert penned the most bitter words
about race that the author has been able to discover in all of
the Alabamian's public and private writing:

> This country I cannot believe will prosper in our day. First
> the free negro is a roguish vagabond & therefore an incubus
> upon the country. Secondly his political status will never be
> settled satisfactorily. The nigger in some shape or other will
> furnish a plank in every National platform while there is a
> nigger that can carry a plank left in the land.[20]

In a later letter he encouraged his father-in-law to join him in
a move to California, writing, "Let us go where we will not
depend upon the solution of the nigger question."[21]

In spite of Herbert's dreams and threats, Alabama was not
to lose one of her future illustrious citizens. The beginning of
her second pregnancy cooled Ella's enthusiasm for a trek across
the country; and subsequently Herbert decided to buy a home
in Greenville.[22] Having decided to remain in Alabama, he applied himself even more arduously to the task of working for
the state's "redemption." In every campaign from 1868 to 1874,
he neglected his law practice—once for three months straight—
and took the stump in behalf of Democratic candidates. All
the while, he refused to offer for any office himself. In later

---

18 Herbert to Washington M. Smith, February 13, 1868, Washington M. Smith
Papers.
19 Herbert to Ella Herbert, n.d. [ca. 1868-1869], Washington M. Smith Papers.
20 Herbert to Washington M. Smith, February 13, 1868, Washington M. Smith
Papers.
21 *Ibid.*, October 4, 1868.
22 *Ibid.*, January 25, 1869.

years Herbert prided himself on his part in the struggle for redemption and felt that in Reconstruction days he had done some of his "most unselfish and effective work."[23] Although Herbert's work was, indeed, "unselfish" in terms of short-range self-interest, in these years he was obviously building up political capital and a reputation of no mean proportions among the people of the district he would later represent for sixteen years in Congress.

Although he moved to Montgomery in 1872 to pursue the practice of law in the capital, Herbert continued his opposition to the Republican program. During the emotional, fraud-ridden campaign of 1874, Walter Lawrence Bragg, the chairman of the state Democratic executive committee, asked Herbert to canvass in mountainous Blount County. Herbert later described his technique of appealing to voters in this section where considerable Unionist sentiment had existed:

> I "hunted the woods," seeking access to every voter. . . . Interest grew and audiences increased. My talks touched on such points as: the conditions in south Alabama; the robbery of our counties and cities; the increase of State taxes, which affected everybody; the decision of the State Supreme Court that it was lawful for negroes and whites to intermarry, threatening to make our descendants a race of mulattoes; the "Civil Rights Bill" with coeducation of the races leading to the same result; the carpet-baggers and the States they hailed from.[24]

Later in this final struggle for redemption, Herbert spoke in his old home town. Addressing the Democratic and Conservative Club of Greenville, he told his friends that the issue of the campaign was clear and simple: whether whites or blacks would rule in Alabama. Herbert bristled with resentment toward the carpetbaggers who had undermined efforts of the Democrats to control the black vote. He explained, "The white people gave barbecues [to the Negro], talked to him on the streets, and did all they could to gain a friendly control over him; but they failed." The only solution now, he exhorted, lay in "the white man's party." Sounding the typical Bourbon

---

23 Herbert, "Reminiscences," p. 242 (back); Herbert, "How We Redeemed Alabama," p. 857; Herbert to Susan Parker Smith, June 11, 1870, Washington M. Smith Papers.

24 Herbert, "How We Redeemed Alabama," pp. 860-861. See also Going, *Bourbon Democracy in Alabama*, p. 14.

theme of absolute party unity, Herbert proclaimed, "The
Democratic and Conservative party is now like an army march-
ing on to victory, and it will not do to break the line."[25]

Like most white Alabamians, Herbert was euphoric when
the Democratic party at last assumed complete control over
the state governmental machinery. For Herbert, the enthusiasm
lasted well after the turn of the century, as evidenced in his
often-cited "How We Redeemed Alabama" written for the *Century Magazine* in 1913. In spite of Herbert's pride in listing himself among the "Redeemers," the objective researcher can only
conclude that his personal role in the struggle to overthrow the
Republicans in Alabama was of no particular significance. He
was never in more than a second-level leadership position in
the Democratic and Conservative party in Alabama. The newspaper of Greenville rarely mentioned him in these years except
in connection with purely local matters of limited interest.

II

Hilary Herbert, nevertheless, has always loomed large in
the story of Reconstruction—larger, in fact, than American
historians have generally realized. Professor C. Vann Woodward has described him as "the editor of the leading apology
for the ultraconservative Redeemer regime, *Why the Solid
South. . . .*"[26] Although virtually unrecognized today even by
specialists in southern history, Herbert's book has had a momentous influence, all out of proportion to its merit as a historical work, on scholarly writing concerning Reconstruction.

The significance of Herbert's *Why the Solid South? or Reconstruction and Its Results*[27] is even more astounding considering the circumstances under which the volume was produced.
In December, 1889, the Republican-controlled 51st Congress,
elected with President Benjamin Harrison, first met. Because
of Democratic manipulation and disfranchisement of black
voters in the South, there was a move among many Republican
legislators to insure the integrity of future federal elections by
placing supervisors and poll-watchers at any ballot boxes where

25 *Greenville Advocate,* Greenville, Alabama, October 15, 1874.
26 C. Vann Woodward, *Origins of the New South, 1877-1913* (Baton Rouge,
Louisiana State University Press, 1951), p. 271.
27 (Baltimore, R. H. Woodward & Company, 1890).

a sufficient number of voters expressed concern over registration procedures, voting, and counting. The measure that embodied this idea, offered in 1890 by Representative Henry Cabot Lodge of Massachusetts, provided for federal supervisors and boards of canvassers to be appointed by petition of fifty to a hundred voters in a given congressional district.[28]

The measure created genuine alarm throughout the South among Democratic leaders who christened it the "Lodge Force Bill." No one was more agitated than Hilary Herbert, who believed that he saw a dark specter from the past rising up to haunt the region. The analogy was so obvious—it would be Reconstruction all over again. For the second time in less than a quarter century, federal officials and finally soldiers would descend on Dixie to meddle in politics.

In his search for a strategy to defeat the measure, Herbert conceived of the idea for his book *Why the Solid South?* It is quite obvious that the volume was hastily executed and was a thinly disguised, although devastating, work of propaganda. While the controversy over the Lodge Bill raged in the House of Representatives in the spring and summer of 1890, the Alabamian rushed his project to completion.

The result of his effort was the most comprehensive and articulate statement of the southern point of view of Reconstruction that had yet appeared. The volume contained an essay on the horrors of Reconstruction in each of the eleven states of the old Confederacy, plus Missouri and West Virginia. The authors of the various essays were all natives of the states about which they wrote; and most of them, not surprisingly, were southern legislators. The list of writers included such men as Senator Zebulon Vance of North Carolina, Congressman John J. Hemphill of South Carolina, Senator Samuel Pasco of Florida, Senator George Vest of Missouri, and Congressman Henry Turner of Georgia. Herbert contributed not only the essay on Reconstruction in Alabama but also the preface, the first chapter entitled "Reconstruction at Wash-

---

28 Paul Buck, *The Road to Reunion, 1865-1900* (Boston and Toronto, Little, Brown and Company, 1937), pp. 278-282; Vincent P. DeSantis, *Republicans Face the Southern Question: The New Departure Years, 1877-1897* (Baltimore, The Johns Hopkins Press, 1959), pp. 198-215; Stanley P. Hirshon, *Farewell to the Bloody Shirt: Northern Republicans & the Southern Negro, 1877-1893* (Bloomington, Indiana, Indiana University Press, 1962), pp. 200-235.

ington" and the last chapter called "Sunrise," a hymn of praise to the New South.

Herbert lost no time in revealing his strategy. The third page of the volume announced a respectful dedication "to the businessmen of the North." In the preface Herbert further elaborated the purpose of the book:

> This work has not been undertaken with any such impracticable purpose as agitating for the repeal of the Fifteenth Amendment, or for the deportation of the negro. Its object is to show to the public, and more especially to those business men of the North, who have made investments in the South, or who have trade relations with their Southern fellow-citizens, the consequences which once followed an interference in the domestic affairs of certain states by those, who either did not understand the situation or were reckless of results. A thorough comprehension of the facts we attempt to portray will, it is believed, at least aid the reader in deciding what ought not to be done by the Federal Government.[29]

Although the book's propagandistic purpose is immediately evident in reviewing the volume today, one must admit that the essays were generally restrained and were coherent in their presentation of a certain point of view. There was no angry denunciation or sustained vendetta which might have alienated northern readers from the start; rather, the volume takes an almost sorrowful tone. Herbert's intent was to woo and convince northern businessmen, to appeal to their self-interest. The final chapter, "Sunrise," using a mass of statistics from Richard P. Edmond's *Manufacturers' Record,* was an effort to authenticate the resurgence of economic prosperity in the South and the value of this recovery to northern businessmen and investors. Any renewal of racial or sectional discord in the South was bound to disrupt this successful and profitable economic relationship. Herbert contended, "Let the reader ponder this fact and then answer the question whether the Congress of the United States can wisely enact any law that would tend to revive the conflict of races in the South."[30]

It is sufficient to say for this chapter that the Lodge Bill failed to become law. Although the House of Representatives

---

29 Herbert, *Why the Solid South?* pp. iii, xvii.
30 *Ibid.,* p. 439.

approved the measure in July, 1890, the proposal never found enough support for passage in the Senate. It is impossible to say whether Herbert's book had any appreciable effect on the outcome of the final votes. Vincent P. DeSantis has contended that many Republican legislators did fear that "revival of Reconstruction tactics would disrupt the community of business interests that had developed between the North and South since the removal of troops in 1877." It is evident also, however, that many legislators were distracted at the time by the tariff and silver issues on which they put a higher priority.[31]

The real significance of Herbert's volume lies in its eloquent and articulate presentation of the southern attitude toward Reconstruction. It is not necessary to present here a comprehensive survey of the book, a body of opinion with which American historians have been familiar for years. Briefly, through his clever ability to seize on words and his uncanny aptitude for finding supporting quotations from northern sources, Herbert attacked the radical Republicans of Reconstruction days as partisan marauders who rode roughshod over a broken and bleeding South, which had already returned submissively and loyally to the Union. The South, Herbert argued, was treated in criminal fashion for the offenses of confining suffrage to whites (as did Connecticut, Ohio, Michigan, Pennsylvania, Kansas, and Minnesota) and for sending representatives to Washington who were mostly Democrats.[32]

To make matters worse, bands of northern meddlers had treked south to debauch southern politics, demoralize the freedmen, and stymie white efforts to control the undisciplined blacks. It was in their agitating about race relations, however, that the misguided northerners had done irreparable damage. They had raised the aspirations of the freedmen until the blacks had begun to assume an unprecedented "tone of defiance." Using the poor blacks only as tools, these meddlers had initiated an era of racial strife which left deep scars on the southern mind. Herbert summed up the white attitude:

> Republican government must be founded on virtue, intelligence, and patriotism. Of all the races in the world the negro alone had been able to hold, always, a whole continent locked

31 DeSantis, *Republicans Face the Southern Question*, pp. 213-214.
32 Herbert, *Why the Solid South?* pp. 8-13.

in the impenetrable mysteries of barbarism. First Egyptian, and then Moorish civilization had assailed Africa from the North; the Asiatics from the East and Europeans from the West had essayed to penetrate it—but Africa was still the dark continent. This was the fight the Africans had fought at home against civilization. Brought from his native land, freed from native influence, as a slave he had greatly developed—he was kindly disposed, docile and faithful. He had cared for the women and children of the South, even when battles were being fought in which his freedom was at stake. For this the Southern people felt deeply grateful, yet they could not think that his training as a slave had fitted him to take part in the government of a state.[33]

In the end, however, Herbert unmistakably turned to the siren song of reconciliation. It was not without design that he chose to call the final chapter of the book "Sunrise," for he intended the stark contrast between Reconstruction and the glorious New South to strike his readers forcefully. He again described the South's long journey into night: "The days during which the reconstruction governments ruled in the several Southern States were the darkest that ever shrouded any portion of our country." In this period he found "nothing but wretchedness and humiliation, and shame, and crime begetting crime. There was no single redeeming feature, except the heroic determination of the better classes in the several states to restore good government."[34] But, then, with the triumph of the Redeemers came the sunrise, the glorious daybreak. With the return of good government, peace and harmony were restored in the Southland. It was a real break in history, Herbert believed; it was as if a people wandering in darkness had found a great light. Never again, he urged, should the American people return to the darkness; never again should they take a horrible lesson "in the school of Reconstruction."[35]

It will be obvious by this time to the student of Reconstruction history that when one allows for Herbert's emotional tone (owing to his involvement as a participant) and for his propagandistic purposes, the view of Reconstruction which he presented it not vastly different from that held by the majority

---

[33] *Ibid.*, pp. 17-18, 37-38.
[34] *Ibid.*, p. 430.
[35] *Ibid.*, p. 442.

of American historians for many years. When Howard K. Beale
wrote his famous revisionist article in 1940, he singled out *Why
the Solid South?*:

> Men of the postwar decades were more concerned with justifying
> their own position than they were with the painstaking search
> for truth. Thus Hilary Herbert and his collaborators presented
> a Southern indictment of Northern policies, and Henry Wil-
> son's history was a brief for the North.

Beale then turned his attention to the "revisionists" who began
to write about 1900:

> A much-needed revision came about the turn of the century,
> associated principally with Rhodes and the "Dunning school."
> For the first time meticulous and thorough research was carried
> on in an effort to determine the truth rather than prove a
> thesis. The emphasis of the Dunning school was upon the harm
> done to the South by Radical Reconstruction. Rhodes and the
> Dunning group drew a picture of the South that—but for out-
> side interference—might have made a happy and practical
> readjustment suited to the new social, economic, and political
> order.[36]

Nevertheless, Beale's description clearly shows in which direction the Dunning scholars moved once the "much-needed re-
vision" was underway. Rejecting Henry Wilson's brief for the
North, the early professional historians lighted firmly on a
position remarkably similar to that which Hilary Herbert had
staked out. The primary difference was in tone of presentation
rather than in substance or interpretation; it was revisionism
all right—southern style.

The dean of the new professional historians himself, William
Archibald Dunning, found occasion to use Herbert's *Why the
Solid South?* citing the volume a half-dozen times in his famous
study of Reconstruction.[37] In his notes, Dunning recognized
the propagandistic quality of the book: "The sketches are of
very uneven quality, and all are strongly partisan in spirit,
seeking to justify the attachment of the South to the Democratic party."[38] Nevertheless, it is possible that Dunning found

---

36 Howard K. Beale, "On Rewriting Reconstruction History," *American Historical Review* 45 (July, 1940): p. 807.

37 William A. Dunning, *Reconstruction: Political & Economic, 1865-1877* (New
York and London, Harper & Brothers, Publishers, 1907), pp. 58, 126, 215, 216.

38 *Ibid.*, pp. 352-353.

much to his liking in the book. A bit of hearsay evidence is presented in a letter to Herbert from John R. Blake, an amateur historian from Baltimore, Maryland, and a correspondent of the Columbia professor. Blake wrote:

> Some time ago I received a letter from Prof. William A. Dunning . . . and in it he mentioned that he has been using your book: "Why the Solid South" for years as an accurate and reliable reference work on Reconstruction in his university work; and he says further that it has done and is doing a good work in furnishing authentic information to political and historical investigators and research workers and authors who write on the subject of that era. His opinion of the book, judging by his letter, is evidently as exalted as my own.[39]

With James Ford Rhodes, the other revisionist leader whom Howard K. Beale mentioned, the record is even clearer. Herbert and Rhodes became good friends and corresponded on occasion. It is not clear whether the friendship influenced Rhodes's objectivity, but at any rate the Boston historian cited *Why the Solid South?* at least a dozen times in the chapters on Reconstruction in the seventh volume of his famous multivolume study.[40] Two letters from Rhodes to Herbert offer a fascinating insight. Herbert, aware that Rhodes was working on his account of Reconstruction, mailed the historian a copy of *Why the Solid South?* In acknowledging the gift Rhodes thanked the Colonel and confessed that he had owned a copy of the book for a good many years, adding: "As I go on with the Hist. of Reconstruction I shall quite likely make considerable use of the book." Rhodes, however, tactfully deflected a thinly veiled suggestion from his friend that he emphasize the dangers of federal intervention past and present as detrimental to sectional reconciliation:

> No work certainly could be holier than one directed to bringing together the South and the North and were I in public life I should keep such an end constantly in mind but as a historian I can write with no conscious purpose. To discern the truth and set it down is my sole aim.[41]

---

[39] John R. Blake to Herbert, August 3, 1918, Herbert Papers.

[40] James Ford Rhodes, *History of the United States from the Compromise of 1850* (New York, Macmillan Company, 1906) 7: pp. 75-79, 84, 97, 140, 167.

[41] James Ford Rhodes to Herbert, November 12, 1904, Herbert Papers.

In slightly over four months, Rhodes wrote again:

> The mind of the North is pretty well made up as regards the
> carpet-bag negro rule of the Southern States and I shall only
> restate from a Northern point of view what you have said in
> your "Why the Solid South?" with my conclusions based on a
> wider range of literary authorities but lacking the personal
> experiences you and your associates had.[42]

It is puzzling that the careful Rhodes would rely on a work
of such dubious scholarly nature, considering the political mo-
tivations behind its publication. As the historian's biographer
has admitted: "The discussion of Reconstruction is in part
based on the monographs of the Dunning school, but it also
draws heavily on sources much less scholarly. Great emphasis
is placed, for example, . . . on a work of special pleading by a
friend of Rhodes, Hilary A. Herbert's *Why the Solid South?
or Reconstruction and Its Results.*"[43]

There is abundant evidence that another of the most eminent and influential of the Dunning scholars relied on Herbert's
book. Walter Lynwood Fleming, whose volume on the war and
Reconstruction in Alabama is generally acknowledged as one
of the finest and most widely used states studies, cited Herbert's
brief essay on Alabama Reconstruction no fewer than thirty-
one times. Moreover, Fleming obviously adopted many of Herbert's interpretations and subjective judgments in addition to
factual material.[44] Herbert's work was given an even more general influence when Fleming produced his famous documentary history, which is still thought by many historians today to
be the best collection available. The reference notes of every
section save one show that the West Virginia professor relied
heavily on *Why the Solid South?* as he made his choice of documents.[45] As the historian Vernon Wharton has stated: "The
fact that Walter Lynwood Fleming would later describe the
work [*Why the Solid South?*] as a 'Democratic campaign docu-

---

42 *Ibid.*, March 25, 1905.

43 Robert Cruden, *James Ford Rhodes: The Man, the Historian, and his Work*
(Press of Western Reserve University, 1961), p. 249.

44 Fleming, *Civil War and Reconstruction in Alabama, passim.*

45 Walter Lynwood Fleming, ed., *Documentary History of Reconstruction*
(Cleveland, Ohio, Arthur H. Clark Company, 1906-1907) 1, 2: *passim.*

ment' did not prevent its being used as a source by Fleming and by many others."[46]

Although he did not document his observation, it was Paul Buck who first recognized the importance of Herbert's book. Buck wrote:

> The book was obviously propaganda intended to establish the thesis that the Lodge bill was a return to the errors of the past. But it made a profound impression in the North. The first detailed representation of the Southern view of Reconstruction to reach a wide audience, the book can be said even to have affected later historiography. "Why the Solid South?" was an important step in the process of historical revision by which judgments were altered and understanding between the sections promoted.[47]

To summarize, then, the evidence is clear that Hilary Herbert is a significant figure in the story of Reconstruction, not for what he did during those years but for what he wrote and compiled about them later. The modern American historian, now a postgraduate of the Freedom Struggle of the 1950's and 1960's, will not have the sympathy for Herbert's racist views that the Progressives of the Dunning era evidenced. The new revisionism has now all but swept the field (in academic circles, at least, if not in the popular mind); and this development is right and proper for our day. From our vantage point we can ascertain that many of Herbert's assumptions were grounded in "myth." There was never actually any threat of "Negro rule" to the South. Politically and socially, at least, white southerners suffered much less than their howling would indicate. Herbert himself even admitted that the Reconstruction process in the county in which he lived was quite mild and that the Republicans were always hard-pressed to find anyone even to stand for offices in the various elections.[48]

Nevertheless, when all our demythologizing is done, when we have related how *we feel* about things from our own historical

---

46 Vernon Wharton, "Reconstruction," in Arthur S. Link and Rembert W. Patrick, eds., *Writing Southern History* (Baton Rouge, Louisiana State University Press, 1965), p. 299. See also Walter Lynwood Fleming, *The Sequel of Appomattox* (New Haven, Yale University Press, 1919), pp. 305-306.

47 Buck, *The Road to Reunion*, p. 281.

48 Herbert, "How We Redeemed Alabama," p. 856.

perspective, it is then an indispensible exercise that we try to understand why Herbert and the men of his day felt as they did about Reconstruction. As Carl Degler has suggested, the southerner's view of the Negro was affected by his deepest racial fears and his past experience with slavery. Perhaps it was too much to expect that southerners would change overnight, or even over a number of decades. It is a matter of record that they did not change, that they were unable to transcend their limited historical experience, and the unfortunate result was, in Degler's words, "a political cold war, one which was more full of hate, bitterness, and misunderstanding than the hot war which preceded it."[49] It is clear also that Herbert and others like him sincerely believed the stories which they contrived about Reconstruction. Although Herbert himself, like many other Bourbon politicians, always capitalized on these myths as political tools in various election campaigns in Alabama, it is also clear from his writing and action that the Reconstruction legends were personal articles of faith with him. Nor must the historian forget that because southerners like Herbert believed in and acted on the basis of the southern Reconstruction legends, they imparted to that twisted body of partly factual and partly fictional material an authenticity and validity which it otherwise would never have had in reality.

As late as 1962, the historian Fawn Brodie, complaining that southern interpretations of the coming of the Civil War had apparently received a triumphant reception, asked the disturbing question, "Who Won the Civil War, Anyway?"[50] Had Mrs. Brodie gone on to include also the story of Reconstruction, the answer would be perfectly clear. For many years, the South won the battle of the books. Hilary Herbert, for better or for worse, fired the major opening shot of that southern victory.[51]

---

49 Carl N. Degler, *Out of Our Past: The Forces that Shaped Modern America* (rev. ed.; New York and Evanston, Harper & Row, 1970), p. 209.

50 Fawn Brodie, "Who Won the Civil War, Anyway?" *New York Times Book Review* 67 (August 5, 1962): pp. 1, 22-23.

51 For an essay elaborating on the implications of Herbert's work for Reconstruction historiography, see Hugh B. Hammett, "Reconstruction History Before Dunning," *Alabama Review* 27 (July, 1974): pp. 185-196.

V. The Rocky Road to Reunion: In Congress, 1877-1893

But there is really no new South. It is the old South coming out in pure, resplendent gold from the furnace of affliction—the old South developing its same old brain and brawn and muscle and pluck . . . that so distinguished it on the battlefield, under new conditions, conditions that give us an even chance in the race set before us. . . .

—Hilary Abner Herbert,
speech to Boston
Merchant Association, 1886

I

IN 1872 when Hilary Herbert moved to Montgomery, he undoubtedly had economic rather than political advancement on his mind. Evidently, he diligently applied himself to building up a large clientele, and his law partnership with Virgil Murphy flourished. In 1875 he moved on to greener pastures, joining the firm of Clopton, Herbert, and Chambers; and within a year it was generally acknowledged in Montgomery that the vigorous young firm was doing the largest law practice in Alabama.[1]

Had Herbert deliberately plotted a scheme to enter politics, he could hardly have come up with a better program than his course over the past years. His political credentials were impeccable: an illustrious family background, a distinguished war record, and yeoman's work in the struggle for "Redemption." Now just barely over forty years of age and well-placed in Montgomery legal circles, Herbert found it much more difficult to stay out of politics than many men do to get in.

In the spring of 1876, the colonel became severely ill with an attack of spinal meningitis that left him incapacitated for almost six months; he had barely recovered when the convention of the Democratic and Conservative party in the Second District

---

[1] *Montgomery Advertiser*, March 1, 1893.

met at Evergreen in Conecuh County to choose a candidate to run for the United States Congress. In spite of his recent illness, Herbert was considered the top prospect for the nomination; and although he had never before run for elective office, he handily defeated E. W. Martin of Conecuh for the honor.[2]

The Conservative press immediately took up Herbert's cause, especially the *Montgomery Advertiser,* the bulwark of Bourbon Democracy in Alabama, and the *Greenville Advocate,* the leading paper in Herbert's old home town in Butler County. Both papers prominently displayed Herbert's name on the masthead, a spot reserved only for Conservative candidates. The colonel launched an aggressive campaign but found it difficult to build much enthusiasm, owing to the failure of the Republicans for many weeks to supply an opponent for him. The Conservative press was alarmed at the Republican tactics and assured the people of the district that trickery was undoubtedly involved and that the opposition would surely launch a "guerrilla fight" at the last minute to try to defeat the Democratic champion. Although he could only fire his cannon at Republicans in general rather than at any adversary in particular, Herbert continued to keep a full schedule of rallies, picnics, and barbecues. At Georgiana in southwestern Butler County, he made an open appeal to the Negroes of the district to support him and the other Conservative candidates.[3] When the election finally came, it was evident that Herbert's vigorous canvass had paid off. He amassed some 11,000 votes to defeat his last minute Republican opponent, Gerald Hall, by around 2,000 ballots.[4]

With his successful election to Congress, Herbert was now recognized as a rising public luminary and, as such, he became even more closely associated with that somewhat intangible political organization and style which historians have usually called "Bourbon Democracy." Most recent descriptions of the leaders of the New South have closely followed the lines sketched out by Professor C. Vann Woodward in his *Origins*

---

2 *Greenville Advocate,* August 31, 1876; Herbert, "Reminiscences," pp. 245-247.

3 *Greenville Advocate,* August 31, October 12, and October 19, 1876. In this period the custom continued that one newspaper might borrow freely from another's columns. The *Greenville Advocate* quite frequently printed excerpts from the larger *Montgomery Advertiser.*

4 *Congressional Directory,* 45th Cong., 1st Sess. (1st ed., Washington, Government Printing Office, 1877), p. 6.

of the New South, 1877-1913. Unlike the rulers of the ante-
bellum regime, the Bourbon leaders (or Redeemers, as Woodward prefers to call them) were generally of capitalist,
industrialist, and middle-class orientation. Dewey W. Grantham
has expressed the same idea; writing of these men, he says:

> Despite the implications of the term "Bourbon," these South-
> erners were not men who had learned nothing and forgotten
> nothing. Their nostalgia for the past glories of their section
> was not strong enough to cause them to spend much time look-
> ing back. Although they paid homage to the beautiful and the
> brave in the ante-bellum South and identified with the roman-
> tic cult of the Confederacy, they urged their fellow Southerners
> to face the future. Convinced that economic progress was the
> key to the South's problems, they associated themselves with
> the business interests and became ardent advocates of Northern
> investments in the South, of Southern industrialization, and
> of sectional reconciliation.

Another historian, William W. Rogers, has addressed himself
even more directly to a definition of Bourbonism in Alabama:

> Bourbonism was reflected in the beliefs of political leaders and
> newspaper editors who, while conservative champions of the
> old South, still admitted industry had its place. Bourbons were
> not bitterly antagonistic toward the Negroes, but demanded
> that they be controlled. Bourbonism was a set of ideals prac-
> ticed and promulgated by a limited group of men who pur-
> ported to, and no doubt did, speak for a large number of
> Alabamians.[5]

There was one characteristic, at least, of Bourbon Democracy
upon which all of its adherents (and all historians) would agree:
a grim determination that events similar to those of Reconstruction would never be repeated. As Professor Woodward has suggested, the only firm base for white unity and party solidarity
was to keep alive the memories of Reconstruction—alien occupation and Negro rule. Woodward says, "The Redeemers
tried by invoking the past to avert the future. The politics of
Redemption belonged therefore to the romantic school, empha-

---

5 Woodward, *Origins of the New South*, pp. 1-20; Grantham, "The Southern
Bourbons Revisited," *South Atlantic Quarterly* 60 (Summer, 1961); pp. 286-287;
Rogers, *The One-Gallused Rebellion: Agrarianism in Alabama, 1865-1896* (Baton
Rouge, Louisiana State University Press, 1970), p. 45.

sizing race and tradition and deprecating issues of economics and self-interest."[6] The *Mobile Register* pointed out that Democrats in Alabama might disagree on many "non-essential questions" but that on "the one great essential question" there was perfect unanimity: "the preservation of State Government here in Alabama in the hands of the white race."[7]

In this respect, at least, Herbert was a southerner and a Bourbon with few equals. The colonel got almost unlimited mileage out of the Reconstruction analogy. In virtually every speech or article of a political nature, he would lead off with his version of the horrors of Reconstruction and brand the events of that time "the most serious crime against free institutions in America." Alabama had suffered particularly, he believed, under the misrule of Radical-Negro government, "child of fraud" that it was.[8] "Home rule" was the positive side of his argument. On one occasion he told an audience in Baldwin County:

> All we ask is the right of local self-government. We don't want to control the affairs of Indiana. They know how to govern themselves in these matters better than we do, and we know how to control our domestic affairs better than they do. We want a fair share in the blessings of honest government.[9]

Inevitably the argument then followed that the only way to assure home rule was to maintain the strictest party unity and discipline. Herbert assured his constituents that during the years in which he had battled for Redemption, the most important lesson he had learned was "the absolute necessity of party organization." He constantly admonished the people of his district to be wary of "independent" candidates, who were actually radicals in disguise, and not to be "led away into strange alliances" where they might become the dupes of the Republicans.[10] As an added garnishment, Herbert might pluck at his hearers' heartstrings with a story or two about the brave boys in gray and their heroic wartime struggle and might even,

---

6 Woodward, *Origins of the New South*, p. 51.
7 Quoted in Allen J. Going, *Bourbon Democracy in Alabama*, p. 27.
8 Herbert, "Reminiscences," pp. 276-277.
9 *Greenville Advocate*, October 14, 1880.
10 *Ibid.*, July 19, 1880.

as modestly as possible of course, speak of his own part in the drama.[11]

It was only after the foregoing litany that Herbert would turn to the subject, to a real issue, on which he had wanted to speak. Unfortunately for the quality of southern politics, however, Herbert—like so many of his colleagues in politics at the time— frequently never got beyond the traditional Reconstruction-solidarity rendition.

In his attitude toward the Negro, Herbert was also typical of the Bourbon leadership. Allen J. Going has suggested that there was little articulated sentiment in Alabama for black disfranchisement before the late 1880's.[12] Although Herbert constantly inveighed against the "Negro rule" of Reconstruction, he never baited or attacked the Negro as a person in his political campaigns, as was the custom of later Alabama politicians in the so-called "Progressive Era." Paternalist that he was, Herbert always was more inclined to view the black man as a tool or dupe of scheming Radical politicians rather than as a menace in and of himself. Nor did Herbert call for disfranchisement in this period. In 1870 he asserted, "It is my individual opinion that negro suffrage is a fixed fact. I do not expect to see the day when negroes will not vote in Alabama."[13]

Most Alabama politicians evidently agreed with the colonel since they confined themselves to efforts to control the black vote rather than totally eliminate it. Many of them succeeded remarkably well in using the Negro vote (in what Professor Woodward calls the "Black-Belt policy") to frustrate the electoral hopes of the lower class whites.[14] Bourbon control of the black vote, especially in the rural areas of the Black Belt, was so adept in many cases that in 1874 one Conservative editor remarked, "The enfranchisement of the colored race, whatever may have been the motives of the dominant party when accomplishing it, has resulted well for all our people."[15]

Hilary Herbert was not successful, however, in building up

---

11 Herbert, "Reminiscences," p. 285.

12 Going, *Bourbon Democracy in Alabama*, pp. 32-36.

13 Quoted in Rogers, *The One-Gallused Rebellion*, p. 38.

14 Woodward, *Origins of the New South*, p. 79; Going, *Bourbon Democracy in Alabama*, pp. 32-37.

15 Quoted in Rogers, *The One-Gallused Rebellion*, p. 46.

a large electoral tally in the Black Belt portion of his district. The Second Congressional District included the counties of Baldwin, Butler, Conecuh, Covington, Crenshaw, Escambia, Montgomery, and Pike. Of these seven, only Montgomery County lay in the state's Black Belt region. The colonel was never able to win many Negro votes in this county because of the well-organized Republican machine in the city of Montgomery, controlled by such men as the "carpetbaggers" Charles Waldron Buckley and Paul Strobach, who could regularly deliver a large bloc of black votes on behalf of their chosen candidates. Nor were the Montgomery blacks, who found strength in their overwhelming numbers, easily intimidated and turned away from the polls by white bullies.

Nevertheless, it was Montgomery County, the obvious chink in Herbert's electoral armor, that ironically provided the key to his eight successive triumphs at the polls. In effect, Herbert built an electoral base on the fears of the white population of his district of the 39,000 Negroes in Montgomery, a black total in a single county that tripled the white population there and more than doubled the number of whites in any of the other seven counties in the district. Terrified by the thought of "black rule" spreading out across the countryside from Montgomery, the frantic whites of Herbert's district stifled meaningful debate, squelched most intra-party opposition, and faithfully plodded to the ballot boxes to return the colonel to Congress every other year. In population the Second Congressional District had around 69,000 blacks to 68,000 whites in 1880. There were more registered white voters, of course; but the whites of the district perceived a real threat of a black victory if Democratic supporters did not consistently turn out en masse on behalf of party candidates.[16] Evidently, the paranoid state of mind of most of the white citizens caused them to accept as gospel Hilary Herbert's ceaseless admonitions that any deviation from party regularity could bring disaster.

Another key to the colonel's success at the polls was the support that he received from the Democratic machine of his district. Because the racial fears of southerners were so strong, even the most mediocre and ignorant legislators were as a

---

[16] The census returns for 1880 are reported in the *Montgomery Advertiser,* February 5, 1881.

matter of course re-elected as long as they continued to be party regulars. If the candidate showed obvious ability and intellect (as did Hilary Herbert), so much the better. As long as he was "right" on the race issue and professed generally to support Democratic principles and policies, Herbert could count on the fidelity of the Democratic organization to return him to his seat until he decided to retire. Within the broad outlines set forth above, it was possible for him occasionally to deviate in his opinions on particular issues and still expect organization support at election time.[17]

In the case of Hilary Herbert, again it was Montgomery County that was the key to his machine support. Faced with a huge Negro majority and a strong Republican machine, the Democrats of Montgomery developed an effective organization of their own. Beset by the ever-present "black menace," the whites of the county felt the need for party unity and electoral solidarity at all costs. Moreover, Montgomery County had the largest white population in the district (between 13,000-14,000) except for Pike County, which totaled about 1,000 more. Therefore, while the Montgomery whites were never able to carry their own county for Herbert in elections, the county delegation (always the largest at the district convention) comprised the largest bloc that consistently supported the colonel for renomination. When he faced severe challenges from within his own party in 1878 and again in 1890, in both instances it was the Montgomery delegation that offered the solid base of convention votes that assured his renomination.[18]

As a final measure to insure the success of their candidate and because efforts to organize and control the Negroes were unreliable (especially in Montgomery County), Herbert's supporters, with his complete acquiescence, agreed that electoral fraud was the next best thing. One must say for Herbert, at least, that although he was not reluctant to accept a victory achieved by dishonest means, he was willing to confess it completely once his political career had ended. Although he made the admission publicly on a number of occasions, a statement which he recorded in his memoirs is worth quoting at some

---

17 For a discussion of the organization and operation of the Democratic Party in the state, see Going, *Bourbon Democracy in Alabama*, pp. 27-40.

18 *Troy Enquirer*, August 4, 1878; *Montgomery Advertiser*, August 17, 1878, and July 31, August 1, 1890.

TABLE 1
SECOND CONGRESSIONAL DISTRICT, ALABAMA, 1880

County	White Population	Black Population
Baldwin	4744	3702
Butler	10,702	8983
Conecuh	6229	6377
Covington	4493	657
Crenshaw	9143	2613
Escambia	4106	1613
Montgomery	13,444	38,948
Pike	14,366	6274
Totals	67,727	69,167

length because it stands as a classic example of the Redeemer rationale by which noble ends were allegedly served by dishonest means. Herbert wrote:

> To rid themselves of the domination of the negro and his allies, who were thus resorting to the most bare-faced frauds to continue their control, the white people of the state had no resource but to fight the Devil with fire. They combined and defeated the Republican party, and then by using the methods forced on them continued to maintain themselves in power. The ballot had theretofore been sacred in the Southern States; nowhere had elections been purer than in the South prior to the civil war. But now the ballot in these southern states had been everywhere corrupted; for what was happening in Alabama was happening in other reconstructed States. It is lamentable that the whites of the South trained to love honest elections could not, as soon as they recovered control, return at once to fair elections; but the negro was still on hand to vote solidly against the white man, and it was not in human nature that Southern Democrats, who in part by false counting methods had now restored honest and economical government, should allow it in State or county to be endangered by fairly counting the ballots of these who had demonstrated their utter incapacity as suffragans.

Speaking specifically of his own elections, Herbert continued:

> The second Congressional district of Alabama, which I represented, was from the date of its formation, in 1875, fairly and honestly Democratic; it had a majority of white voters. Only in one county, Montgomery, did the negro predominate. Here he was largely in the majority. I could easily be elected by a fair count of all the votes cast, black and white, but in some

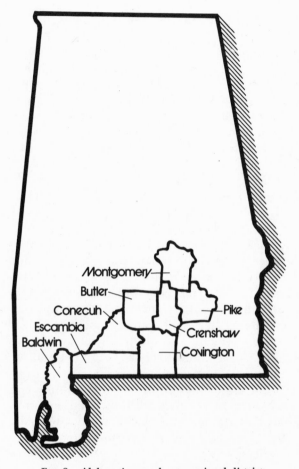

Fig. 2. Alabama's second congressional district

of my elections prior to my canvass with Rice [1882] a portion of the negro vote in Montgomery County had been suppressed by inspectors.[19]

Although Herbert exemplified Bourbon purpose and practice in racial matters, in one way he differed markedly from the commonly accepted description. Professor Woodward has described the capitalist-industrialist orientation of so many of the New South Redeemers. In Alabama he found well-developed links between the Redeemer regime and the railroad and

19 Herbert, "Reminiscences," pp. 278-279.

industrial interests, especially the Louisville and Nashville
Railroad, which had by 1874 thoroughly identified itself with
the Conservative cause. Woodward also pointed out, however,
that some of the men who took their places in the Conservative
regime were "more strongly associated by their point of view
and leadership with the ante-bellum order."[20] Hilary Herbert
more properly belongs in the latter, minority group.

There is no record that the colonel ever had any business or
industrial connections. Unlike numerous politicians of the era,
his influence was not for sale at any price; and unlike many
others, Herbert gained no material wealth from his twenty
years in public service. When he left the Navy Department
in 1897, his assets consisted of less than $1,000 in the bank, a
house and lot in Montgomery, and several hundred acres of
wilderness land of little value in Butler County, Alabama. It
was only after his return to law practice in Washington in
1897 that Herbert acquired his first stock, ten shares in the
United States Steel Corporation which netted him about sev-
enty dollars annually.[21] It is, incidentally, an interesting com-
mentary on the mysteries of southern politics that the same
man whose high principles would never let him accept a bribe
from an industrialist would freely admit to defrauding Negroes
to win elections.

Not only did the colonel avoid personal business connections
but also on occasion he evidenced an agrarian's suspicion of
big business and the city. Speaking at the University of Virginia in 1887, he described the alarming tendency which he
saw in American society:

> Wealth accumulates in private and corporate hands, and pop-
> ulation crowds into the cities. There the very poor and the very
> rich are placed side by side. Luxury and want confront each
> other, breeding discontent and inviting in the words of Dr.
> [Josiah] Strong, mobocracy on the one hand and plutocracy on
> the other.[22]

---

20 Woodward, *Origins of the New South,* pp. 8-11, 20.

21 Hilary A. Herbert, "Ex-Secretary of the Navy Urges Preparedness," *New
York Times Magazine,* December 12, 1915, p. 7; Herbert, "Reminiscences," pp.
366-367.

22 Hilary A. Herbert, *An Address Delivered before the Society of Alumni of
the University of Virginia on Commencement Day, June 29, 1887,* pamphlet
(Lynchburg, Va., J. P. Bell & Co., 1887), p. 13.

Moreover, Herbert's distrust of powerful industries and trusts increased throughout his years in public life. His experience with the "Robber Barons" and their constant clamor for subsidization by tariffs or even by more direct means caused him grave concerns. At the University of North Carolina in 1902, he warned that lack of concern for the consumer had become the characteristic feature of American business. Already the United States led the world in the proliferation of trusts and combination of industries. He added, "These trusts are constantly multiplying, reaching out their tentacles in every direction to gather in for the profit of monopolies whatever the American consumer's necessities compel him to have." The time had come, Herbert concluded, for the government to act decisively to protect its citizens. In spite of his lifelong devotion to *laissez faire,* he argued that "corporations should be regulated and compelled to stop short of monopoly," and he added that "no monopoly should by law be allowed to rob its own people."[23]

Herbert was not anti-business, as such. For the most part, he hoped to return to an older, simpler day—to the free market, to *laissez faire.* Although the remedy of government intervention to curb the trusts might have appeared to a man of his conservative philosophy to be a drastic solution, Herbert feared that unless forceful action were taken to give the people relief and restore the free market, the public would rise up and demand government ownership of all industry. If such a solution were ever to become popular, he warned, then "the abyss of socialism is before us."[24]

In analyzing the colonel's strictures against the proliferation of monopolies, one must not get the idea that he was a hopeless reactionary who opposed the economic prosperity and material advancement that the term "New South" came to signify in the ante-bellum years.[25] Indeed, when Herbert spoke before the Boston Merchants Association in December, 1886, he facetiously assured his audience that earlier that month another

23 *Charlotte Observer,* Charlotte, North Carolina, June 5, 1902, Vol. 11, Herbert Papers.
24 *Ibid.*
25 See Paul M. Gaston, *The New South Creed: A Study in Southern Myth-making* (New York, Alfred A. Knopf, 1970) for the most extensive treatment of New South ideology.

southerner had hijacked the very speech that he had intended
to give. Referring to the address which Henry Grady of Atlanta
had made to the New England Society of New York on December 2 (which had already made Grady a popular southern hero),
the Alabamian assured his delighted audience that Grady had
spoken "not for himself alone, but for the whole South." In
fact, Herbert boasted, his home state of Alabama was the
epitome of what Grady had described; the state was construct-
ing "more furnaces, more railroads, and more cities than any
other state in the Union." Alabama, he insisted, was in the
"vanguard of progress" and was "splendidly typical" of what
Grady had meant by the "New South."[26]

For Herbert, however, the greatest thing about the New
South was not the extraordinary material advancement as exemplified by the roaring steel furnaces of Birmingham; rather,
it was the new spirit of reconciliation, of patriotism and loyalty to the nation. More than anything else, Herbert saw the
New South as the reconciled South. Speaking at a memorial
banquet in honor of General Grant in 1894, he assured his
New York audience that "a mighty revolution in public sentiment" had swept the South; southerners had now completely
accepted the results of the war. Throughout his service in
Congress, the Alabamian had sounded the same theme and had
been recognized as a leader among those who were valiantly trying to drag the South back into step with the nation.[27]

Although Herbert delivered his share of New South rhetoric,
he is properly not listed among the leading New South propa-
gandists whom Professor Paul M. Gaston has so perceptively
described. For one thing Herbert was too old; too much of the
Old Regime was in him. Except for Henry Watterson, the
prominent ideologists of the New South were men born after
1850, men to whom the days before the war were only faded
childhood memories.[28] These younger men were more attuned
to the reorientation that was necessary for the region to join
in the industrial bonanza. For his part, Herbert was never
quite willing to participate in the criticism of the Old Regime

---

[26] Reported in the *Greenville Advocate*, January 5, 1887.

[27] Hilary Herbert, "Address before Grant Memorial Society, New York City,
April 27, 1894," in correpsondence, Herbert Papers; Going, *Bourbon Democracy
in Alabama*, pp. 31-32.

[28] Gaston, *The New South Creed*, p. 48.

that the New South men inevitably found imperative if they were to clear away the ante-bellum ruins of society and custom so that a new order could be constructed. Herbert summed up his dual approach to the Boston merchants, explaining what the term "New South" meant to him:

> If by that is meant that the South has put away all its past, forgotten its statesmen and its heroes, forgotten its hospitality, its high sense of honor, and its chivalry, so much derided, forgotten Washington, Jefferson, Madison, the Pinckneys and Calhoun, or that it repudiates Robert E. Lee, Stonewall Jackson and the brave soldiers who died upon the thousand battlefields of the civil war, then we repudiate the term. But if it means, simply, that we have put away secession and wear the Union in our hearts, that we have put away slavery and fling forth gladly the banner of freedom, that we have put away, wherever it lingered here and there among us, any idea that labor was not ennobling, if it means that, rejoicing now in the music of the axe and the spindle, the hammer and the saw, we recognize fully that true progress can be wrought out only by the God given law of labor, then we accept the term "The New South."[29]

In trying to assess Herbert as a Bourbon politician, one must conclude that he fits the generally accepted description only in part. Only recently William J. Cooper, Jr., who has intensively studied Bourbon Democracy in South Carolina, published his conclusion that the Conservative leaders in that state, unlike other Redeemers, were older men of ante-bellum and planter heritage. These South Carolina Bourbons did not become "self-serving agents and associates of Northern financial inter-ests." Led by Wade Hampton they were able to accept the Negro franchise because of their "self-assurances in dealing with Negroes" and the "Conservative confidence in their racial superiority." Cooper says of them:

> The theme of the Confederacy and of times past pervaded the Conservative mind. The South Carolina Conservatives looked forward not to a better world but to a re-created one. For them, the best of all possible worlds had existed in ante-bellum South Carolina.

Undoubtedly, Hilary Herbert was much closer in ideology and practice to the South Carolina Bourbons than to the Redeemers whom Professor Woodward has described.

---

[29] *Greenville Advocate,* January 5, 1887.

One final qualification must be made, however. Unlike the
South Carolina Conservatives, who clung to their tattered Confederate banners and faded uniforms as symbols of the only important thing that ever happened to them and as ample evidence of their fitness to lead in the postwar years, Herbert was
not a man given to "thinking in the past tense."[30] The dichot-
omy or dualism in Herbert's rationale prevailed. In looking
at the South, he often idolized the past; in viewing the nation,
he customarily cast his eyes toward the future. He sought, in
effect, the best of both worlds. One Alabama paper caught his
spirit: "Mr. Herbert is a thorough southerner by birth and
training, not forgetting nor apologizing for the past. Yet no
American enters more thoroughly into the spirit of the present
day of progress."[31] The historian Hugh Charles Davis has
graphically portrayed the colonel as even symbolizing this dualism in his own body. With one hand, he always reached out on
behalf of progress and reconciliation; at the same time, however, the arm that had been shattered at the Wilderness remained limp at his side, symbolic of older days and values
which he would never forget.[32]

II

It required time, of course, for even so masterful a Bourbon
strategist as Hilary Herbert to consolidate his political base in
his home state. On eight occasions he went before the electorate
of his district; the most crucial contests were those of 1878,
1880, 1882, and the trying election of 1890 when the Farmers'
Alliance launched against the colonel the most bitter political
attack of his entire career.

Originally, Herbert had promised his law partners that he
would serve only one term in Congress before returning to the
firm. But when the District Congressional Convention, meeting at Pollard on August 15, 1878, was unable to choose a
candidate among a field of seven hopefuls, the exhausted delegates turned to Herbert on the 180th ballot. The colonel grate-

---

30 See Cooper, *The Conservative Regime in South Carolina, 1877-1890* (Baltimore, Johns Hopkins Press, 1968), pp. 13-20.

31 *Birmingham Age-Herald*, February 24, 1893, Vol. 7, Herbert Papers.

32 Davis, "Hilary A. Herbert: Bourbon Apologist," *Alabama Review* 20 (July,
1967): p. 225.

fully accepted the honor once more. The Conservative press, as expected, was overjoyed at the nomination and immediately began forecasting certain victory at the polls.[33]

Not everyone was as happy at the outcome of the nominating convention. The editor of the *Troy Enquirer*, Frank Baltzell, assumed the leadership of a dissatisfied faction which charged that not only had one delegate sent to the convention as a proxy disobeyed his instructions in voting for Herbert but also that the congressman had maneuvered behind the scenes to secure the nomination again for himself, while at the same time claiming that he did not seek it. Baltzell used his editorial page to warn of "trouble brewing" and of widespread indignation against Herbert because of "the manner in which his nomination was brought about." Baltzell charged that the colonel had only "personal aggrandizement" rather than the "welfare of the party at heart." Especially angered, the Troy editor reported, were delegates from Pike and Covington counties whose favorites had been defeated by the machinations of the Montgomery ring when it delivered its solid bloc of votes for Herbert at the crucial moment in the district convention.[34]

When Frank Baltzell then offered himself as an independent candidate in opposition to the incumbent, the Democrats were faced with a grave crisis; a split in the white vote could easily mean a Republican victory. The harried Democratic executive committee of the district immediately convened an emergency hearing to clarify the matter and scotch further rumors and talk. After receiving much testimony, as expected the body acquitted the colonel of any duplicity in seeking the nomination. The session ended with a fervent appeal for party unity.[35]

There is no way now to know with absolute certainty whether Hilary Herbert had secretly sought the nomination once more; for the sake of party solidarity the committee would have probably absolved him in any case. In retrospect, the evidence does not appear to be on the side of his accusers. In his private letters to his friend Robert McKee, the editor of the Selma *Southern Argus*, the greatest initiative that Herbert took during the weeks before the convention was to hedge away from

---

33 *Montgomery Advertiser*, August 18, 20, 1878; *Greenville Advocate*, August 22, 1878.
34 *Troy Enquirer*, August 17, 24, 1878.
35 *Greenville Advocate*, August 29, September 17, 1878.

his absolute refusal to accept the nomination (if tendered) toward a position of agonizing uncertainty. Confessing to Mc-Kee that he was "awkwardly situated," the colonel continued to be reluctant to re-enter the contest. Ella Herbert confided to a close friend that she had encouraged her husband to make the race once his law partners had voluntarily released him from his promise to return to the firm; his reluctance to enter the field, Ella remarked, was solely the result of what she called "an over-strained sense of honor."[36]

The most interesting person, however, in the entire episode is Herbert's would-be opponent Frank Baltzell. Baltzell's story is an illustration in miniature of how the "Solid South" worked. The Troy editor came under the most severe censure for his deviation and was pressured intensely to withdraw his candidacy. The editor of the *Troy Messenger*, Baltzell's competitor, wrote sarcastically:

> Now comes Baltzell, editor of the Troy *Enquirer*, who crept into this state about five years ago, from God only knows where, probably Maine, proclaiming himself an Independent candidate for Congress and maliciously denounces Col. Herbert a fraud, a knave, and a political hypocrite. This same squatter is unworthy to black the boots of Hilary A. Herbert. The trimmings of Herbert's finger nails would make a better man every day in the week. . . .[37]

Writing of Baltzell later, the editor of the *Greenville Advocate* branded him a "chronic growler," "a Judas," and accused him of "giving aid and comfort to the enemy" while professing to be a Democrat. The *Troy Messenger* observing that Baltzell was "a small and dangerous individual," contended that he was not an Independent at all but, rather, the unofficial Republican candidate whose platform was "subversive of every material interest of the country."[38]

Under the heavy buffeting, Baltzell finally capitulated. In his cryptic statement of withdrawal, he confessed that his charges against Herbert may have been in error, but he still maintained that "serious grievances have been inflicted upon the

---

36 Herbert to McKee, July 10, August 8, 1878, McKee Papers, Alabama Archives; Ella Herbert to Mrs. [Mark] Lyons, October 1, [1878], Herbert Collection, Alabama Archives.
37 *Troy Messenger*, September 5, 1878.
38 *Greenville Adovcate*, October 3, 1878; *Troy Messenger*, October 24, 1878.

people." His letter closed with the revealing statement, "Political necessity is a strong and exacting demand, and I yield to it under protest."[39]

With the threat from Baltzell out of the way, Herbert had relatively calm sailing. His opponent, the Greenbacker James P. Armstrong, received the support of the Republican machine in Montgomery but suffered an embarrassing blow when the Greenback Club of Butler County, apparently tinged with Bourbonism, came out for Herbert. When the election returns were reported, Herbert had amassed 8,364 votes to 6,505 for Armstrong. The colonel carried every county except Montgomery, which gave him only around 2,000 ballots as compared to 4,000 for the opposition.[40] Even in Pike County, the home of Frank Baltzell, Herbert rolled up a large majority in what *Troy Messenger* chronicled as "the vindication of the grand principles of Caucasian Democracy." The few votes that Armstrong did receive in the county, according to the report, were "at the hands of ignorant and prejudiced Africans manipulated by a few sore-headed white brethren."[41] Commenting also on the returns, the *Greenville Advocate* reported that "the Negroes came up in squads, and nearly all voted as they had been told by Radical leaders, for Mr. Armstrong" and that only a few "honorable exceptions" cast their ballots for Herbert.[42]

In the exciting contest of 1880, Herbert was pitted against none other than Paul Strobach himself, a "carpetbagger" of Austrian descent and a chief leader of the Montgomery Republican machine. The Conservative leadership in the white counties especially was extremely uneasy during this contest, and many of the Democratic papers were warning that only the heaviest turnout in the rest of the district could overcome the certain 4,000-vote majority that the Republicans would roll up in Montgomery. The *Greenville Advocate,* beside itself with alarm, printed such headlines as "Wolf! Wolf! Wolf!" and warned that "even the cold stones would almost rise up and curse us if we let Strobach beat Herbert." Herbert, the paper exclaimed, was an "*honor* to the second district," while Stro-

39 *Troy Enquirer,* September 21, 1878.
40 *Montgomery Advertiser,* November 13, 21, 1878; *Greenville Advocate,* September 19, October 13, 17, and November 14, 1878.
41 *Troy Messenger,* November 14, 1878.
42 *Greenville Advocate,* November 7, 1878.

bach was a "*dishonor* to savages."[43] Interestingly enough, the
leading Bourbon organ in Montgomery was more calm. When
Herbert had been renominated early in August, the *Advertiser*
told its readers that "the nomination of Col. Herbert is equiva-
lent to his election."[44] Although as the election approached
the paper intensified its barrage of insults aimed at Strobach,
the Montgomery party leaders evidently were certain that Herbert could easily defeat any avowed Radical.

The contest was widely reported, even in the North. The
New York Times carried a graphic description of the efforts
of the colonel's supporters to disrupt a rally for Strobach in
Pike County. From the audience the Democrats harassed the
Republican candidate with catcalls and abusive remarks, tried
to drown him out by beating a drum, and even set up a nearby
platform where an auctioneer attempted to lure away the black
audience by distributing candy, pencils, and cheap jewelry.
When all else had failed, the Democrats drove Strobach from
the platform with rotten eggs; and in the ensuing fight, two
Negroes were stabbed and many beaten with clubs.[45]

When the ballots were counted in November, Herbert
emerged with an easy victory, 13,271 votes to 8,884 ballots for
Strobach.[46] In a letter to the *New York Times,* Herbert's opponent charged that the victory had been achieved by wholesale dishonesty and intimidation. The paper's correspondent
affirmed that with "unblushing fraud" the election officials had
counted some 4,000 Republican votes for Herbert. In a number of Republican precincts, the Democratic managers had delayed the voting or simply refused outright to open the polls.
Black voters were threatened with violence and the loss of their
jobs, and in several instances persistent blacks were arbitrarily
arrested for trying to vote.[47]

As a result of the fraud-ridden election of 1880, the seats of
four of the Representatives from Alabama were under dispute;
Herbert's district had not been singular in turmoil at the ballot box. Extensive hearings were conducted by the House Committee on Elections, chaired by William H. Caulkins of In-

---

43 *Ibid.*, October 21, 28, 1880.
44 *Montgomery Advertiser,* August 12, 1880.
45 *New York Times,* October 25, 1880.
46 *Montgomery Advertiser,* November 12, 1880.
47 *New York Times,* November 8, 10, and December 13, 1880.

diana and heavily stacked with Republicans. For reasons which the committee did not publish, after days of hearings and deliberation the body recommended that the seats of Joseph Wheeler and Charles M. Shelley be declared vacant but that Herbert and William C. Oates be allowed to retain their places in the House.[48]

Herbert always considered the campaign of 1882 to be personally the most exciting of his electoral contests. His opponent was Judge Samuel Farrow Rice, one of the most able but most inconsistent men ever to participate in Alabama politics. Rice, a brilliant and witty lawyer, was a former newspaperman, state senator, and chief justice of the State Supreme Court. Although he had been a secessionist in 1861, the judge's political record was spotty. In the early thirties he had been a State Rights Democrat, then a Whig, then a Know-Nothing, then a secessionist in 1861, and a Democrat for Seymour in 1868. Finally in 1869 the judge defected to the Republicans, arguing that the Democracy was incapable of governing for a time and that the only way to assure decent government in Alabama was for good practical men to go into the Republican party and try to control it. Indeed, in 1869 the judge had approached Herbert and asked the young lawyer to join him in entering the Republican ranks.[49]

Although Judge Rice now professed to be a Liberal Republican, he announced that he was entering the race against the colonel as an Independent. In an effort to gain more attention for his own views, Rice invited Herbert to canvass with him jointly so that the people might hear both men in debate on the same platform.[50] Although Rice was reputed to be "the wittiest man in Alabama," Herbert readily accepted the challenge to the joint appearances. The judge, in spite of his toying with the Republicans, was considered an honest, respectable man.

48 Chester H. Rowell, ed., *A Historical and Legal Digest of All the Contested Election Cases in the House of Representatives of the United States from the First to the Fifty-Sixth Congress, 1789-1901* (Washington, Government Printing Office, 1901), pp. 262-268. For the testimony in the Herbert-Strobach case, an emotion-packed document of 413 pages, see *House Miscellaneous Documents,* 47th Cong., 1st Sess., No. 17.

49 Herbert, "Reminiscences," pp. 261-262; Herbert, "Additions to 1903 Memoirs," 1917, Vol. 6, Herbert Papers; Sarah Van Woolfolk, "Five Men Called Scalawags," *Alabama Review* 17 (January, 1964): pp. 47-49; Going, *Bourbon Democracy in Alabama,* pp. 51-52.

50 *Greenville Advocate,* October 5, 1882.

Herbert later confessed, "I was afraid to let Judge Rice canvass by himself; he would get audiences that no other Republican speaker could draw and might do damage if no one should be there to answer him."[51] In spite of Rice's intellectual and rhetorical prowess, Herbert was able to hammer again and again on the judge's most vulnerable spot. One paper described the failure of Rice's strategy:

> His game is one at which two can play, and Herbert is playing it for all it is worth. Herbert repels his opponent's attacks and then turns his attention to that opponent's own record. Rice's glaring inconsistencies are shown up. He is described now as a Whig, now as a Know-Nothing, now as a red-hot Democrat, unwilling to be reconstructed, and in these latter days as a straight Republican with Independent variations.[52]

On one occasion Herbert assured his audience that Judge Rice could not be completely mistaken in his politics since he had been "a member of every political party that ever existed in the state of Alabama during his residence here, and that he therefore must have been right at some time or other."[53]

Once again the standard of party unity was hoisted. Rice's status as an Independent was seriously damaged when the Montgomery Republicans, including one Negro, issued a signed circular endorsing his candidacy. The *Montgomery Advertiser* continually harped on the race theme. In reporting a debate in the city between Herbert and his opponent, the paper observed that it was "evident that Judge Rice was sustained by the body of negroes and Federal officials while Col. Herbert had the sympathy of the great body of white people." A week before the election the *Advertiser* flatly branded Rice the "negro supremacy candidate"; and when the judge protested that the Herbert forces were stirring up sectionalism and racism, the paper dismissed the charge as "nauseating." When the ballots were counted in November, the colonel received approximately 12,000 votes to defeat Judge Rice by around 3,000 ballots. As usual, the Montgomery machine returned ballots two to one favoring Herbert's opponent.[54] In regular fashion,

---

51 Herbert, "Reminiscences," pp. 261-262.
52 *Greenville Advocate*, October 5, 1882.
53 Herbert, "Reminiscences," p. 263.
54 *Montgomery Advertiser*, October 1, 27, November 5, 1882; *Greenville Advocate*, November 15, 1882.

the "Solid South" was kept intact in the Second Congressional District.

With his triumph over Judge Rice, Herbert appeared virtually unbeatable. The elections of 1884, 1886, and 1888 went off without serious challenge. In 1886 one paper reported, "Very few negro votes were cast and the whites were so well assured of the result that only a few appeared at the polls."[55] Herbert's own campaign expenses remained low; he was proud that he was never forced to buy any votes, a practice that later became quite common in the district.[56] It was only in 1890 that Herbert was again challenged. At that time he met the most severe test of his entire career in Alabama politics, a story which is reserved for the last section of this chapter.

III

Except for insight into the style of one particular Bourbon leader and for affairs in the Second Congressional District, a study of Herbert's career touches only rarely on state politics in Alabama. Aware that his concentration would have to be on national rather than regional affairs if he were ever to have any influence in the Congress, Herbert made a conscious effort to avoid the rough and tumble of state politics. Although he constantly worked at keeping his political fences in repair, he usually refrained from being drawn into controversial issues of purely local concern. His policy occasionally elicited criticism from those who wanted him to speak out, such as in 1882 when the *Evergreen News* supported Judge Rice because the colonel refused to take a stand on the present state election laws to which the paper was opposed.[57]

Hilary Herbert arrived in Washington in the fall of 1877, accompanied by his wife Ella and his two daughters, Leila, then nine years old, and Ella, seven. He established the family in comfortable quarters in a boarding house, an inexpensive accommodation similar to that rented by many congressmen of limited means. Ella helped save expenses also by acting as a part-time secretary. The first year in the capital was brightened

---

[55] *Greenville Advocate,* November 10, 1886.
[56] Herbert, "Reminiscences," p. 287.
[57] Reported in the *Greenville Advocate,* October 26, 1882.

by the birth of a son, christened at Ella's insistence Hilary Abner Herbert, Jr.[58]

Herbert took his seat in the House of Representatives on October 15, 1877, at the special session of the 45th Congress. Washington still buzzed with the talk of the bitter presidential electoral dispute between Rutherford B. Hayes and Samuel J. Tilden that had occurred only a few months earlier. Many Democrats in the House of Representatives were still extremely bitter over the outcome of the election. Interestingly enough, Herbert found that his southern colleagues, many of them ex-Confederates, were for the most part reconciled to the settlement and were visibly relieved that it had transpired without violence. Herbert personally never harbored any ill feelings toward the Hayes administration, and in later years he described it as "patriotic, clean and perfectly honest."[59]

Like the careers of most congressmen, Herbert's tenure in the House began in inauspicious fashion. Informed that freshmen representatives were to be seen and not heard, he meekly took his seat in the back and listened as the veterans conducted the business. As did every other new legislator, he quickly learned that his constituents at home demanded a great deal of his time; and he soon found himself answering letters, filing petitions and requests for claims and pensions, mailing seeds and documents, and performing chores and favors in different governmental departments. He was not too busy, however, to join in the social life of the capital city. He and Ella became well-known figures at dances, receptions, the theater, and parties of various sorts.[60]

The happy times of the early days of Herbert's years in Washington did not last indefinitely. Always inclined to be sickly, Ella Herbert, after an extended illness, died in 1885 of a lung infection. Herbert was reported to be "well-nigh inconsolable"; and by his own admission it took him two years to recover from her loss. He later wrote, "From my election to Congress in 1876 until her death, at Washington, March 14,

---

58 Herbert to Susan Parker Smith, October 10, 1877, and [April, 1878]; Ella Herbert to Susan Parker Smith, April 13 [1878], all in Washington M. Smith Papers; Herbert, "Reminiscences," p. 247.

59 Herbert, "Reminiscences," pp. 248-254; *Congressional Record*, 45th Cong., 1st Sess. (1877), pp. 50-51.

60 Emma Francis Lee Smith, "Personal Recollections of a Noble Man," *Confederate Veteran* 27 (July, 1919): pp. 246-248; Herbert, "Reminiscences," p. 255.

1885, no constituent ever came to my house or met her in Washington or elsewhere, without being a better friend of mine for it."[61]

The years in which Herbert served in the Congress, 1877-1893, have not been noted by historians for the quality of their political life. The record is clear that many contemporaries as well as later writers found little to admire in most of the public men of the time. The Russian lawyer and political scientist Moisei Ostrogorski, who visited frequently in the two decades after 1880, came to the conclusion after observing American politicians that "ideas, convictions, character, disqualify a man from public life."[62]

The Democratic party had won control of the House of Representatives in 1874 and retained a majority after the election of 1876. During the eight congresses in which Herbert served, 1877-1893, the Democrats kept control of the House during six of his terms while the Republican party was able to organize the chamber only in the 47th Congress (1881-1883) and in the 51st Congress (1889-1891). The Senate remained Republican—but usually only by the barest majorities—throughout the period, except during the second half of the Hayes administration, 1879-1881. On the executive side during the period, the Democratic party won the presidency only twice with the triumphs of Grover Cleveland. No president of the time, however, from Hayes to the end of Cleveland's second administration (1893-1897) had a full term in which his party was in control of both branches of Congress. Although Leonard D. White has called his masterful administrative history of the period *The Republican Era*,[63] the point is that neither of the two parties enjoyed a commanding position in federal politics during these years. Whether of shoddy or distinguished character, the public policy of the time was of necessity bipartisan.

Congressional politics of the period consisted in large measure of histrionics, sectional denunciation, and hot air. Very little of this verbiage was expended on meaningful issues or on relevant remedies for the myriad problems that beset the coun-

---

[61] *Greenville Advocate*, March 18, 1885; Herbert, "Reminiscences," p. 240.

[62] Quoted in John A. Garraty, *The New Commonwealth, 1877-1890* (New York, Harper & Row, Publishers, 1968), pp. 220-222.

[63] White, *The Republican Era: A Study in Administrative History, 1869-1901* (New York, Macmillan Company, 1958).

try. It was not, however, that the politicos of the times were on the average less intelligent, conscientious, or moral than those of other days. Professor John A. Garraty has explained one problem that they faced:

> The parties, closely balanced, hesitated to take clear positions on controversial questions lest by so doing they destroy the precarious balance of power. New voters found no compelling reason not to identify with the parties of their parents or, in the case of immigrants, with the party that their local compatriots appeared to prefer. These conditions produced "the most spectacular degree of equilibrium in American history." Control of Congress and the White House shifted back and forth, not because of drastic alterations in voter opinion, but because the balance between the parties was so delicate that minor changes and chance events easily tipped it one way or the other.[64]

The House of Representatives was especially noted for its ineffectiveness. In reading through the record of the debates, even the student familiar with scandalously ineffective practices and procedures in our present-day Congress cannot help but be amazed at the confusion, commotion, obstruction, and general lack of serious purpose which animated the daily routine of the lower chamber. Time for debate was extremely limited; and, therefore, most important business was worked out in committee. The chairmen of the few important committees were the most powerful men in Congress; and because of the press of business, they were sometimes able to railroad through even the most comprehensive bills with little debate.

In this process that many historians have considered for the most part a continuous parade of irrelevancies, the most insignificant and uninfluential of all the marchers were the men from Dixie. The southern representatives were always at the center of the continuing sectional debate, the most irrelevant and yet the most frequently discussed of all the issues in these years. Dubbed the "Confederate Brigadiers," they were often the butt of ridicule and of vicious recrimination concerning their personal loyalty to the nation.[65]

---

64 Garraty, *The New Commonwealth*, p. 226.
65 Theodore Clarke Smith, *The Life and Letters of James Abram Garfield* (New Haven, Yale University Press, 1925) 2: p. 657.

As late as 1905, Philip Alexander Bruce wrote of the poor quality of internal southern politics and the continued decline of southern influence in national affairs. Bruce attributed the eclipse of southern leadership to three factors: (1) the destruction as a result of the Civil War of the old "rural gentry" from whom so many statesmen had come; (2) the distraction of the race issue, subordinating every other consideration; (3) the tendency for young men to choose business or education rather than politics as a profession.[66] Five years later William Garrott Brown penned a devastating critique of the problem. The South, Brown contended, had spent the half-century since the Civil War in "political isolation." Brown asserted:

> Even the fact that the South has had, since Reconstruction, its fair proportional representation in Congress, may be misleading. For the South has not had the actual weight in legislation which the fact might indicate. Southern men in Congress have not had as much power as men from other quarters. Most of the time, the party to which all but a few of them have belonged has been in the minority. When it has controlled one house, it has seldom had either the other or the presidency. . . . Moreover, whether in the majority or the minority, and whether as individuals or as a group, Southerners in Congress have not exercized such power as they did before the war. They have not seemed to feel that they had full freedom of initiative. Certainly, they have not often taken the initiative effectively. If for fifty years there has been a single great general law or policy initiated by Southerners or a Southerner, or which goes or should go by any Southerner's name, the fact escapes me.

Brown contended that only a small part of the reason for the South's poor showing was the natural desire of northerners to remain in the ascendancy. The roots of the problem, he stated, lay in the region itself: illiteracy and ignorance; poverty (the lack of the "political leverage of wealth"); and the "Negro problem," which shackled the minds of southerners and incessantly gnawed away at their spirits, making them less free and, therefore, weak.[67]

---

66 Bruce, *The Rise of the New South* (Philadelphia, George Barrie & Sons, 1905), p. 443.

67 William Garrott Brown, "The South in National Politics," *South Atlantic Quarterly* 9 (April, 1910): pp. 103-115.

It was under this severe sectional handicap that Hilary Herbert entered Congress in 1877. The Alabamian embarked upon his duties with a dual purpose constantly in mind. First, he determined to work for sectional reconciliation; but second and even more important, this reunion would have to come on terms acceptable to the South—in particular, the right to deal with the race issue in its own way. Herbert later recorded:

> During my public life, twenty years at Washington, my prime purpose was, and I never lost sight of it, the recovery by the Southern States of their autonomy—the right to govern themselves, which as a result of the civil war and by the Republican plan of Reconstruction, they had practically lost.

Herbert realized, of course, that "home rule" (his symbol for white supremacy) and sectional reunion were inseparable corollaries. He counseled fellow southerners to refrain, even under the severest provocation, from intemperate responses which might alienate northern opinion. Recalling his own record in a moment of self-indulgence, he boasted, "I pride myself on the fact, in which I will be sustained by the *Congressional Record,* that at no time did I ever utter any word or sentences in debate, or indeed while I was in public office, that was calculated to keep alive sectional strife."[68]

Because the Democrats controlled the House of Representatives during much of this period, it was in the lower chamber that southerners (who made up the largest part of the party's voting bloc in Congress) could play an enlarged and meaningful role in federal politics. Two southerners, John G. Carlisle of Kentucky and Charles F. Crisp of Georgia, held the coveted position of Speaker during portions of Herbert's tenure in the House, although neither man was noted for the control that he exercised over the assembly. It seems safe to assert as axiomatic that southern influence in the House increased in proportion to the increase of years since the events of the war and Reconstruction. For example, in 1886 the *New York Times* reported that of the 184 Democrats in the House, 108 were from the South. The southerners held the chairmanships of nearly two-thirds of the committees. On the more important committees, of the seventy-seven Democratic members, forty-

---

68 Herbert, "Reminiscences," pp. 2-4.

seven were from the South as opposed to twenty from the West and ten from New England.[69]

Like those of most new congressmen, Hilary Herbert's committee assignments in the early years in the capitol were of little consequence. By the end of 1883 when the 48th Congress met, Herbert had evidently proved his capability and loyalty and had been accepted as a party regular by the leadership. In return for his support of John G. Carlisle (whose views on tariff reform paralleled those of the colonel) for the speakership, the Alabamian was rewarded with his first assignment to a prestigious committee, the powerful Committee on Ways and Means. A roll call of the group included the names of some of the most important public men of the time: William R. Morrison of Illinois, James H. Blount of Georgia, Abram S. Hewitt of New York, William McKinley of Ohio, Thomas B. Reed of Maine, and John A. Kasson of Iowa. Ironically, Herbert's two years on the Ways and Means Committee were among the most uneventful of his tenure in the House. Finally, in 1885 at the start of the 49th Congress, Herbert assumed the chairmanship of the Committee on Naval Affairs, an assignment which occupied practically all of his attention in the following eight years.[70]

Undoubtedly it was Herbert's temperate manner and conciliatory attitude that allowed him to move gradually to the front ranks of the House leadership. Although he studiously avoided agitating the sectional issue merely for spite, he was constantly on the lookout for ways to undo some of the damage which he felt that the war and Reconstruction had inflicted upon his region. Along with other southerners he worked ceaselessly (although without conspicuous success) to repeal legislation that allegedly bore inequitably on the South in the matter of jury laws, the conduct of federal marshals, and the allotment of veterans' pensions.

By far the most explosive sectional measure to come before the House during Herbert's tenure in office was the Lodge Election Bill in 1890. The measure, which has been discussed at some length in the fourth chapter, occasioned the publication of the book *Why the Solid South?* of which Herbert was

---

69 *New York Times*, February 17, 1886.

70 *Congressional Record*, 48th Cong., 1st Sess. (1883-1884), p. 223; 49th Cong., 1st Sess. (1885-1886), p. 538. See also the *New York Times*, December 25, 1883.

the editor and chief contributor. The political and propagandistic nature of the book is best illustrated by the appearance of at least four of its chapters in the *Congressional Record* during the House debates. In spite of the considerable time demanded by Herbert's extensive writing and editorial activities, the Alabamian also found time to take the floor of the House himself to denounce the Force Bill as a return to Reconstruction, a revival of sectionalism and bloody shirt politics, and a renewal of northern occupation.[71]

Actually, Herbert spent very little time on sectional legislation, preferring instead to give most of his attention to issues of national scope. Aside from his reputation as a champion of the Navy, Herbert was best known in the Congress as a persistent crusader for limited, economical, and efficient government.

In the very first Congress in which he served, Herbert staked out his ideological position in such dramatic fashion that he created, for a freshman congressman at least, a minor sensation. The occasion was the colonel's speech during the lengthy debate over Tom Scott's Texas and Pacific Railroad, a question which many considered one of the most important to come before the 45th Congress.[72] The railroad venture had been launched in 1872 when Scott, then president of the Pennsylvania Railroad, began laying in Texas tracks that were eventually to reach the Pacific to challenge the transcontinental monopoly of the Union Pacific and Central Pacific lines. The doughty entrepreneur managed to secure in excess of 16,000,000 acres of public land in California, Arizona, and New Mexico along the proposed route of the road and, additionally, to finagle large land grants and a $6,000,000 bond issue from the Texas legislature. With the panic of 1873, however, the project ran onto hard times; and chief engineer Grenville M. Dodge was forced to halt construction. Faced with certain financial disaster without federal aid to bail out the enterprise, Scott and Dodge embarked on a whirlwind campaign to mobilize public opinion in the South in support of a subsidy. Glowing

---

71 *Congressional Record*, 51st Cong., 1st Sess. (1889-1890), pp. 6761-6768. The chapters of *Why the Solid South?* that appear are Herbert's general essay and those on Georgia, Arkansas, and Texas; see pages 6715-6720, 6775-6779, 6806-6810.

72 *New York Times*, February 22, 1878.

propaganda releases projected at least four branches of the line to run eastward from the Mississippi terminus in order to catch votes in most southern congressional districts. The Old Guard was not neglected; Scott obtained endorsements from Jefferson Davis, Alexander Stephens, and General Beauregard.[73]

The tribulations of the Texas and Pacific, made famous by Professor C. Vann Woodward's *Reunion and Reaction,* are well known to students of American history. In brief, Woodward concluded that the Great Compromise of 1877 had been achieved because a group of southern Democrats, as a result of clandestine agreement with the Hayes forces, acquiesced in the decision of the electoral commission to award the disputed presidential election of 1876 to the Republican contender rather than to Samuel J. Tilden. The political commitment of the southern side included the completion of the electoral count for Rutherford B. Hayes, the election of James A. Garfield as Speaker of the narrowly Democratic House of Representatives, and a vague pledge to work for a strong Republican organization in the South under conservative (mostly former Whig) leadership. Aside from the removal of the last federal troops from the South and a southern representative in the cabinet (policies Tilden would have implemented anyway), the Hayes managers implied to the southerners that they could count on Republican support for a large program of internal improvements, specifically to include a subsidy for the Texas and Pacific Railroad.[74]

The Redeemers apparently took the president's initial encouragement seriously. In three months in 1877, they introduced 267 subsidy bills in the House of Representatives and forty in the Senate.[75] Scott and Dodge met with marvelous success in depicting their scheme as a "southern measure" in the capital-hungry region. Hilary Herbert later recalled the feeling in the South:

> There was scarcely a town or city in all the Southern States that was not to be greatly benefited by having the riches of China and Japan, teas, silks, etc., pouring into and through it in great train-loads, spreading everywhere the blessings of trade.

---

[73] Woodward, *Origins of the New South,* pp. 31-34.
[74] Woodward, *Reunion and Reaction: The Compromise of 1877 and the End of Reconstruction* (Garden City, Doubleday & Company, Inc., 1951), pp. 166-185.
[75] *Ibid.,* p. 253.

Congress had subsidized a transcontinental road for the North;
now was to come the turn of the South.

Nevertheless, as the subsidy bills piled high in the House hop-
pers and the petitions favoring the Texas and Pacific scheme
rolled in from his district, Hilary Herbert became increasingly
uneasy. After weeks of mental agony he determined that conscience demanded that he speak out on the issue; and because
Speaker Samuel Randall also objected to the subsidy, Herbert
was given his opportunity.[76]

On June 6, 1878, Herbert took the floor of the House, os-
tensibly to speak in the general debate on a routine deficiency
appropriations bill. To the shock of those present, the Alabamian addressed himself to the subject of the Texas and
Pacific Railroad. Asserting that his purpose was to answer the
arguments that so many other southern Democrats had advanced for the railroad, the colonel launched a merciless attack
on the idea that the scheme was a southern measure. Tom Scott
was a Pennsylvanian, he pointed out, as were the first vice-
president, the secretary, the treasurer, and six of the fifteen
directors. Of the other directors, three were from New York
and one each was from Ohio, Maryland, California, Tennessee,
Kentucky, and Texas. The chief engineer hailed from Iowa,
and the executive offices of the corporation were in Philadelphia. It was absurd, Herbert argued, to call the project a
southern measure when few southerners owned any stock at
all and none would handle any of the money. Herbert then
trained his guns on Tom Scott's record as a manipulator and
monopolist and ridiculed as ludicrous the notion that the entrepreneur's altruistic motive was to break down the monopoly
of the Union Pacific Railroad and thus assure competition in
transcontinental traffic. Herbert listed over eighteen separate
lines which Scott's Pennsylvania Railroad controlled with "tentacles all over the Northwest" and suggested that Scott, one of
the greatest monopolists in the nation, was a strange convert
indeed to the idea of free competition.

The political transparency of the scheme infuriated Herbert
the most. Tom Scott, he asserted, was playing the southern
people for dupes. In all his propaganda, the railroad baron had
steadfastly refused to fix the exact point of the Mississippi ter-

---

76 Herbert, "Reminiscences," pp. 255-256.

minus of the line in order to keep up the hopes of the people of virtually every congressional district that one of the eastern spurs might come near them. The Alabamian also pointed out that Scott had made no plans for a bridge across the Mississippi. Herbert then aired his suspicions that, once the subsidy was approved, Scott would tie in the Texas and Pacific with the rest of the Pennsylvania system at St. Louis. In short, the railroad might not even come near the South. Herbert explained:

> Although the company does not own or profess that it will own a foot of road in the Southern States east of the Mississippi; although its track is of a different gauge from the southern roads; although it does not propose to bridge the Mississippi, yet today it is being heralded throughout the South as a great transcontinental southern railway.

Herbert then acknowledged that he was painfully aware of the overwhelming sentiment in his own district supporting the scheme and also readily admitted that he was disobeying the request of the Alabama legislature that he vote for it. Nevertheless, he explained, behind all the arguments that he had already marshalled against the measure was a matter of principle. Concluding his remarks with a lecture on the functions of democratic government, the colonel elaborated a strong personal conviction that he would take throughout his remaining years in public life. He explained:

> One of the things government ought not to do is to tax one portion of its people for the benefit of another—take A's money without his consent and expend it for the benefit of B. I believe the Government should clean out its rivers and harbors. They belong to the public. Every man has equal rights upon them. They can never become enemies of the Government. But to tax the people for the benefit of the owners of a railroad corporation is another thing. It is to take the people's money and give it to private individuals.

The building of a railroad, Herbert argued, was the business of private enterprise. The pursuit of federal subsidies for such projects had already turned the legislative function into a "game of grab." His final thoughts were directed to fellow southerners:

> Sir, we have something else to do besides resting in fancied security and talking about which section has had the lion's

share of public plunder. The Government was never made to
be plundered or to be the means of plundering its people.
It was not made to build railroads by taxing the many for the
benefit of the few. It was not made to build great works to
testify like the pyramids of Egypt to the powers of the rulers
and the slavery of the people. When it becomes perverted to
these ends, farewell to liberty.[77]

Understandably, many of Herbert's southern colleagues were
not impressed favorably with his remarks. The next day, Representative James R. Chalmers of Mississippi entered into the
record a searing attack on the freshman congressman. Rebuking
the Alabamian for pretending to know more about the sentiments of the southern people than the veteran legislators from
the region, Chalmers chided, "If he seeks national fame at the
expense of our section, let him answer that to his own constituents. Time will tell which of us has represented best the
interests and sentiments of our people." The attack by Chalmers
not only left Herbert unbowed but also called even more attention to his speech than it was already receiving.[78]

News of Herbert's speech created general and outspoken indignation in his district in Alabama. A vengeful Tom Scott sent
two lobbyists into the Second District who were able to get two-
thirds of the leading men to sign a petition demanding that
their congressman change his mind. For his part, Herbert immediately had hundreds of printed copies of his remarks distributed throughout the district and then returned home to
man the parapets in person.[79] Once the people had time to read
the colonel's eminently sensible remarks, the abuse gradually
ceased. Opinion began to shift markedly to his side. Charles C.
Langdon, the respected former mayor of Mobile, publicly
praised Herbert's "moral courage" for standing by his convictions in the face of overwhelming public pressure.[80] By the
middle of July, Herbert was able to write to his wife in light-
hearted fashion from the town of Pollard, "My T & P speech
has had great effect here. The people are with me it seems

---

77 *Congressional Record*, 45th Cong., 2nd Sess. (1877-1878), pp. 4210-4216.

78 *Ibid.*, 45th Cong., 2nd Sess., Appendix, p. 246. *Washington Post*, June 7, 1878.

79 Herbert to Robert McKee, July 10, August 8, 1878, McKee Papers.

80 *Montgomery Advertiser*, September 21, 1878.

unanimously. One old gentleman of fine intelligence wants to vote for me for President."[81]

A brief glance at Herbert's district in Alabama during the Texas and Pacific crisis is fascinating. Illustrative of the nature of regional politics and of how the "Solid South" worked is the shifting position of the *Montgomery Advertiser* during the agitation over the railroad scheme. William W. Screws, the editor of this leading Bourbon daily, had been an enthusiastic booster of the Scott plan. In January, 1877, Screws promised that the Texas and Pacific would "bring the rich resources and immense natural wealth of the South into direct and close communication with the markets of the world." Even the construction of the road itself, Screws argued editorially, would be a vital stimulus to many lagging southern industries.[82] In June, however, it became Screws's embarrassing duty to report that his paper's favorite congressman had just delivered a damning speech opposing the railroad subsidy. The editor was obviously keenly diappointed but manged to take a sporting tone about the conflict. The *Advertiser* observed that Herbert was "decidedly wrong" but at the same time called the colonel's address a magnificent speech that exhibited "careful preparation" and was, in fact, the "very best one that has been made against the road."[83]

The agony of the *Montgomery Advertiser* was greatly compounded by time and circumstance. Herbert's surprising remarks had come just five months before the congressional elections of 1878. With the time for balloting perilously close, the last thing the Democratic party needed was a bitter internecine feud over a transcontinental railroad. When the colonel was renominated in August, the *Advertiser* omitted any mention of the railroad controversy and pronounced Herbert a "safe, sound legislator." A month later the paper dutifully backed off from its support for the Texas and Pacific scheme, voicing its suspicion that involved were "adroit and skillful manipulators" who were laboring on behalf of "Eastern interests." Herbert's opposition to the plan, the paper now advised, showed "how

---

81 Herbert to Ella Herbert, July 9 [1878], Washington M. Smith Papers.
82 *Montgomery Advertiser*, January 20, 1877.
83 *Ibid.*, June 19, 1878.

scrupulously and ceaselessly he watches the interest of his constituents."[84]

The truth did not come out until the rival *Troy Enquirer*, edited by Frank Baltzell, began to taunt the *Advertiser* for its inconsistent support of Herbert in view of its earlier stance on the railroad controversy. The pained reply out of Montgomery is especially revealing. Wallace Screws admitted frankly that he favored a transcontinental railroad by a southern route —by the Texas and Pacific scheme if it were honest and if not by some other plan. Nevertheless, the editorial continued, the railroad was not of "paramount importance." More important at the time was the unity of the Democratic party. Should that solidarity be broken, the paper solemnly intoned, then the darkness of Reconstruction might descend upon the South once more. With graphic images the editorial continued:

> The bayonet, with its banner of blood, will again step to the front. Rings and rascals of every grade will, like Egyptian locusts, cover the entire land, and the TOM SCOTTS and HUNTINGTONS and their schemes will be as specks upon the wall, compared with the distress of the people.[85]

In accordance with its policy, the *Advertiser* also suppressed until after the November election a letter rebutting Herbert's arguments from John C. Brown, a vice president of the Texas and Pacific Railway Company. Nor is it surprising to note that within a month and a half after Herbert was re-elected the paper once again gave the Texas and Pacific plan its strong endorsement.[86]

The incident of the Texas and Pacific speech is significant for several reasons. First, it presents the fascinating example of one Bourbon politician who was adamantly opposed to a major part of the Redeemer compromise of 1877. It shows also that the present-day historian ought not to let his fascination with Professor Woodward's brilliant reconstruction of evidence in *Reunion and Reaction* obscure the recognition that what is common knowledge to us was not commonly known at the time.

---

84 *Ibid.*, September 21, 1878.
85 *Ibid.*, October 1, 1878.
86 *Ibid.*, November 7, December 17, 1878.

Like most southerners, Hilary Herbert evidently did not know about the "Great Compromise" either in detail or in broad outline. In Hilary Herbert's case, at least, considering his philosophical objections it is doubtful that he would have approved even had he been apprised of the complex, secret arrangement. In the Second District of Alabama, moreover, Herbert's point of view won out. Public opinion dramatically swung to his side, and even those who disagreed with him could hardly help but admire his courage. The colonel undoubtedly felt vindicated when he won re-election for a second term. When the railroad was completed several years later (with private funds), as Herbert had predicted, it did not come close to the district. Finally, the speech was important as Herbert's first major statement in public life concerning his philosophy of government. He would carry these old-line conservative principles with him until the day of his death in 1919.

Herbert's attack on the railroad subsidy was only the beginning of a consistent assault on all subsidy legislation throughout his congressional career. For example, on a number of occasions he strongly condemned shipping bills that proposed to provide substantial bounties to shipbuilding corporations for enlarging the American merchant marine. Although Herbert enthusiastically favored a strong merchant fleet, he believed that private enterprise and not the government should construct it. He lamented that special interests were trying to extend to the sea the very same system which he believed had been so harmful on land. In the 51st Congress he denounced one shipping bill as typical of Republican policy and contrasted it with his own faith:

> I stand upon the doctrines of the old Democratic party. . . . That party demands equal and exact justice to all men and special favors to none. The Democrat who does not plant himself here, he who departs from this great foundation principle, he who demands for any set or class of men privileges or favors from the government can not stand here as I stand, and as I have always stood, denouncing any and all legislation that takes the fruits of one man's labor and gives it to another.[87]

---

[87] *Congressional Record,* 51st Cong., 2nd Sess. (1890-1891), Appendix, pp. 19-24; 47th Cong., 2nd Sess. (1882-1883), pp. 1020-1025.

During the congressional years, Herbert's most sustained criticism was leveled at the subsidy that he considered to be the most gigantic and unconscionable of all, the tariff. Although he accepted the traditional Democratic goal of a "tariff for revenue only," for Herbert opposition to prohibitive duties was more than merely a partisan issue. At stake again were foundation principles of government. The federal government, he believed, should no more subsidize great corporations through the tariff than it should build transcontinental railroads for the South. The Alabamian argued on a number of occasions (although never with notable success) that the nation's industries were no longer in need of excessive tariff protection. In the final analysis, he argued, it was the little man, the consumer, who was hurt when prohibitive duties increased the prices that he had to pay for manufactured goods.[88]

In only one minor incident did Herbert depart from his strict adherence to *laissez faire* government. In April, 1886, in the wake of devastating floods throughout parts of rural Alabama, Herbert introduced a joint resolution calling for an appropriation of $150,000 to aid distressed and displaced families. Herbert's own district had been hit especially hard. Although the great majority of the sufferers were Negroes, pleas had come to Congress from groups of both white and black citizens. Arguing that the sufferers were unable to cope with the emergency by private resources, the colonel joined with his colleague William H. Forney, also from the state, in pushing for an emergency appropriation. Unfortunately in this case, racism triumphed over humanity. Another Alabamian, William C. Oates, took the floor and insisted that conditions in the state were not nearly as bad as Herbert and Forney had pretended. He then offered several newspaper editorials supporting his view that federal aid would do more harm than good by demoralizing the Negro laborers who would simply cease work and live off government handouts. When Oates suggested that Herbert's position tainted the purity of his constitutional faith, the colonel hotly retorted that in the face of brutal suffering he did not intend to be "more rigid in the construction of the Constitution than John C.

---

88 *Ibid.*, 47th Cong., 1st Sess. (1881-1882), pp. 3520-3526. See also 48th Cong., 1st Sess., pp. 3226-3232; 50th Cong., 1st Sess. (1887-1888). Appendix, pp. 571-578; and 51st Cong., 1st Sess., pp. 5038-5045.

Calhoun," who had always supported this kind of legislation. To Herbert's dismay, he was never able to push the measure through over Oates's protestations.[89]

To Hilary Herbert, good government was not only limited but was also economical. Early in his career he established himself as a sharp-eyed watchdog of the public purse. He warmly praised Grover Cleveland's determination to hold down federal spending and was always among those who sustained the president's vetoes of extravagant projects and pensions. Within the House, the colonel's reputation for parsimony was almost legendary. His philosophy of limited, economical government is perhaps best illustrated by his attack on the United States Geological Survey. In 1884 the Alabamian was appointed to membership on a joint congressional commission, headed by Senator W. B. Allison of Iowa, to investigate and report on the Signal Service, the Coast and Geodetic Survey, the Geological Survey, and the Hydrographic Office of the Navy Department. The investigation lasted more than two years, and accounts of hearings filled 1,200 pages of printed testimony. Before the matter was put aside, Hilary Herbert almost singlehandedly created the most severe crisis in the history of one of the bureaus.[90]

It was the Geological Survey of the Department of Interior that gave the colonel the most concern. Since its founding in 1879, the Survey had mushroomed from a staff of forty scientists to around 200 men and had steadily increased the scope of its operations at an annual cost of around $500,000. When the Cleveland administration assumed office in 1885, however, the Survey came under careful scrutiny. As one historian has noted, "Cleveland Democracy was restrictive in its attitude toward federal bureaus, advocating frugality and hoping for as little government as possible." It is not surprising that men of this conservative stripe should come into profound disagreement with those who hoped for an expansive program of government science. The president himself was notably unenthusiastic about the work of the Geological Survey in particular.[91]

---

89 *Ibid.*, 49th Cong., 1st Sess., pp. 3208, 3216, 3585-3589.

90 *Ibid.*, 48th Cong., 1st Sess., p. 6174. For the complete transcript of the committee hearings see *Senate Miscellaneous Documents*, 49th Cong., 1st Sess., No. 82.

91 Thomas G. Manning, *Government in Science: The U.S. Geological Survey, 1867-1894* (Lexington, University of Kentucky Press, 1967), pp. 122-127. This

Hilary Herbert summed up his own attitude to O. C. Marsh, a survey paleontologist:

I am radically democratic in my views; I believe in as little government as possible—that Government should keep its hands off and allow the individual fair play. This is the doctrine I learned from Adam Smith & Mill & Buckle, from Jefferson, Benton, and Calhoun.[92]

On behalf of the joint investigative committee in May, 1886, Herbert submitted a report to the Congress that severely criticized the operations of the Survey; and in June, he sought to have an appropriation of $400,000 for the bureau slashed by $25,000. Additionally, he proposed that the Survey be limited by law to its original work of classification of public lands, examination of national mineral resources, and preparation of geological maps. The bureau, he exclaimed, had moved into the realm of pure science with its publications on "living oysters," "birds with teeth," volcanoes in the Sandwich Islands, and at least five different books on the Comstock Lode alone. Such studies, Herbert argued, were more properly the task of the universities and private scholars. Although there was little evidence to support his charge, Herbert maintained that the Geological Survey was becoming a powerful political organization, reaching out to control scientific inquiry into geology all over the country.[93]

The colonel's attack on the Survey brought down on his head a storm of protest from the scientific community. The influential magazine *Science* predicted distaster for the Survey should Herbert's views prevail. The work of the bureau was also capably defended by its director J. W. Powell, who cogently argued that the record was perfectly clear that private scholars had not rushed to take up this vital work in the past nor was there any reason to think that in the future any group of men with the inclination, dedication, and financial resources would be willing to assume the effort. Before the episode was over, Herbert's opponents had managed to label him an anti-intellectual sensa-

---

excellent monograph contains a full account of the controversy from the point of view of the Survey.

92 Quoted in *ibid.*, p. 133.

93 *Congressional Record*, 49th Cong., 1st Sess., pp. 6295-6300. For Herbert's report see *House of Representatives Reports*, 49th Cong., 1st Sess., No. 2214.

tionalist. Although every member of the investigating committee had originally agreed with many of Herbert's criticisms of the Survey, in the aftermath of the scientists' uproar only Senator John Tyler Morgan, also of Alabama, was willing to sign his colleague's report. Other congressmen rallied to the side of the Geological Survey and, ironically, the episode only augmented its influence and assured its status as a permanent government agency.[94] Undaunted, Herbert continued in future congresses to try to reduce the scope of the bureau's activities. In 1892 he won a minor victory for his philosophy of government when he managed to have the Survey's appropriation reduced to stop its work in paleontology.[95]

The contemporary reader, accustomed to the almost infinite scope of governmental science today, will undoubtedly see as quaint and, perhaps, amusing Herbert's attempts to station himself foresquare in the path of progress to block the onward march of science and history. Wallace Stegner, a professor of English who has written on the Survey, describes the colonel as an "anti-intellectual States' rights politician" whose attacks on the bureau "do not give him a high rating for prophecy, or even for intelligence."[96] The historian, however, must make an effort to view an historical figure in the context of his own time and values. Herbert was neither anti-intellectual nor anti-scientific. Speaking at the University of Virginia in 1887, he advocated increased public assistance to the universities so that they, rather than government bureaus, could carry on scientific research. It was precisely because Herbert had impressive intellectual credentials of his own that his attacks struck so much fear in the scientific community and could not be simply ignored or brushed aside. His presentations were inevitably based on careful research and were cogently presented. Senator Matthew Ransom of North Carolina on one occasion described the colonel as the "best scholar in the House of Representatives."[97] What was at stake for the Alabamian in this controversy

[94] Manning, *Government in Science,* pp. 134-150.

[95] *Ibid.,* pp. 206-209; *Congressional Record,* 52nd Cong., 1st Sess. (1891-1892), pp. 4389-4396.

[96] Stegner, *Beyond the Hundredth Meridian: John Wesley Powell and the Second Opening of the West* (Boston, Houghton Mifflin Company, 1954), pp. 280-281, 290.

[97] Baltimore *Sun,* February 25, 1893, in Vol. 8, Herbert Papers; Hilary A. Herbert, *An Address Delivered before the Society of Alumni of the University*

was the principle of *laissez faire* government. His philosophy was one which looked back to a simpler day with less complicated governmental forms. Nor was he alone in these views; most of the prominent men of the era professed (when convenient and profitable) a devotion to *laissez faire* as an ideological article of faith. Herbert is notable in that he was so much more consistent than most.

In battling for economical and limited government, Herbert always believed that he was effectively representing the interests of his Alabama constituency. As the election of 1890 approached, however, the colonel received a rude shock. A growing body of his constituents did not share his philosophical and ideological commitment. At home in Alabama the farmers had fallen on hard times, and many of the agrarians came to feel that men who lacked the necessities of life could ill afford pure constitutional principles. In Herbert's district, as elsewhere throughout the South, the talk was about the desirability of subsidies for a newly organized interest group, the farmers. It was at their hands that Hilary Herbert was treated more roughly than ever before in Alabama politics; and it was as a result of their crusade, indirectly at least, that the colonel was finally run out of his congressional seat.

IV

Hilary Herbert was undoubtedly surprised and dismayed at the severity of the farmers' barrage. Prior to this time he had considered the agrarians in his district to be among his staunchest political friends. Whenever he had spoken on the tariff, he had tried to demonstrate that prohibitive duties were hurting the farmer most of all. Herbert recognized that overproduction of farm commodities and a decline in prices were inevitable, given the spate of technological improvements and the opening of fertile western lands since the Civil War; moreover, he accepted these results as an understandable operation of the free market. The farmers' problem, Herbert reasoned, was that the prices of manufactured goods had not fallen correspondingly, because of continued government tampering with the free market by means of tariff subsidies to manufacturing.

---

of Virginia on Commencement Day, June 29, 1887, pamphlet (Lynchburg, Va., J. P. Bell & Co., 1887), pp. 6-7.

The tariff, then, he argued, was "monstrous in its discrimina-
tions in favor of the rich and against the poor." The blame for
this policy he placed squarely on the Republican party.[98]

Except for his fight against the tariff, however, there is little
else in his record to suggest that Herbert was a champion of
agrarian interests. In 1882 and again six years later, the colonel
opposed bills to make the Department of Agriculture an executive department of cabinet rank. Apparently his arguments
against change for its own sake and against putting politicians
in charge of the bureau rather than businessmen were designed
to cover his deeper fears that the organized farmers would be
too powerful an interest group. Although he avowed that he
did not desire to "keep the farmer out of politics," Herbert
maintained that agriculture as a particular occupation was no
more deserving of special cabinet representation than any other.
He argued, "All the departments of this Government should be
for the benefit of the farmers as well as of all the people." He
did not believe that it would dignify the farmer to thrust him
into politics and the vicious scramble for spoils and "special
legislation."[99]

In 1890 Representative John A. Pickler of South Dakota
introduced a bill to establish a subtreasury system of federal
grain elevators and warehouses in which farmers might store
non-perishable crops (such as tobacco, wheat, cotton, and corn)
and receive from county subtreasury offices loans worth eighty
per cent of the market value of the crops. The crops could then
be sold when prices on the world market were favorable; and
the short-term credit would, according to agrarian leaders, allow
producers to break out of the insidious crop-lien system. Although Hilary Herbert dutifully submitted several petitions
favoring the Pickler Bill from farmers throughout his district,
he refused to support the measure himself.[100]

An organization called the Farmers' Alliance became the chief
instrument of the colonel's chastisement. The Southern Farmers'

---

[98] Hilary A. Herbert, *The Tariff, the Republican Party, and the Farmer*,
pamphlet in miscellaneous clippings and pamphlets, 1883-1914, Herbert Papers.
This booklet is actually the copy of a speech Herbert made in the House on
May 20, 1890; see *Congressional Record*, 51st Cong., 2nd Sess., pp. 5038-5046.

[99] *Congressional Record*, 47th Cong., 1st Sess., p. 3764; 50th Cong., 1st Sess., pp.
4477-4481.

[100] *Ibid.*, 51st Cong., 1st Sess., p. 7085.

Alliance had its origins in Texas about 1875. After a decade of stumbling, the movement caught fire around the middle 1880's and began spreading throughout the South. Alabama was one of the first five states to be organized by agrarian missionaries from Texas and Mississippi. By late 1889 the Alliance leadership in Alabama, headed by the dynamic state commissioner of agriculture Reuben F. Kolb, claimed to have 100,000 members in more than 300 lodges. At first the organization concentrated on social and educational activities. Gradually the Alabama Alliance began to move into politics and finally embraced the St. Louis platform of the national Alliance, calling for anti-trust legislation, tariff reform, free silver, government ownership of the railroads, abolition of the national banking system, governmental economy, tax reforms, prohibition of alien ownership of land, and a subtreasury system.[101]

At first the Conservative leaders and newspapers in the state played along with the Alliancemen. The Bourbons became increasingly alarmed, however, as the farmers' political objectives were revealed. When the powerful *Montgomery Advertiser* denounced agrarian politicking, it got into a heated and acrimonious exchange with Kolb and his organization. The Alliance leaders finally became so exasperated at the paper's constant sniping that in January of 1890 they announced a boycott, admonishing agrarians to refuse to read the contaminating columns of the *Advertiser* and to return any copies which arrived in the mail.[102] By the middle of 1891, no less a personage than the prestigious Senator John Tyler Morgan felt it necessary to take to the parapets of Bourbonism. In a national magazine Morgan denounced the platform of the Alliancemen as "class legislation" that would be "destructive of our theory of government" and that was akin to "race advantages in legislation" sought by the Negroes.[103]

Indeed, most disturbing of all to the Bourbon leaders were

---

[101] Woodward, *Origins of the New South,* 188-198; William Warren Rogers, "The Farmers' Alliance in Alabama," *Alabama Review* 15 (January, 1962): pp. 6-11; Charles G. Summersell, "Kolb and the Populist Revolt as Viewed by Newspapers," *Alabama Historical Quarterly* 19 (Fall and Winter, 1957), pp. 382-383.

[102] *Weekly Advertiser,* Montgomery, January 16, 1890.

[103] John Tyler Morgan, "The Danger of the Farmers' Alliance," *Forum* 12 (November, 1891): pp. 408-409. See also Summersell, "Kolb and the Populist Revolt," p. 386, and Going, *Bourbon Democracy in Alabama,* p. 106.

the first halting efforts of the white farmers to work with the Negro Farmers' Alliance, which placed its membership in the state at around 50,000. The *Alabama Sentinel* of Birmingham, the official organ of the Alabama Knights of Labor, warmly endorsed the Alliance platform and strategy. At the same time the paper bitterly described the Conservative tactics:

> The Bourbon Democracy are trying to down the Alliance with the old cry "nigger." It won't work though. The wool has been pulled from off our eyes and we don't propose to be swerved from our purpose of political reform by that old cry. The Bourbon Democracy have used the negro very successfully in keeping their supremacy over us and By —— our lady! we propose to use him in turn to down them for the good of whites and blacks alike.[104]

The Alliancemen did not passively accept the Conservative onslaught but returned in full measure and intensity the charges leveled at them. Throughout the state even the most firmly entrenched incumbents, including Hilary Herbert, were told that they would be measured by the "Alliance Yardstick." The colonel's district was a hotbed of Alliance activity in 1889 and 1890. In November, 1889, the Farmers' National Congress, a meeting that led up to the national convention at St. Louis in December, was held in Montgomery. The capital city also became the site of several Alliance hotels, and in 1889 the Alabama State Exchange was established there. In Butler County the organization established a manufacturing and commercial firm with a capitalization of $250,000. In Butler County alone there were thirteen Negro Alliances, and six more groups were organized in Montgomery County. In Montgomery, Frank Baltzell, an old adversary from Herbert's campaign of 1878, established the *Alliance Herald,* the newspaper that was to become the principal thorn in the colonel's side.[105]

Events in Butler County at the end of April, 1890, gave an indication of trouble in the Second District. At the meeting to

---

104 Quoted in the *Weekly Advertiser,* January 9, 1890. See also William Warren Rogers, "The Negro Alliance in Alabama," *Journal of Negro History* 45 (January, 1960): p. 41.

105 *Greenville Advocate,* March 12, 1890; Rogers, "Negro Alliance in Alabama," p. 41; Rogers, "Farmers' Alliance in Alabama," pp. 12-18. See also Theodore Saloutos, *Farmer Movements in the South, 1865-1933* (Berkeley and Los Angeles, University of California Press, 1960), p. 103.

select delegates to the district congressional convention, there
was strong opposition to the customary procedure of instructing
the representatives to vote for Herbert. Disgruntled agrarians
pushed through a motion instructing the delegates to vote for
the colonel only if he gave satisfactory promises that he would
go back to Washington and support legislation which would
"bear equally on all classes." By the middle of June, rumors
were rife throughout the county that the people were fed up
with Herbert.[106] During the summer Captain Ariosto A. Wiley
of Montgomery, who had eagerly embraced every plank in the
Alliance platform, announced his intention to oppose Herbert's
candidacy in the coming convention. The colonel tried to keep
up a brave front with such statements as, "For one I am glad the
farmers of the country are looking around to find out the causes
of their distress." Nevertheless, he was obviously distraught.
Frank Baltzell, editor of the *Alliance Herald,* chortled that although Herbert had promised to remain at his post of duty in
Washington, he had already rushed home three times on various
pretexts.[107]

On July 31, 1890, Baltzell published the results of Herbert's
measurement by the "Yardstick" in the form of a series of
answers that the colonel had given to questions put to him in
an open letter by the Reverend John L. Stewart. Most of the
Alliancemen found Herbert's suggestions for government regu-
lation of the railroads rather than actual ownership satisfactory
and, likewise, accepted his vague advocacy of an expanded currency as a suitable reply on the silver question. On the matter
of a subtreasury system, however, Herbert did not equivocate.
The Pickler Bill, he asserted, was subsidy legislation on behalf
of a special interest group; and as such it was dangerous, im-
practical, and unconstitutional.[108] In a pamphlet that was widely
distributed in the district, Herbert further elaborated his opinion. Branding the subtreasury plan as "unjustifiable class legislation," he wrote:

> The wrong of which the farmer complains is that discrimina-
> tion has been made against him. Shall the farmer discriminate

---

106 *Greenville Advocate,* April 30, June 11, 1890.

107 *Ibid.,* July 11, July 30, 1890; *Alliance Herald,* July 31, 1890, Vol. 8, Herbert
Papers.

108 *Alliance Herald,* July 31, 1890, Vol. 8, Herbert Papers; *Greenville Advocate,*
August 29, 1890.

now against his brother farmer or shall the farmers as a class
discriminate now against everybody else? Shall they sanction
class legislation by asking other class legislation?[109]

Once again Herbert had come face to face with his principle of
laissez faire government, but on this occasion it was the agrarians
rather than the industrialists who challenged his convictions.
Once again the old warrior could see no other choice but to
fight behind the breastworks he had constructed fourteen years
earlier. Later he explained his dilemma:

How can you constantly oppose high tariffs as class legislation and then with your very next breath demand class legislation for yourselves? Can two wrongs make a right?[110]

Unfortunately the quality of Herbert's logic and conviction
were completely lost on the economically embattled farmers.
The Reverend John Stewart wrote to the *Covington Times* in
Andalusia to report that Hilary Herbert and his congressional
colleague William C. Oates had been measured by the Alliance
"Yardstick" and were found wanting. Stewart exclaimed,
"Down with these old plutocratic colonels. Let us send men of
our own class to represent us in our national government. They
will know better how to represent our interest than any of those
plutocratic lawyers."[111] In July the press reported that the state
commissioner of agriculture Reuben F. Kolb, the most powerful agrarian leader in the state, had publicly called for the
defeat of Congressman Herbert. Even many of Herbert's former
supporters were now reluctant to stand with him in the increasing gale. The *Standard Gauge* of Brewton reported that he was
in deep trouble in both Pike and Montgomery counties, where
schemes to turn him out of office were already well advanced.
The Troy papers teemed with anti-Herbert sentiment that resulted in the endorsement of Herbert's opponent, Ariosto A.
Wiley, by the Pike County convention.[112]

The most bitter assaults on Herbert were launched by the
Alliance Herald of Montgomery. In a caustic point by point

---

109 Herbert, *The Tariff, the Republican Party and the Farmer*, pamphlet in
miscellaneous clippings and pamphlets, 1883-1914, Herbert Papers.

110 *Montgomery Advertiser*, November 24, 1891.

111 *Covington Times*, May 31, 1890.

112 *Montgomery Advertiser*, July 26, 1890; *Standard Gauge*, May 8, 1890;
Weekly Advertiser, May 1, 1890; *Troy Messenger*, May 1, 1890.

attack on the colonel's answers to the Stewart letter, Frank Baltzell concluded that the replies all revealed either "stupidity,
demagoguery, or artful dodging." The editor wrote:

> The all-important question . . . was, if you disapprove of the
> subtreasury bill, "what plans do you propose by which the
> agricultural classes shall be relieved of their present distress?"
> That is the heart of the question. It comes from the hearts of
> two-thirds of the constituents of Col. Herbert with anxiety
> and solitude. What does he answer? "An increase in the cir-
> culating medium and a reduction of taxation." The same old
> song he has sung for fourteen years. Supplement it with a lot
> of whoop-up about "the impending crisis" that arises every two
> years, "that threatens popular liberty by the centralizing ten-
> dencies of the republican party," and the regular assortment
> of machine politics is on hand.
> He has had fourteen years to increase the circulating medium.
> He has never introduced a bill for that purpose. . . .[113]

On another occasion, Baltzell found it strange that such an
avowed friend of the farmers should have opposed the measure
to give agricultural interests a voice in the cabinet by making
the Agriculture Department a cabinet-level agency. It was the
editor's final conclusion that the colonel had done absolutely
nothing for the farmers; and although his own ideas had borne
no fruit, Herbert adamantly refused to try a new program.
Baltzell wrote:

> A representative dependent upon the will of the people he pro-
> poses to serve, who has had time enough, ample opportunity
> and every facility he could desire to accomplish a certain result,
> who has either tried or seen attempted for twenty years a cer-
> tain way to do it and knows it has failed and will ever fail,
> yet refused to try a different plan or a different way to accom-
> plish it, either is too stupid to be further sent on the same
> mission or too arrogant and bigoted to be longer the servant
> of the people.[114]

Considering the severity of the Alliance attack, Herbert
demonstrated an amazing strength at the district congressional
convention early in August. The delegates from Montgomery

---

113 *Alliance Herald,* July 31, 1890, Vol. 8, Herbert Papers.
114 *Alliance Herald,* undated clipping entitled "The Alliance Yardstick," Vol. 8,
Herbert Papers.

and Crenshaw counties were instructed for him; those from Pike for A. A. Wiley; and those from Baldwin, Butler, Conecuh, Covington, and Escambia were uninstructed. Nevertheless, the colonel had the large delegations; twenty-four of the twenty-eight votes necessary to win renomination were already committed to him. When the Herbert forces were able to carry a motion that forbade any delegate from bolting his instructions, the demoralized Alliancemen, realizing that the fight was lost, did not even enter Captain Wiley's name in opposition.[115] For the sake of Democratic unity to which the Alliance was still giving nominal allegiance, Reuben F. Kolb, halfheartedly counseled the farmers to support Herbert in the November election over the Republican, the Reverend Stephen Pilley of Troy. The *Montgomery Advertiser* promptly labeled Pilley "the choice of the negroes of this District"; and although a few of the farmers supported the Republican, Herbert handily won re-election for an eighth term.[116]

In spite of another triumph at the polls, Herbert's victory was undoubtedly soured by the vindictiveness and persistence of his opposition. The campaign left him feeling embittered and unappreciated. In December the press carried the news that agrarian forces in South Carolina had swept aside the respected conservative Senator Wade Hampton as though he had never been important at all. Throughout Alabama the undaunted Alliancemen continued to gird themselves for the election of 1892.[117]

The colonel undoubtedly saw the handwriting on the wall. Pleading that his salary as a congressman had now become insufficient to provide adequately for his family, Herbert announced in June, 1891, that he planned to retire from politics at the end of his term and return to the practice of law in Alabama. Although a number of the Conservative papers graciously asserted that he could have easily won re-election, Herbert's announcement was accepted as final; and no move developed to draft him as a candidate again. So uncertain, in

---

115 *Greenville Advocate*, August 6, 1890.

116 *Montgomery Advertiser*, October 24, 1890; *Greenville Advocate*, October 22, November 5, November 12, 1890.

117 Joseph C. Manning, *The Fadeout of Populism* (New York, T. A. Hebbons, Publisher, 1928), p. 23. See also a note written by Herbert, June, 1915, in scrapbook, Vol. 8, Herbert Papers.

fact, was Herbert of his political position by the fall of 1891 that he was advised by friends to cancel a speech in his old hometown of Greenville lest he be embarrassed by a rude and hostile reception.[118] Within a few days of Herbert's withdrawal as a candidate for re-election, Ariosto A. Wiley again announced that he would seek the congressional seat. Interestingly enough, with the colonel's vulnerable record no longer at issue, the Conservatives the following year were able to fill the vacancy with one of their own, Jesse F. Stallings of Butler County.[119]

In spite of his personal plans, Hilary Herbert's political career did not end in 1893. Although it may have appeared to his agrarian constituents that he had failed them, close observers of congressional affairs were well aware that the Alabamian had made a monumental contribution to the national interest. As a result of his work in the Congress, Herbert was drafted by Grover Cleveland to serve as a member of the cabinet in the president's second administration. In assuming the position of Secretary of the Navy, however, Herbert was in a real sense only continuing the work of rebuilding the American Navy to which he had so vitally contributed during his last eight years in the House of Representatives. His congressional contribution to the growth of the New Navy is the subject of the next chapter.

---

118 Herbert to Governor Thomas Goode Jones, January 30, 1892, Jones Papers, Alabama Archives.

119 *Greenville Advocate,* June 3, 10, 17, and November 9, 1892.

VI. "The Congressional Secretary of the Navy"

> It makes no difference with me upon a question
> of this kind whether the Administration is Demo-
> cratic or Republican and it seems to me that it
> ought not with any other gentleman. It is a great
> national question what sort of Navy we should
> have. . . .
>
> —Hilary Abner Herbert,
> speech in House of
> Representatives, 1890

I

THE opening of the 49th Congress in December, 1885, found the Democratic party once again in control of the House of Representatives. In the White House sat Grover Cleveland, the first Democratic president since James Buchanan. The Speaker of the House of Representatives, now beginning his second term, was John G. Carlisle of Kentucky.

In the process of alloting committee assignments, Carlisle showed Hilary Herbert the courtesy of inquiring as to what appointment the Alabamian would like. Although the colonel had served on the prestigious Ways and Means Committee in the last Congress, he requested that the Speaker appoint him to the Committee on Naval Affairs.

The Alabamian was motivated by two considerations. For one thing, he recognized that sentiment had been steadily growing among both Republicans and Democrats in the Congress for the rehabilitation of the United States Navy. Although he was only superficially aware of the magnitude of the problems the decrepit fleet faced at the time, Herbert shared the feeling that the navy ought to be returned to its proper function as a a vital and dynamic instrument of national policy. A second and, perhaps, even more important consideration for the colonel at the time was his hope that the example of a southern man working energetically for the national mili-

tary forces might help reduce criticism of southern patriotism
and hasten the end of the sectional debate. In other words,
having found his ride on the rocky road to reunion a hard and
frustrating ordeal, the Alabamian concluded that he might try
sailing in the direction of reconciliation for a time. To Herbert's delight Speaker Carlisle, with the encouragement of the
new secretary of the navy William C. Whitney, appointed the
southerner to be the chairman of the Committee on Naval
Affairs.[1]

There was very little newspaper comment on Herbert's
initial appointment. Although he had been a capable and efficient congressman to this time, he was virtually unknown to
the public; and he was not considered a principal leader in
the House. The *Philadelphia Press* did applaud the selection:

> In selecting Mr. Herbert as chairman the Speaker has made an
> admirable choice. . . . He is intelligent, capable and a gentleman
> of the highest integrity. He will enter upon the discharge of
> his duty without bias for or against any scheme that may be
> presented for naval construction. He favors upbuilding the navy
> and can be relied upon to preside over the committee with
> judgment and discretion.[2]

Herbert always believed that one of his greatest assets in coming to the position was his almost total lack of preconceptions
concerning the naval establishment. The first to admit his
grave deficiencies, he set out with characteristic vigor to remedy
the situation. He later recalled:

> My ignorance I was not ignorant of, and so set to work at once
> to inform myself, reading, studying, and talking. I sent for
> prominent naval officers and had them visit me in my rooms
> at night, telling each as he left that all his naval friends would
> be welcome; and they all came, one after another, perhaps
> nearly or quite every naval officer in Washington, for naval
> officers always have views, and these they are quite ready to give
> to those who may be expected to have any power or influence
> in carrying them out.

---

[1] *Congressional Record,* 49th Cong., 1st Sess., 538; Baltimore *Sun,* February 25,
1893, Vol. 8, Herbert Papers; Herbert, "Reminiscences," pp. 4-5. See also
George H. Davis, *A Navy Second to None: The Development of Modern American Naval Policy* (New York, Harcourt, Brace and Company, 1940), p. 89.

[2] Quoted in the *Greenville Advocate,* July 13, 1886.

During this process of education, Herbert was struck not only by the quantity and quality of the opinions that he heard but also by their diverseness and divergence. He noted:

> Nearly every one of my advisers had his own idea of the character and classes and proportions of classes of ships, guns and torpedoes, of the equipment in navy yards and stations, the value and uselessness of marines, etc., etc.; but this was all the better for me, because arguments on all sides of every question gave me opportunity to form views of my own.[3]

In spite of the wide range of views among Navy men, on one issue there was virtual unanimity. By the early 1880's, even the most optimistic observers were forced to admit that the navy was a mere "shadow fleet," consisting primarily of decayed wooden hulks of Civil War vintage. Practically useless for modern warfare, the rickety fleet was vulnerable to destruction by the ships of even the weakest advanced naval powers, including several of the Latin American nations. American ships were too weak to fight and too slow to flee from an enemy.

As was the case with many of the severe problems that beset the nation, the low quality of politics in the postwar years may in great measure be held accountable for the decline of the navy. While the politicians mismanaged, delayed, and obstructed—in an era of rapid technological change in naval progress—the American fleet became obsolete. During the Grant years, under Secretary George M. Robeson, a few wooden vessels had been completed; and construction was begun on five large, double-turreted monitors, all powerfully armed and heavily armored for harbor defense. When the Hayes administration took office, however, because of suspicions of graft in the awarding of the contracts for the monitors, Secretary Richard W. Thompson suspended work on the five new vessels.

For the six years after 1875, the Democratic party was able to organize the House of Representatives. Traditionally given to a "little navy policy" and generally antagonistic to the Republican administrations, the Democrats refused to appropriate any funds for the monitors or for new ships. Nevertheless, huge sums were expended to keep the rickety old fleet in repair. The *Kearsarge,* for example, which had been built in

---

[3] Herbert, "Reminiscences," pp. 5-6.

1861 for only $286,000, was the greedy beneficiary of repair work amounting to more than $1,100,000 in subsequent years. With considerable justification the Democrats accused the Republicans of mismanagement that resulted in the spending of $385,000,000 on a worthless navy. At this same time, the Republican control of the White House gave the opposition party the excuse that it needed to reject proposals for an adequate program of naval expansion. In the final analysis both parties were to blame for the low estate of the fleet, and each one was ready to use it as a political tool at every convenient opportunity.[4]

Even before the Grant years had ended, several farsighted political leaders had expressed concern about the perilous condition of the nation's naval arm. Among the Democrats in the House of Representatives, Congressman W. C. Whitthorne of Tennessee waged a lonely campaign to inform his comrades about the navy's condition, as did Benjamin W. Harris and Eugene Hale, both Republicans from Maine; Hale carried his pro-navy views with him when he went to the Senate in 1881 and for many years was the fleet's best friend in the upper chamber. Another respected Republican leader, John A. Kasson of Iowa, who had served as minister to Austria-Hungary during the Hayes administration, added his pen to the navy's cause. In Europe, Kasson viewed with alarm the intense acceleration of the swirling currents of imperialism. Realizing that the United States would have to sail through these troubled waters, he also knew that the decaying American navy could never survive the ordeal. Over and over again, Kasson insisted that the United States could resist the force of rising European imperialism only by the creation of a powerful fleet which would give the nation a chance in the expansive competition. With the nation's phenomenal economic expansion abroad, a revitalized navy was essential to protect America's commerce and prosperity. Additionally, Kasson warned that the United States would never be able to defend the Monroe Doctrine without a fleet that could serve as a dynamic instrument of diplomacy. By the start of the Garfield administration, then, in 1881, a few politicians and statesmen had begun to lay the

---

[4] Leon B. Richardson, *William E. Chandler: Republican* (New York, Dodd, Mead & Company, 1940), pp. 286-289; Davis, *A Navy Second to None*, pp. 16-22.

political and intellectual foundations for the resumption of a vigorous naval policy.[5]

The breakthrough came in 1881 as a result of the report of a Naval Advisory Board, which Secretary William H. Hunt had taken it upon himself to appoint. On the basis of the recommendations of the board, Hunt proposed the addition of thirty-eight unarmored steel cruising vessels to the navy. Although the eight largest of the projected ships were to vary between 4,500 and 5,800 tons displacement, thirty auxiliary vessels were to consist mostly of torpedo craft. The secretary told Congress:

> The condition of the Navy imperatively demands the prompt and earnest attention of Congress. Unless some action be had in its behalf it must soon dwindle into insignificance. . . .
>
> We have been unable to make such an appropriate display of our naval power abroad as will cause us to be respected. The exhibition of our weakness in this important area of defense is calculated to detract from our occupying in the eyes of foreign nations that rank to which we know ourselves to be justly entitled.[6]

The year in which Hunt had entered the Navy Department was propitious for naval expansion. By 1881 the depression of the seventies was behind; the treasury was showing a large surplus; the growth of American manufactures and commerce had sparked a renewed interest in the merchant marine and a fleet to protect it; there was increasing public awareness of the growing naval prowess of foreign nations; and for the first time in six years the Republicans controlled both houses of Congress.[7]

Although Secretary Hunt remained in office only one year, the new president, Chester A. Arthur, and Hunt's successor at the Navy Department, William E. Chandler, strongly supported the idea of naval expansion. After one false start, the renewed interest in the administration and in the 47th Con-

5 Edward Younger, *John A. Kasson: Politics and Diplomacy from Lincoln to McKinley* (Iowa City, State Historical Society of Iowa, 1955), pp. 292-295; Davis, *A Navy Second to None*, pp. 20-23.

6 United States Navy Dept., *Annual Report of the Secretary of the Navy*, 1881 (Washington, Government Printing Office, 1881), pp. 3, 29-30. See pp. 27-81 for the complete report of the Naval Advisory Board.

7 Harold and Margaret Sprout, *The Rise of American Naval Power, 1776-1918* (Princeton, Princeton University Press, 1939), pp. 183-186.

gress led to the Navy Act of 1883. To facilitate the process of junking the old fleet, the measure provided that none of the navy's obsolete vessels were to receive repairs amounting to more than twenty per cent of the cost of a new ship of the same size. Most important, the act authorized the first four ships of the "New Navy" (as it came to be called): one steel cruiser of 4,300 tons displacement; two cruisers of approximately 3,000 tons displacement; and one dispatch boat. The four vessels were to become the protected cruisers *Atlanta, Boston,* and *Chicago,* and the dispatch boat *Dolphin;* known to the public as the "ABCD's" or the "White Squadron," these ships formed the nucleus of the New Navy.[8]

In spite of the hopeful beginning, events in the following Congress revealed graphically to naval supporters the enervating effect that partisan strife could have on the expansion program. Although sentiment for the navy was growing within their party, the Democratic leaders of the House of Representatives remained inclined toward caution and economy. Many of the representatives wanted time to observe the progress of the first four ships of the New Navy before sinking any more money into the program. The Republican Senate, frustrated by the protracted delay, took matters into its own hands. Spurred on by the zealous Eugene Hale of Maine, the senators usurped the prerogative of the lower chamber to initiate all appropriations measures and passed a bill providing for the construction of seven new vessels. The Democratic House, however, indignantly rebuffed the Senate measure and adamantly refused any compromise whatsoever. Not even President Arthur's vigorous intervention could budge the grimly determined Democrats; and the naval appropriation in 1884 contained no authorization for increase of the navy. It was only after the election of 1884 with Grover Cleveland bound for the White House that the Democrats relented and approved the addition of two cruisers and two gunboats in the Navy Act of March 3, 1885.[9]

---

8 U.S. Navy Dept., *Navy Yearbook,* 1911 (Washington, Government Printing Office, 1911), pp. 9-12; Walter R. Herrick, Jr., *The American Naval Revolution* (Baton Rouge, Louisiana State University Press, 1966), pp. 28-29; Davis, *A Navy Second to None,* pp. 37-41.

9 Davis, *A Navy Second to None,* pp. 41-43; Navy Dept., *Navy Yearbook,* 1911, pp. 37-38.

Hilary Herbert assumed the chairmanship of the House Committee on Naval Affairs at a momentous time in the history of the fleet. Although the Garfield and Arthur administrations had made an excellent beginning, the New Navy was still in its infancy. With a Democratic administration now in the White House, the crucial question was whether the party of Jefferson and Jackson could shake off the shackles of its traditional small navy policy and launch a constructive program of expansion.

Herbert's position as head of the Navy Committee gave him an almost unparalleled personal opportunity to affect the future of the American fleet. Beginning with his tenure as chairman in the 49th Congress in 1885, the Committee on Naval Affairs for the first time wrested from the powerful Appropriations Committee the right to control its own appropriations bills. (It was not until January, 1899, that the Navy Committee in the Senate won the right to consider money measures.) Moreover, after the debacle over the naval appropriations bill in the 48th Congress, the Senate resigned itself to waiting on the House to initiate measures for naval increase.[10]

As the chairman of a major House committee in a period when Congress was the dominant member in the executive-legislative relationship, Hilary Herbert would often have been in a position to pursue whatever program he desired in his area of concern with little reference either to the president or to the Navy Department. Writing as a historian Woodrow Wilson described the powerful committee chairmen in these years as "petty barons" who "may at will exercise an almost despotic sway within their own shires, and may sometimes threaten to convulse even the realm itself."[11] Fortunately for national policy, Herbert did not relish power for its own sake and was able to form a cooperative and harmonious working relationship not only with the new secretary of the navy, William C. Whitney, but also with his Republican successor Benjamin F. Tracy four years later. Because of the scope and complexity of naval problems in an era of rapidly changing technology, the Navy Department was in a strong position to

---

10 White, *The Republican Era*, p. 65; David J. Rothman, *Politics and Power: The United States Senate, 1869-1901* (Cambridge, Harvard University Press, 1966), p. 66; Samuel W. McCall, *The Business of Congress* (New York, Columbia University Press, 1911), p. 28.

11 Quoted in White, *The Republican Era*, p. 50.

push its policies with the Committee on Naval Affairs; and, in turn, the chairman and the other most knowledgeable members of the committee were usually able to press their ideas on their poorly informed colleagues in the House. Hilary Herbert served as chairman of the body throughout the four years of Cleveland's first administration. Although he was replaced by the Republican Charles Boutelle of Maine from 1889 to 1891, the Alabamian remained as the ranking Democrat on the panel. With Democratic control of the House once more in the last two years of the administration of Benjamin Harrison, Herbert resumed his place at the head of the committee. Long before the colonel left Congress in 1893, the Committee on Naval Affairs had come to be considered part of the prestigious "House aristocracy," along with the committees on Rules, Ways and Means, Appropriations, and Military Affairs.[12] One of the most knowledgeable naval historians has written:

> Since 1881 the business of the naval committees in Congress has greatly grown in volume and importance, and appointments to them have come to be highly prized. They are among the chief "working committees" of Congress, and are powerful factors in determining the naval policy of the country. Their decision upon the numbers and types of vessels in the shipbuilding program each year is usually final. Their views upon any measure which the department wishes to have enacted into law must be reckoned with, for their opposition will prevent its passage. . . . The chairmen of these committees often acquire an extensive knowledge of the navy.[13]

Herbert's first and most important task as chairman of the Committee on Naval Affairs was to convince fellow Democrats of the necessity of an expansive naval policy. Within the executive branch, little persuasion was necessary; fortunately both President Cleveland and Secretary Whitney were "easterners with the prevailing seaboard attitude toward the Navy."[14] In

---

12 Robert Seager, "Ten Years Before Mahan: The Unofficial Case for a New Navy, 1880-1890," *Mississippi Valley Historical Review*, 40 (December, 1953): pp. 498-499; Charles Willis Thompson, *Party Leaders of the Time* (New York, G. W. Dillingham Company, Publishers, 1906), pp. 166-171.

13 Charles Oscar Paullin, *Paullin's History of Naval Administration, 1775-1911: A Collection of Articles from the U.S. Naval Institute Proceedings* (Annapolis, U.S. Naval Institute, 1968), pp. 375-376.

14 H. and M. Sprout, *Rise of American Naval Power*, p. 189.

his first annual message the president pointed out that the nation did not possess a single ship that could successfully engage a first-class vessel of any important naval power. Moreover, the appalling state of the fleet had a debilitating effect on the nation's foreign policy. He explained:

> The nation that cannot resist aggression is constantly exposed to it. Its foreign policy is of necessity weak, and its negotiations are conducted with disadvantage because it is not in condition to enforce the terms dictated by its sense of right and justice.

Cleveland then asked the Congress to turn its full attention to reconstruction of the fleet. The Navy Department, he concluded, ought no longer to be simply "a shabby ornament to the Government."[15] Additional impetus for a shift in the party's attitude came in 1885 as a result of the encouragement of the old chieftain, Samuel J. Tilden, who began to advocate publicly that the Democrats support naval rehabilitation.[16]

Within the House of Representatives, however, enthusiasm for the navy did not run as high. As a result of the bitter feuds with the Republicans concerning naval expenditures in earlier years, many Democrats in the lower chamber retained a healthy hostility toward large appropriations for the fleet. Indeed, Hilary Herbert's greatest problem in shepherding his appropriations bills through the House in the succeeding years was in getting the measures past obstructionist members of his own party. In 1887, for example, the *New York Times* commented on the difficulty that beset Herbert and other administration supporters as they tried to press naval legislation through the House:

> There are Democrats, and not a few of them, who have not outgrown the habit of acting as a party of obstruction and opposition. They do not readily learn that they belong to the majority and should be on the affirmative side when discussing suggestions from the Administration.[17]

Hilary Herbert's mission, then, involved the navigation of perilous legislative straits. On one side of the aisle of the House

---

15 James D. Richardson, ed., *A Compilation of the Messages and Papers of the Presidents* (Washington, D.C., Published by Authority of Congress, 1898) 8: p. 351.
16 *New York Times*, December 28, 1885.
17 *New York Times*, January 10, 1887. See also Davis, *A Navy Second to None,* p. 17; Herbert, "Reminiscences," p. 5.

sat a vigorous Republican opposition, always ready to vote large funds for the navy, yet unable as the minority party to carry any bill on its own. Around Herbert sat a large number of Democrats, chiefly from the Midwest and the South, who relished any excuse to vote little or nothing for naval increase. Of necessity, naval legislation would have to be bipartisan; innumerable compromises on both sides were inevitable. Herbert's tricky assignment was to frame appropriations bills which were of sufficient size and scope to win Republican support while at the same time were cautious and conservative enough to get past economy-minded Democrats. In devising his strategy, the colonel finally came to the conclusion that his only hope of success was in a policy of gradual but constant expansion. This approach was remarkably in tune with his own conservative nature. He recalled, "My task with my own party was not an easy one, and it soon became apparent that to 'go sure' it was necessary to 'go slow.' "[18]

One last expression is necessary before turning to a discussion of naval expansion in the years 1885-1893. In his excellent monograph *The Congress Founds the Navy, 1787-1798,* Marshall Smelser makes an important point about the origins of the first American navy which is just as applicable to the American naval renaissance in the two decades after 1880. Smelser says:

> Naval historians have usually given little attention to the political shaping of the national naval policy, and political historians (a more numerous species) have generally presented only the final decisions of naval policy without much investigation of the policy-making process. The result of these approaches to the study of American naval history has been the writing of a good deal of apolitical narrative, with emphasis on strategy, operations, technology, heroism—even patriotic slogans—but with very little on what the nation expected of the Navy and how the judgments on its mission were arrived at.
>
> Because these methods have been followed a number of gallant naval officers have been elevated to the rank of fathers of the Navy, among them Jones, Truxtun, Barry, and some of their illustrious contemporaries. These gentlemen were fathers of naval customs and tactical practices but they were not the founders of the Navy. The United States Navy, like other

---

18 Quoted in George F. Parker, *Recollections of Grover Cleveland* (New York, Century Company, 1909), p. 396.

navies, was not founded by sailors but by politicians, and the story of its founding must deal with politics.[19]

In the popular mind, all too often the rebirth of the United States fleet has been associated with the writings of Captain Alfred Thayer Mahan. Even Leonard D. White's thorough administrative history of the period calls Mahan the "intellectual architect of the new navy."[20] Certainly, one does not want to take away from the captain any of the credit due him; he was a masterful naval publicist and propagandist, and Mahan did personally influence the direction of American strategic thinking both during and after the Harrison administration. Nevertheless, one should not forget that the nativity of the New Navy occurred in 1881, almost ten years before Mahan published his pathbreaking *The Influence of Sea Power Upon History, 1660-1783*. The historian Robert Seager has elaborated this point with his findings that the 1880's were a period of essential preparation for the more dynamic and expansive policies of the next decade. Seager has discovered a number of indications that responsible national leaders had already begun to recognize the relationship between seapower and world power. In effect, Mahan and his close associate Secretary of the Navy Benjamin F. Tracy jumped on a bandwagon that had already been rolling for some time. Seager concluded:

> In retrospect, it seems more accurate to regard Tracy and Mahan as codifiers of concepts already in circulation in naval and legislative circles rather than innovators. While their propagandistic function is not to be dismissed lightly, considerable evidence points to the conclusions that neither Tracy nor Mahan initially added much that was new either to naval theory or to naval attitudes. Considered together, their views at the outset of the new decade were a summing up rather than a bold new departure.[21]

To conclude, the credit for the naval renaissance after 1880 belongs to several groups. The admirals, led by Mahan, deserve a share as do the exceptionally able administrators of the Navy

---

[19] Smelser, *The Congress Founds the Navy, 1787-1798* (Notre Dame, University of Notre Dame Press, 1959), p. v.
[20] White, *The Republican Era*, p. 161.
[21] Seager, "Ten Years Before Mahan," pp. 491-493, 511.

FIG. 3. WILLIAM H. HUNT
1881-1882.
Courtesy of U.S. Navy Department.

FIG. 4. WILLIAM E. CHANDLER
1882-1885.
Courtesy of U.S. Navy Department.

FIG. 5.   WILLIAM C. WHITNEY
1885-1889.
Courtesy of U.S. Navy Department.

FIG. 6.   BENJAMIN F. TRACY
1889-1893.
Courtesy of U.S. Navy Department.

SECRETARIES OF THE NAVY, 1881-1893
Along with Hilary Herbert, these men helped create the New American Navy

Department, secretaries Hunt, Chandler, Whitney, Tracy, and Herbert. Nevertheless, as Marshall Smelser suggests concerning the first navy, a lion's share of the praise must go to the naval advocates in Congress, practical politicians who pushed through the authorizations and appropriations that allowed the new fleet to become a reality. Because the role of the Congress in building the New Navy has never been adequately assessed, the next section traces in some detail the course of naval legislation and the predominant part played by Hilary Herbert.

II

With the opening of the 49th Congress in December, 1885, the important question for the Navy was whether the Democratic House would be willing to follow the leadership of the Cleveland administration and accept an enlarged naval commitment. Although the president could hardly be called a "big-navy man," he evidenced from the start a desire to have a navy capable of defending the national interest.[22] The first report to the Congress by Secretary William C. Whitney was a forceful and carefully conceived presentation, comprising two volumes of documents. Studiously avoiding a partisan tone, Whitney emphasized the necessity of sound business principles to assure economy and efficiency in the operation of the Navy Department. Within the report of the Bureau of Construction and Repair was a request for seven new ships, ranging from two small vessels of 800 tons displacement to a seagoing armored cruiser of 7,500 tons; the report also suggested that the five monitors begun by Secretary Robeson be completed. When Secretary Whitney appeared before the House Committee on Naval Affairs on February 12 and 13, 1886, he particularly stressed the need in the long-range building program for fast cruisers of 3,000-5,000 tons displacement to act as commerce destroyers. Departing somewhat from the suggestions of the Bureau of Construction and Repair, the secretary now recommended the authorization of two armored cruisers of 6,000 tons (actually second-class battleships) and four torpedo boats.[23]

---

22 Horace Samuel Merrill, *Bourbon Leader: Grover Cleveland and the Democratic Party* (Boston and Toronto, Little, Brown and Company, 1957), pp. 82-83.
23 Mark D. Hirsch, *William C. Whitney: Modern Warwick* (New York, Dodd, Mead & Company, 1948), pp. 294-301; Navy Dept., *Annual Report*, 1885.

As chairman of the Navy Committee, Hilary Herbert introduced two bills in March, 1886. The first bill was the customary appropriations measure to provide for regular naval expenditures for the fiscal year ending June 30, 1887. The second measure, a separate bill entirely, was to provide for the increase of the navy and was the first bill of this type framed by the Committee on Naval Affairs rather than the Appropriations Committee. The regular appropriations bill, Herbert's first presentation, had deceptively clear sailing. The Alabamian spent much of his time talking about reforms not even directly related to the bill at hand. Charles Boutelle, the leading Republican on the Navy Committee, warmly praised the bill. Indeed, with a measure on the floor that provided for no new ships at all, everyone—Republican and Democrat alike—was the navy's friend. Much of the wrangling over the bill, in fact, involved disputes over which party had shown the greater support for the fleet in the past. In June the measure passed the House substantially as Herbert had presented it, and within a month the Senate had accepted the measure. The Navy Act of July 26, 1886, authorized almost $13,000,000 for the ordinary expenses of the fleet.[24]

With the regular naval appropriation out of the way, Hilary Herbert began to press for discussion of his bill for increase of the navy. Herbert's report to accompany the measure was a carefully prepared and closely reasoned document, containing enough of a dash of sensationalism to shock the legislators out of their lethargy. Herbert pointed out that, although the United States had once been secure in this hemisphere, the appalling situation now existed in which the country was woefully lacking adequate means of defense. While other nations had been incorporating modern technological innovations into ship construction, the American fleet had actually regressed, with the result that at present American ships carried no guns that could pierce the armor of the newest enemy warships.

---

24 *Congressional Record*, 49th Cong., 1st Sess., pp. 4778, 5830-5839, 5870-5877, 5968, 7223-7224, 7405-7407; *House of Representatives Reports*, 49th Cong., 1st Sess., No. 2497, pp. 1-2; Navy Dept., *Navy Yearbook*, 1911: pp. 39-48, 721. Because of deficiency appropriations and the complexities of naval accounting which allowed the shifting of items to various accounts, the researcher will find that appropriations figures used in congressional debates and reports may vary slightly from those in Navy Department reports. For the sake of consistency, when possible in this manuscript the totals given in the *Navy Yearbook* are used.

Additionally, the country had no coastal forts that could withstand the guns of modern naval vessels. Herbert then added punch to his argument by listing all of the major American coastal cities which stood naked and defenseless before the modern ships of even such small powers as Chile and Brazil. He then summarized:

> We are therefore absolutely helpless against an invasion from the sea, so helpless that your committee would hesitate to publish the fact to the world, were it not already everywhere else better known than to the people of America.

Of the eighty-six vessels then in naval service, Herbert explained, only thirty-eight were fit for sea duty at all; and of these not one had modern armor or machinery. The American fleet was slow, ill-protected, and fitted with obsolete weapons. To remedy the situation, immediate action was necessary. Herbert recommended a total appropriation of approximately $6,500,000 for new ships: two second-class battleships of 6,000 tons each, three protected cruisers of 3,500-5,000 tons each, four first-class torpedo boats, and a torpedo cruiser of about 800 tons displacement. Additionally, he requested funds for completion of the Robeson monitors.[25] Commenting on the report, the *New York Times* expressed delight at the new Democratic interest in the navy. The paper remarked, "From refusing to give the country any fighting vessels at all, Congress is apparently proceeding to turn them out in profusion."[26]

When he began pressing for consideration of his bill, Herbert rapidly learned that a committee chairman had to be nimble and shrewd to get through the "unknown jungle," the apt characterization given by one historian to the House rules.[27] To his dismay the colonel found that many of the fleet's avowed "friends" melted away once they saw the size of the committee request. On three different occasions the Navy Committee petitioned for a day to take up consideration of the bill, but Herbert's pleas fell on deaf ears among the House leadership. Particularly adept at obstructing consideration was Democratic Representative William S. Holman of Indiana, a staunch midwestern isolationist. After sounding out many of his colleagues

---

25 *House of Representatives Reports*, 49th Cong., 1st Sess., No. 993.
26 *New York Times*, February 27, 1886.
27 White, *The Republican Era*, p. 50.

on the Democratic side, Herbert reluctantly concluded that he would never be able to bring before the chamber a bill carrying so large an appropriation. Democratic sentiment on behalf of the navy had not progressed as far as the chairman had hoped. As the time remaining in the session waned, the Alabamian was driven to drastic action. Reconvening the Navy Committee he led the Democratic majority in slashing the request from $6,500,000 to $3,500,000. The substitute measure retained appropriations for the two battleships but asked for only one protected cruiser, one torpedo boat, and a dynamite pneumatic cruiser. Shortly afterwards, the obstruction ceased; and on July 24, 1886, the measure for increase of the navy came up for consideration.[28]

Unfortunately, the rough sledding for Herbert had only begun. In his explanation of the bill he recapitulated the committee report and asserted that the substitute request which he now made was an extremely modest proposal. Admitting that the nation did not need the largest fleet in the world, he argued nevertheless that a strong navy was necessary to maintain the peace. "Our true policy," he said, "is peace, but a defenseless nation often finds it difficult to maintain neutrality in time of war." Nudging his Democratic colleagues, he called up "the old Democratic idea, expressed by James K. Polk, . . . that our Navy should be increased in proportion 'to the growing interests to be protected' by it." The chairman closed with a forceful bipartisan appeal to both sides of the aisle to eschew parliamentary tactics and unnecessary amendments in the interest of the passage of so moderate a measure.

Once Herbert had maneuvered past efforts by Representative Holman to extend debate, certain death for the bill with so little time remaining in the session, the colonel was berated by the Republican opposition for the reductions that the committee had made. Charles Boutelle of Maine, the ranking Republican member of the Committee on Naval Affairs, branded the parsimonious substitute measure an affront to the public, considering the perilous state of the fleet. In the ensuing exchanges, the embarrassed Herbert was all but forced to

---

28 *House of Representatives Reports,* 49th Cong., 1st Sess., Nos. 1470, 2619, 2648; *New York Times,* July 17, 1886; *Congressional Record,* 49th Cong., 1st Sess., pp. 7474-7478.

admit publicly that it was the sentiment in his own party which had forced him to back down and, in Boutelle's words, accept "half a loaf." Although Herbert might have persuaded a small group of Democrats to fuse with the Republican minority to pass a larger appropriation, he could not accept the inevitable political consequences of a Republican claim that the naval appropriation was their bill. To ensure the passage of this and of future measures with Democratic votes, the colonel had no choice but to go with the substitute recommendation. On a strict party vote the chamber disposed of Boutelle's amendment favoring the original section of the bill and then passed the substitute provisions substantially as Herbert had presented them. The Senate, desiring to stimulate the growth of armor manufacture and make the American building program self-sufficient, accepted the bill after adding an amendment that all armor used in the new ships be of domestic manufacture. With the concurrence of the House and the president's signature, the measure carrying an appropriation of $3,500,000 for naval expansion became law on August 3, 1886.[29]

Having learned many lessons from his first hard experience with a naval expansion bill, Herbert began requesting a day for consideration of his next appropriations measure even before the first session of the 49th Congress adjourned. Shortly after the start of the second session in December, 1886, Herbert offered the regular naval appropriations bill which, as in the last session, omitted any mention of naval increase. He quickly realized, however, that his separate measure for expansion of the fleet might well suffer the same fate as had his last attempt. The Alabamian carried the problem to Speaker Carlisle, who fortunately had become more sympathetic to the naval program. The two men finally agreed that the committee should simply incorporate a section for naval increase into the regular appropriations bill (which had to be passed each session to keep the navy in pay, supplies, and repair). The major problem with this approach was that some opponent of naval expansion would undoubtedly raise the point of order that the House rules forbade the inclusion of new projects in general appropriations bills. Speaker Carlisle finally made a secret bargain to appoint a presiding officer who would decide disputed points in Herbert's favor.[30]

When the appointed day arrived for discussion of the regular naval appropriations bill, Representative James B. McCreary of Kentucky was in the chair. Discussion on the measure had hardly begun when Joseph D. Sayers of Texas offered an amendment that sounded suspiciously like the very provisions for naval increase on which the Herbert committee had been working for some time. The Sayers amendment called for the construction of two cruisers of 4,000 tons each, four gunboats of 1,700 tons each, and a swift torpedo boat. When William Holman of Indiana raised the predicted point of order, McCreary ruled that the ships proposed in the amendment were not part of any new project but, rather, were simply extensions of the work of naval expansion which the Congress had initiated in past sessions. Although Holman indignantly appealed to Speaker Carlisle, the Speaker joined with former Speaker Samuel Randall in declaring McCreary's ruling to be proper.[31] The significance of the precedent set by the McCreary ruling can hardly be overemphasized. From that time on, provisions for increase of the New Navy were to be considered simply as a part of the regular naval appropriations bills.

Regrettably, Herbert's neatly laid scheme was attacked from an unexpected quarter even before the Sayers amendment could be brought to a vote. Speaking for the Republican opposition, Charles Boutelle attacked the amendment as too limited and stingy. Boutelle then advanced an amendment of his own, calling for no fewer than ten protected steel cruisers to cost approximately $20,000,000. In the ensuing debate the isolationist William Holman, having lost his point of order, bitterly attacked both amendments. Seconded by Richard P. Bland of Missouri and William C. Oates of Alabama, Holman expressed his deep suspicions of a large military establishment. The nation, he contended, had not needed a huge fleet before and did not need it now. He decried the work of the naval advocates

---

[30] Parker, *Recollections of Grover Cleveland*, pp. 397-398; *New York Times*, August 16, 1886. See also *Congressional Records*, 49th Cong., 2nd Sess., pp. 955, 1244.

[31] Parker, *Recollections of Grover Cleveland*, pp. 397-398; Herbert Bruce Fuller, *The Speakers of the House* (Boston, Little, Brown and Company, 1909), pp. 211-212.

as the "beginning of a revolution, silent as it may be, that aims at placing this Republic on a military footing."[32]

Once again, Herbert and William McAdoo of New Jersey, who was emerging as the chairman's chief lieutenant on the Navy Committee, were able to take the moderate course. The Sayers amendment, Herbert insisted, was a cautious approach to naval expansion, calling for an authorization of just under $5,000,000. The danger of a crash program like that suggested by the Republicans was that American builders might rush to completion an obsolete fleet that did not utilize the spate of technological innovations and advances that were resulting each year from experimentation in Europe. Herbert's arguments evidently seemed reasonable to his colleagues; the appropriations bill was passed with the Sayers amendment. Although the Senate amended the House bill, the results of the conference on the measure were not too far from what Hilary Herbert had wanted in the first place. The Navy Act of March 3, 1887, carried a total expenditure of almost $26,000,000 for all naval purposes, including appropriations for two steel cruisers and two gunboats.[33]

An analysis of the battles over naval appropriations in 1886 and 1887 is instructive because the two episodes reveal the pattern that would often prevail in these debates during the remainder of Hilary Herbert's tenure in the House. On one side, William Holman, followed by a small group of midwestern and southern Democrats, hoped to sabotage any expenditure for the expansion of the fleet. On the other side, the Republicans, led by Charles Boutelle and his assistant Henry Cabot Lodge, incessantly demanded larger expenditures. Hilary Herbert and William McAdoo took the middle ground, pressing for gradual but constant naval increase. Interestingly enough, signs were already apparent that Charles Boutelle was beginning to recognize that although Herbert's approach was slow, it was the only sure way to keep the drive for naval expansion alive in the Democratic-controlled House. Gradually, Herbert and Boutelle came to an excellent working relationship; and the mastery of naval matters that the two men attained earned

---

[32] *Congressional Record*, 49th Cong., 2nd Sess. (1886-1887), pp. 2336-2339; 2343-2345, and Appendix pp. 96-99.

[33] *Ibid.*, 49th Cong., 2nd Sess., pp. 2337-2339, 2347-2352, 2539, 2724-2727; Navy Dept., *Navy Yearbook*, 1911: pp. 53-68, 721.

for them unchallenged leadership within their own parties on questions of naval policy. In the 50th Congress, in fact, one colleague referred to them as the "two eminent sailors in the House" and asserted that once they had both spoken on any piece of naval legislation, the House had very nearly heard all it needed to know.[34]

In the first session of the 50th Congress in 1888, Herbert presented another comprehensive report on the state of the American navy. He reported that the end of the wooden fleet was now in sight. The committee was gradually reducing appropriations for its repair, and within ten years the useless antique armada would disappear entirely. Quickly, the colonel turned to offer the House a comprehensive review of the progress of the New Navy. Of the first four vessels authorized, the cruisers *Atlanta* and *Boston* were already in commission, as was the dispatch boat *Dolphin*. The *Chicago,* the largest of the first four ships, would be ready in a few weeks. The cruisers *Newark* and *Charleston* and the gunboats *Yorktown* and *Petrel,* all authorized in 1885, were in various stages of completion. Contracts had been let on the craft approved in 1886, the second-class battleships *Texas* and *Maine,* the cruiser *Baltimore,* and a dynamite gun cruiser (to become the *Vesuvius*). The Robeson monitors were also in various stages of completion, but the work had been delayed by the difficulties of securing armor plate of domestic manufacture. Contracts had also been let on the last four vessels authorized, the cruisers *San Francisco* and *Philadelphia* and the gunboats *Concord* and *Bennington.*

Turning to the committee's recommendations for the coming fiscal year, Herbert pointed out that the proposed measure totalled just under $20,000,000, of which about one-third was to go for new vessels. In concluding the encouraging report the Alabamian requested specifically four new ships: an armored cruiser of 7,500 tons (technically an armored cruiser but actually a second-class battleship), another cruiser of 5,300 tons, and two cruisers of 3,000 tons displacement.[35]

The debate on the measure which incorporated the committee request revealed not only Herbert's growing mastery of naval legislation but also the evidence of a bipartisan accord

---

[34] *Congressional Record,* 59th Cong., 1st Sess., p. 2122.
[35] *House of Representatives Reports,* 50th Cong., 1st Sess., No. 2617.

between the chairman and the Republican leader Charles Boutelle. The appropriations bill passed the House in approximately twenty minutes without significant Democratic or Republican opposition. Except for its insistence that the measure be amended to add three small gunboats, the Senate also accepted the proposals from the Herbert committee. The Navy Act of September 7, 1888, carrying a total authorization of almost $20,000,000 undoubtedly pleased the Secretary of the Navy. Although William C. Whitney had recommended only five cruisers, the measure approved seven ships in all, four cruisers and three gunboats.[36]

Herbert's report on naval appropriations in 1889 recommended only two new ships to the second session of the 50th Congress. Benjamin Harrison had already been elected president and was in the process of forming his cabinet. Secretary of the Navy Whitney, in his usual display of caution and good sense, had even promised to leave the matter of contracting for the seven vessels approved in 1888 to his Republican successor. With so large a number of craft already being carried over to the new administration, Hilary Herbert and Charles Boutelle agreed that the Navy Department could not conceivably superintend more than two new vessels properly. The report is significant, however, because it contains one of Hilary Herbert's most concise statements concerning his strategy of a gradual but consistent approach to naval expansion:

> With regard to a new navy, Congress seems to have settled upon a policy of appropriating toward its construction about $6,000,000 per annum. Your committee believes that this will build a navy as fast as prudence dictates. Our Navy Department and our ship-builders are utilizing, as far as may be, by every means in their power the knowledge acquired from the costly experience of other nations, but they must acquire experience of their own. Too great haste on the part of the Government would inevitably result in confusion and waste, and most probably in combination instead of competition among ship-builders. Besides, it would be an easy matter in this country to build ships more rapidly than we could supply them with armament of domestic manufacture.[37]

---

[36] *Congressional Record*, 50th Cong., 1st Sess., pp. 5499-5506, 6714-6730, 6785, 7836-7839; Navy Dept., *Annual Report*, 1887: p. xxii; Navy Dept., *Navy Yearbook*, 1911: pp. 85-86, 721.

[37] *House of Representatives Reports*, 50th Cong., 2nd Sess., No. 3796.

Without trying to detract from the stimulating monograph concerning the building of the New Navy, *The American Naval Revolution* by Professor Walter Herrick, Jr., it would seem slightly more accurate to call the naval expansion in these years an evolution. The process of building the new fleet did not include the sudden, radical, and complete change that the term "revolution" popularly implies. Had the Republicans been able to form a working majority in the House of Representatives, they might well have revolutionized American naval policy. As matters stood, however, Hilary Herbert, ever the convinced expansionist but at the same time realistic and economy-minded, kept a firm but sure hand on the evolution of the new fleet.

In the ensuing debate on Herbert's report, the House followed the precedent of the previous year and passed the naval appropriations bill on the same day it was presented. The agreement between Herbert and Charles Boutelle to eschew partisan bickering was clearly in operation. Although the Maine congressman took the occasion to praise the role of the Republican minority in the passage of naval legislation, he ended his remarks with a firm bipartisan appeal: "The country recognizes the treatment which has been accorded to the Navy by the two political parties of the country, and, gentlemen, the country is going to hold political parties on both sides of this Chamber responsible for carrying on the good work." The Senate accepted the two cruisers for which the House had provided and then added three smaller craft of relatively low cost. The Navy Act of 1889 provided five additional ships for the New Navy.[38]

With the close of the Cleveland administration, Hilary Herbert could look back with pride on the record of the past four years. In taking the chairmanship of the Committee on Naval Affairs, he found eight vessels of the New Navy already approved. In only four years, his committee had spearheaded the authorization of twenty-one new craft for the fleet in addition to taking up work on the Robeson monitors. With a number of the new ships well on the way to completion, the American

---

[38] *Congressional Record*, 50th Cong., 2nd Sess. (1888-1889), pp. 1428-1450, 1743-1750, 2459-2474, 2678-2679. See also *New York Times*, February 21, 1889; Navy Dept., *Navy Yearbook*, 1911: pp. 103-105, 721.

navy was rapidly nearing the place that it would be a respectable fighting force.[39]

As a result of the election of 1888, the Republicans won control of the House of Representatives as well as the Senate and the presidency. Because of Hilary Herbert's commitment to naval expansion, Benjamin F. Tracy, the new secretary of the navy, requested that Speaker Thomas B. Reed leave the Alabamian on the Committee on Naval Affairs. Accordingly, over the next two years, the colonel was the ranking Democrat and leader of the loyal opposition within the group.[40]

The policies formulated during Benjamin F. Tracy's administration of the Navy Department are important because they signaled a shift in strategic thinking concerning the role of the navy. Although the Congress had been moving perceptibly in the direction of larger and larger ships, it was not until the Tracy years that a battleship policy was definitively revealed. During the first decade of the history of the New Navy, because of both political and economic considerations, legislators and policymakers had emphasized the fleet's defensive role. Naval advocates commonly held the view that the United States had no need of a seagoing fleet; strategists envisaged the nation as taking a passive, defensive role in any maritime conflict. There was little thought that America would ever desire to be the offensive rival of any major naval power. Therefore, the two types of vessels that were emphasized were coast defense craft, such as monitors, torpedo craft, and rams; and, secondly, swift unarmored cruisers to prey on enemy commerce. During the Harrison years, however, Secretary Tracy began to utilize the ideas of his friend and adviser, Captain Alfred Thayer Mahan. Pressing on the Congress the need for a battleship fleet which could engage the enemy in mid-ocean, Tracy argued that America's coasts and cities were best defended by a powerful offensive fleet that would be able to destroy an enemy before he came close enough to the American mainland to do any damage.

---

[39] For a spirited defense of the Democratic record, see Hilary Herbert, "The Navy," in William L. Willson, ed., *The National Democratic Party: Its History, Principles, Achievements, and Aims* (Baltimore, H. L. Harvey & Co., Publishers, 1888), pp. 515-572. This book is actually the Democratic campaign manual for 1888.

[40] *Greenville Advocate*, December 18, 1889; *Congressional Record*, 51st Cong., 1st Sess., p. 379.

The secretary's first annual report recommended an ambitious program of eight battleships and eight other auxiliary craft.[41]

The report of the House Navy Committee to the first session of the 51st Congress was presented by the chairman Charles Boutelle. Drawing on the strategy enunciated by Secretary Tracy, Boutelle pointed out that the nation possessed no vessels that could hold their own against the first-class battleships of foreign powers. If war were to come, he explained, the United States Navy would inevitably have to face these huge enemy monsters. To remedy the situation in part, Boutelle requested appropriations for three "sea-going, coast-line battleships" equipped with the heaviest armor. (The curious designation "coast-line" was inserted to make it easier for the adherents of the old strategy to accept the new ships.) Each of the proposed vessels was to have a displacement of about 8,500 tons and was to cost no more than $4,000,000. Boutelle also recommended one armored cruiser of 7,300 tons.[42]

The debate on the naval appropriations bill in 1890, one of the most important in the history of the New Navy, put to a test the willingness of the Congress to accept the new strategy. With the Navy Committee recommending larger and more expensive ships with an obvious offensive capability, it was inevitable that sentiments on behalf of isolationism and economy would surface once again. The Democratic opposition sprang on the Boutelle bill with relish. Representative Joseph D. Sayers of Texas, once a good friend of the fleet, criticized the measure as an expansive and radical departure from the sane Democratic policy. Like Sayers, many other southern Democrats were beginning to balk at further advance. William Holman of Indiana, the powerful arch-foe of naval expansion, called the bill a scheme "to enter upon the construction of a navy of such magnitude as would have appalled any Congress in our former history." Holman then moved to strike the enacting clause of the entire bill. Moreover, the normally strict Republican discipline began to break down. On behalf of a group of midwestern Republicans, Representative Samuel R. Peters of Kansas attacked the measure as extravagant and unnecessary,

---

41 Herrick, *The American Naval Revolution*, pp. 10-11; White, *The Republican Era*, p. 158; Paullin, *Paullin's History*, pp. 337-338; Navy Dept., *Annual Report*, 1889: pp. 10-14.

42 *House of Representatives Reports*, 51st Cong., 1st Sess., No. 1178.

assuring his colleagues with classic midwestern provincialism that "naval warfare . . . is a thing of the past."[43]

Hilary Herbert's speech on the second day of the debate was crucial. With the split in the Republican ranks, Charles Boutelle's bill had no chance of passage unless Herbert, whose word was considered gospel among the pro-Navy Democrats, approved it. Taking the floor, the colonel dissented from the committee report, not in strategy but in tactics. Evidencing his customary moderation and emphasis on economy, the Alabamian advocated two rather than three large battleships. When the Democratic foes of the bill tried to get Herbert to condemn the battleship strategy on principle, the colonel countered with an eloquent appeal for the type of ships that Boutelle sought. A limited number of battleships was essential to national security, he insisted. Launching a scholarly lecture on the various types of vessels in world navies, Herbert explained that the ships which the committee recommended were actually smaller than some presently being built in Europe. Herbert declared that he harbored no reservations about building such vessels except that the work should not proceed so rapidly that it would be improperly supervised.[44]

Although his own suggestion failed to win the necessary votes, Hilary Herbert joined with Charles Boutelle to marshal the pro-navy forces and stave off the isolationist onslaught from midwestern and southern representatives. Fifteen Republicans defected from the navy's cause, but Herbert managed to hold thirty democrats in line (ten of them southerners). Once again the bipartisan coalition provided for the enlargement of the fleet. The Navy Act of 1890 authorized the three battleships that were crucial to the new strategic thinking of the Harrison administration.[45]

The passage of the naval appropriations bill for 1892 was uneventful. Chairman Boutelle asked for only one ship, a protected cruiser of 7,300 tons displacement. Owing to maturing obligations on a number of ships already authorized, the committee explained that the Navy Department already had enough

---

43 *Congressional Record*, 51st Cong., 1st Sess., pp. 3161-3169 and Appendix, pp. 175-178.

44 *Ibid.*, 51st Cong., 1st Sess., pp. 3256-3258.

45 *Ibid.*, 51st Cong., 1st Sess., pp. 3395-3397, 5298, 6493-6496; Navy Dept., *Navy Yearbook*, 1911: pp. 107-126, 721.

to keep it busy. Once again, Herbert and Boutelle spoke almost as one. When several Democratic congressmen attacked the bill they were answered by Herbert rather than the Republican chairman. With a smaller appropriation for new ships, the colonel was able once again to sway a number of southern Democrats to desert their isolationist friends and accept the committee proposals. The Senate accepted the House measure which appropriated around $30,000,000 for naval expenses.[46]

When the Democrats were again able to organize the House at the start of the 52nd Congress in 1891, Hilary Herbert resumed his place as head of the Committee on Naval Affairs. In both of Herbert's two final reports on appropriations he was able to call only for a small naval increase. While warmly praising Secretary Benjamin F. Tracy for his capable administration of the Navy Department, Herbert pointed out that unavoidable delays on the part of domestic contractors had created a situation in which appropriations had far outstripped the capabilities of American yards to complete the ships.[47] Therefore in Herbert's last two years as chairman of the Committee on Naval Affairs, the Congress approved appropriations only for one additional battleship, an armored cruiser, and three light-draft gunboats.[48]

In trying to evaluate Hilary Herbert's work in the Congress on behalf of the New Navy, the historian will find the colonel's last report on naval appropriations illuminating. The statistics speak for themselves. As Herbert left the committee, nine of the vessels authorized in his eight-year tenure were already completed. A total of twenty-five other ships, including four first-class battleships, two second-class battleships, two heavy armored cruisers, and eight light cruisers were in various stages of completion. When Herbert joined the committee in 1886, the United States ranked nineteenth among world naval powers; when all the ships authorized during his tenure were completed, the nation would rank seventh—behind only Great Britain,

---

[46] House of Representatives Reports, 51st Cong., 2nd Sess., No. 3339; Congressional Record, 51st Cong., 1st Sess., pp. 1773-1781, 1793-1801, 1814-1820, 3228-3230; Navy Dept., Navy Yearbook, 1911: pp. 127-145, 721.

[47] House of Representatives Reports, 52nd Cong., 1st Sess., No. 621; 52nd Cong., 2nd Sess., No. 2489.

[48] Congressional Record, 42nd Cong., 1st Sess., p. 6179; 52nd Cong., 2nd Sess. (1892-1893), pp. 2564-2567; Navy Dept., Navy Yearbook, 1911: pp. 147-186, 721.

France, Italy, Russia, Germany, and Spain.[49] Not the least of the Alabamian's contributions was the prodding of a large element of the Democratic representation in Congress away from the traditional small navy policy to a grudging acceptance, at least, of the necessity of a modern steel fleet. Recognizing his emergence as a leader in the House, in 1892 the *New York Times* noted, "Among the Southern men in Congress there is no member whose opinions are more thoroughly respected than Col. Hilary A. Herbert of Alabama."[50]

Of course, a number of men share with Herbert the distinction of being founders of the New Navy. Secretaries Hunt, Chandler, Whitney, and Tracy were among the finest administrators ever to hold the naval portfolio. The work of Charles Boutelle of Maine can hardly be overestimated. In the House of Representatives also, William McAdoo of New Jersey among the Democrats and young Republican congressman Henry Cabot Lodge of Massachusetts often spoke forcefully on naval legislation. In the Senate, Eugene Hale of Maine emerged as the navy's most vocal champion.

Nevertheless, it was in the House of Representatives that the first crucial battles on behalf of the New Navy were fought and won. Secretary Benjamin F. Tracy publicly recognized the two men chiefly responsible for the advancement in his last *Annual Report*. In mentioning by name Hilary Herbert, a member of the opposition party, the retiring secretary paid the Alabamian an unparalleled compliment. Boutelle and Herbert, according to the secretary, had "sustained by their clear perception of our naval necessities, and by unremitting devotion . . . the work of naval reconstruction," and it was to their efforts that "the success of the past eight years is largely due."[51] Perhaps the greatest compliment of all to the colonel as a legislative leader came from fellow-Democrat William McAdoo as the representative from New Jersey left the Naval Committee in 1891. McAdoo stated:

> I know of no better authority in this House or out of it than the able, painstaking, careful, and conservative gentleman from Alabama [Mr. Herbert]. In taking leave of the committee,

---

49 *House of Representatives Reports,* 52nd Cong., 2nd Sess., No. 2489.
50 *New York Times,* March 5, 1892.
51 Navy Dept., *Annual Report,* 1892: p. 31.

after eight years of continuous service upon it, I wish to say
of him that I consider him, speaking generally, as safe a man
to follow upon all questions relative to the Navy as any one
who has ever served in this House; and in saying this I wish
in no way to disparage the ability and zeal of other members
of the committee. Having no personal or special local interest
in naval rehabilitation and reorganization, his broad and catholic patriotism and robust Americanism entitle him to the highest honorable designation of statesman. His stand on this
question does infinite credit to the farseeing statesmanship and
splendid nonsectional spirit of the Southern people in their
phenomenal and unrivaled progress.[52]

III

During his eight years on the Committee on Naval Affairs,
Hilary Herbert spoke on a multitude of other naval matters
in addition to appropriations bills. Two pieces of this other
legislation are especially interesting because the problems involved continued to confront the Alabamian when he left the
House for the Navy Department.

One of Herbert's greatest disappointments as chairman of the
Navy Committee was his inability to win approval for a measure to reorganize the bureau system of the Navy Department.
The administration of the department itself was one of the
most vexing problems faced by the builders of the New Navy.
The disease afflicting the department, according to the historian Leonard D. White, resulted from eight "over-powerful
bureaus, each jealously guarding its respective prerogatives, un-
willing to yield authority to secure coordination, professionally
arrogant, and unmindful of the needs of the Department as
such." Accordingly, the Navy Department was a hodgepodge
of divided authority and competing organization.[53]

Everyone in the Navy knew that the bureau system needed
reform. As early as 1878, a rising young naval officer, Stephen B.
Luce, wrote to Congressman W. C. Whitthorne advocating
consolidation of the bureaus. Ten years later at Annapolis,
Rear Admiral Luce argued that the system showed an "utter
incapacity for dealing with problems of war or military ques-

---

52 *Congressional Record*, 51st Cong., 2nd Sess., pp. 1789-1801.
53 White, *The Republican Era*, pp. 162-163.

tions in general."[54] The dilemma, however, was that no one knew how to get reform past the powerful bureau chiefs. Secretary William E. Chandler had initiated an attempt at consolidation but had backed away when he encountered hostile opposition from the chiefs and their well-placed friends. With the advent of the Cleveland administration with its emphasis on efficiency and economy, the system again came under attack. Secretary Whitney appeared before the Herbert committee on February 16, 1886, and testified that the system had far outlived its usefulness. He recommended that the eight rival bureaus be concentrated into three more manageable and natural divisions: military operations, construction activities, and accounting and supply operations.[55]

As a result of Whitney's appearance, Herbert introduced a bill for the consolidation of the bureau system. The colonel's report on the measure recounted the problem of bickering and lack of coordination within the department. He explained:

> In other words, these eight Bureaus have become eight little Navy Departments. As the business in and about which they are engaged is, to so great an extent, one business, this division of powers and duties brings about many conflicts of authority and results in much needless expenditure of money.[56]

Nevertheless, the sensible proposal by Whitney and Herbert was destined to fail. For one thing, to dramatize the necessity for reorganization, the Democrats had no choice but to criticize past practices in the department. For example, Herbert pointed out that in a time when the value of sail power for modern ships was under serious question, the Navy Department had accumulated 657,000 yards of canvas—enough to outfit every ship in the British Navy twice. Unfortunately, the Republicans, who had administered the Navy Department since the Civil War, viewed the criticism of the department's record as a partisan attack. Even friends of Secretary Chandler, who had once endorsed a reorganization measure himself, rushed

---

54 Albert Gleaves, *Life and Letters of Rear Admiral Stephen B. Luce: U.S. Navy* (New York, G. P. Putnam's Sons, 1925), pp. 227-231.

55 "Memorandum on Consolidation of the Bureaus of the Navy Department," Files of the Committee on Naval Affairs, House of Representatives, 49th Cong., Legislative Records, National Archives; Hirsch, *William C. Whitney*, pp. 289-292.

56 *House of Representatives Reports,* 49th Cong., 1st Sess., No. 1469.

to vindicate his administration by opposing the reformers. The Republicans were joined by friends of the influential bureau chiefs, who personally lobbied against the measure incessantly. The *New York Times* reported, "If the bill is beaten the defeat will undoubtedly be attributed to the adverse influence of the navy circles and the friends of those in the bureaus proposed to be wiped out." Herbert was never able to gather enough votes to overcome the determined opposition bloc. The badly needed consolidation was not effected during Herbert's tenure in the House.[57]

One other issue with which Hilary Herbert dealt was that of the Naval War College, which had been established on the initiative of Secretary William E. Chandler in 1884. The brainchild of Commodore Stephen B. Luce, the college had been designed to offer for naval officers a "postgraduate" course of instruction in the higher naval sciences and in international law and history. In spite of the high hopes of Luce and his young energetic staff member, Alfred Thayer Mahan, the infant institution was not able to win the friendship of Hilary Herbert. In fact, it was only in spite of the powerful committee chairman that the school stayed alive at all. The colonel was not in the least opposed to the intellectual infusion that Luce and his supporters wanted to give the navy. He did believe, however, that this process should take place at Annapolis at the Naval Academy. His opposition, he explained, rested primarily on grounds of economy:

> It does seem to me that at this time when our old fleet is passing away, when it will soon live only in history, now when we need money so much for the building of warships and new guns, now is not the time for the establishment of another naval college.[58]

In 1887, Herbert successfully blocked any appropriation for the school. A. T. Mahan went to Washington to try to win the Alabamian's support. Mahan recalled:

> I went to Washington, and pleaded with the chairman of the House naval committee, Mr. Herbert; but while he was per-

---

[57] *Congressional Record*, 49th Cong., 1st Sess., pp. 5830-5839; 50th Cong., 1st Sess., p. 5055; *New York Times*, December 13, 1886, January 7, 1887.

[58] *Congressional Record*, 49th Cong., 1st Sess., pp. 5830-5839. See also Richardson, *William E. Chandler*, p. 307; Gleaves, *Life and Letters of Luce*, pp. 148-178.

fectly good-natured, and we have from then been on pleasant terms, whenever he saw me he set his teeth and compressed his lips. His argument was: Once establish an institution, and it grows; more and more every year. There must be economy somewhere, and nowhere is economy so effectively applied as to the beginning.[59]

Undoubtedly, the colonel was still bitter about his experience with the Geological Survey, an institution that he believed had got out of hand.

Mahan, having decided the next year to navigate around Herbert if he could not enlist his support, returned to Washington. With the grudging permission of Secretary Whitney, who also was rather unenthusiastic about the college, Mahan launched a sustained lobbying effort directed at the other members of the Committee on Naval Affairs. The indomitable officer succeeded in winning all but three members of the group to his side, and his efforts saved the college during the remainder of Herbert's congressional years. Later Mahan recalled:

This was quite an achievement in its way, for, as one of the members said to me, "It is rather hard to oppose the chairman in a matter of this kind. Still, I am satisfied it is a good thing, and I will vote for it." So we got our appropriation by a big majority. Mr. Herbert was very nice about his discomfiture. That a set of influential naval officers should so unexpectedly have got the better of him, in his position, had a humorous side which he was ready to see; though it is possible we, on whose side the laugh was, enjoyed it more. He afterwards, when Secretary of the Navy, came to think much better of the College, which flourished under him.[60]

One final aspect of Herbert's development during his congressional years is notable: his evolving views concerning foreign policy. As a member of the House of Representatives, a body that usually touched on foreign affairs only in a tangential way, Herbert spoke infrequently on matters of diplomacy. Clearly, however, in his early years in the House, he evidenced that same conservative approach toward diplomacy which char-

---

[59] A. T. Mahan, *From Sail to Steam: Recollections of Naval Life* (New York and London, Harper & Brothers Publishers, 1907), pp. 294-297. See also Nelson W. Aldrich to Admiral S. B. Luce, May 17, 1886, Early Records (NWC AC8), Naval War College Archives.

[60] Mahan, *From Sail to Steam*, pp. 298-299.

acterized all of his opinions and actions. From 1878-1880 the De-Lesseps Company of France undertook to build an interoceanic canal across the Isthmus of Panama. President Rutherford B. Hayes objected to the scheme, however; and citing the Monroe Doctrine, Hayes told the Congress that the United States could never relinquish to a foreign company the right to control a Central American canal. Shortly afterwards, the Hayes administration tried to put teeth into its objections by requesting an appropriation to build a naval and coaling station at the Isthmus. In the finest tradition of conservative nineteenth-century diplomacy, Hilary Herbert took the floor to denounce the administration's scheme. The colonel reminded his comrades in the House that the Monroe Doctrine had grown out of "peculiar circumstances." It originally had only one specific purpose: to prevent Europeans from imposing their form of government on American nations. The original doctrine, Herbert admitted, was necessary and wise; but he could not see that it had any positive application to the canal policy of the Hayes administration. He continued:

> No occasion has risen to cause any alarm for the safety of our Government. No attack is threatened on republican institutions. The alarm has been sounded by President Hayes simply because some enterprising Frenchmen propose to dig a canal across the Isthmus, and these Frenchmen not only work under a charter from the republic to which the Isthmus belongs, but they are themselves citizens of a sister republic, the republic of France. Sir, Mr. Monroe never intended to advance the absurd or dangerous doctrine that the United States of Colombia, a foreign nation, might not charter, if it saw proper, an interoceanic canal within its own borders and permit the subjects of any foreign nation at its pleasure to take stock in and carry on such enterprise.

In concluding, the Alabamian counseled against jingoism and against meddling in the business of others. The business of the United States, he added, should be "attending to our own affairs and leaving other peoples and other nations to attend to theirs in their own way." Although the House rejected Herbert's advice at the time and voted the necessary appropriation for the bases, the Arthur administration dropped the issue after it came into office.[61] Herbert again revealed his cautious tem-

---

61 *Congressional Record*, 46th Cong., 3rd Sess. (1880-1881), pp. 2154-2155; Navy Dept., *Annual Report*, 1881: pp. 24-25.

perament when the Arthur administration instructed John A. Kasson, the American minister in Berlin, to attend the Congo Conference in 1884-1885. The meeting, called by France and Germany, was to discuss free commerce in the Congo Basin, free navigation of the Niger and Congo rivers, and orderly procedures for the establishment of future African colonies. The administration, believing that American trade interests might be involved, felt that it would be wise to have an American representative present. A number of congressmen, Hilary Herbert included, were disturbed at this departure from America's policy of non-involvement. Herbert offered a resolution bluntly requesting that the president explain to the House what particular American interests were involved in the Congo. The resolution called the administration action "a departure from the traditional policy of the Government of the United States" and questioned whether the nation should become involved in "erecting and maintaining a new state on the continent of Africa." Herbert's resolution was not reported back from the Committee on Foreign Affairs; but because other congressmen shared his concern, the House requested and received from President Arthur all documents and correspondence concerning the mission.[62]

In spite of his basically conservative record, throughout his career in Congress, the Alabamian apparently was moving toward the view that naval power and world power were intimately connected. It would be a mistake, however, to describe either Herbert or most of the other Cleveland Democrats in this period as imperialists, expansionists, or jingoists. It is only in the Republican-controlled Senate during this time that one can find incipient expansionist sentiment in the form of talk about "manifest destiny" (with one Democrat, John Tyler Morgan of Alabama notable for his participation).[63] Nevertheless, Hilary Herbert could not help but be aware that the growth of American naval power had monumental international implications. He apparently accepted, even if unconsciously, the idea that the expansion of the navy paralleled an expansion of American interests, especially in the Far East. In 1889, for example, he incorporated into the naval appro-

---

62 *Congressional Record*, 48th Cong., 2nd Sess., pp. 446, 580; David M. Pletcher, *The Awkward Years: American Foreign Policy Under Garfield and Arthur* (Columbia, Mo., University of Missouri Press, 1962), pp. 314-320.

63 *New York Times*, July 28, 1888.

priations bill the sum of $100,000 to construct a naval base on Pago Pago harbor on the island of Tutuila, Samoa. Citing specifically the decade of friction with Germany over the islands, Herbert explained that the Navy Committee wanted to remove all doubt that the United States would permanently occupy this base in the islands. The New Navy also would allow the nation to defend more aggressively its diplomatic interests. In January, 1891, Herbert told the House Democrats that their party had always favored "a vigorous foreign policy and . . . a Navy which would enable us to enforce that policy." When a serious dispute with Chile erupted near the end of the Harrison administration, Herbert evidenced his complete support of whatever naval operations Secretary Tracy felt necessary to defend American interests and honor.[64]

IV

With the approach of the election of 1892, Hilary Herbert was nearing the end of his career in the United States Congress. Although he planned to leave public life, he returned to Alabama one last time to do battle with the Farmers' Alliance. On this occasion he went not for his own sake but on behalf of the Democratic presidential nominee, Grover Cleveland. Predictably, the colonel was the lone member of the Alabama congressional delegation to find the time and courage to confront the angry farmers on Cleveland's behalf. It was a personal victory for Herbert as well as Grover Cleveland when the Democrats won Alabama's electoral votes in November.[65]

As Cleveland was selecting his cabinet in January and February of 1893, it was only natural that he should consider Hilary Herbert for the naval portfolio. The colonel had been too valuable to the navy and to the Democratic party to allow him to retire into the obscurity of law practice in Montgomery. Nevertheless, the Alabamian was not Cleveland's first choice. The president-elect was initially inclined to give the Navy Department to a man from New England, the region that had always evidenced the greatest support for the fleet. Cleveland was also

---

64 *Congressional Record,* 50th Cong., 1st Sess., pp. 1428-1435; 51st Cong., 2nd Sess., pp. 1773-1781; Herbert, "Reminiscences," pp. 310-313.

65 *New York Times,* March 5, 1892; Grover Cleveland to Herbert, March 27 and August 30, 1892, in Herbert Papers.

fearful that the selection of a former Confederate officer to head one of the national military departments might bring severe censure upon him in many of the northern states. According to Cleveland's close aide and adviser, George F. Parker, the colonel was originally considered for another post (which Parker did not identify). When several New Englanders, including Richard Olney who took the attorney generalship, refused the Navy Department, Grover Cleveland determined at last to offer it to the most logical man in the Democratic party.[66]

Several weeks before Cleveland announced his final choice, the newspapers printed rumors that Hilary Herbert would be the next secretary of the navy. The *New York Times* advised: "He has been the best Democratic friend of the Navy in Congress for many years." The *Boston Herald* was almost embarrassingly ardent in its advocacy of Herbert's cause:

> The navy will lose its best friend among Democrats in Congress when Representative Hilary A. Herbert voluntarily closes his service in the House. It is not strange that discriminating naval officers, who appreciate Representative Herbert's services to the navy, should unite with discriminating public men who recognize Mr. Herbert's peculiar fitness for the place in hoping that he may be the secretary of the navy in Mr. Cleveland's cabinet.

Calling Herbert "the congressional secretary of the Navy," the paper asserted that "he has dedicated himself more assiduously to the improvement of the navy than any other man in either house of Congress."[67]

The pattern for the reception of the news of Herbert's appointment was set on the morning it was announced. As soon as the colonel entered the chamber of the House of Representatives, the assembly erupted into a spontaneous ovation from both the Democratic and Republican sides of the aisle.[68] Grover Cleveland soon learned that in this case he had over-

66 Parker, *Recollections of Grover Cleveland*, pp. 177-178, 307-312; Cleveland to Daniel S. Lamont, February 19, 1893, in Allan Nevins, ed., *Letters of Grover Cleveland 1850-1908* (Boston and New York, Houghton Mifflin Company, 1933), p. 318.

67 *New York Times*, February 15, 1893; *Boston Herald*, February 15, 1893, Vol. 8, Herbert Papers.

68 *Congressional Record*, 52nd Cong., 2nd Sess., p. 2063; *New York Times*, February 24, 1893.

estimated the durability of sectionalism. The appointment was warmly praised in papers in both the North and the South. The *Review of Reviews* called it the "most popular appointment" that Cleveland made. The *Nation* declared that the choice was "not only . . . an excellent thing in itself" but was also especially significant in showing that the sectional issue was finally dead. Naval circles were elated also. *Harper's Weekly* suggested that "no appointment could be more popular with the officers of the service than Mr. Herbert's." The *Army and Navy Register* agreed that "seldom . . . has a cabinet appointment received more unanimous applause."[69]

Ironically, only in Alabama, a state which had never before received a cabinet appointment, was there grumbling. The Alliance elements were still bitter about their defeat in 1892 and the part that Herbert had played. The *Alliance Herald* grouched that the Colonel was "Cleveland's lackey" and was "a pliant and ready tool of Wall Street." The paper declared:

> The appointment of Col. Herbert as secretary of the navy seems to have been awarded to him as a reward for his perfidity and treachery to the people of this district in the manner in which he betrayed them on free silver, and a recognition of his pliability in the hands of Wall street spoilators [*sic*].[70]

Nevertheless, the Alabama dissidents could no longer hurt Herbert. The Conservative press rushed into the breech and drowned out the growling with paeans of praise for Herbert's record.

Perhaps the most interesting contemporary assessment of the choice came from an ambitious young professor at Princeton University, Woodrow Wilson:

> Mr. Herbert has long had a very important part in administering the Navy Department. No one has had a more influential share than he in the legislation by which Congress has of late years sought to build up the navy into real effectiveness; and as chairman of the Committee on Naval Affairs in the House of Representatives of the Congress which has just ex-

---

69 *New York Times,* February 24, February 27, 1893; *Review of Reviews,* Editorial, 7 (April, 1893): p. 262; *Nation,* Editorial 56 (March 2, 1893), pp. 151-152; *Harper's Weekly,* Editorial, "The Cabinet," 37 (March 4, 1893): pp. 198-199; and *Army and Navy Register,* n.d., Vol. 8, Herbert Papers.

70 *Alliance Herald,* March 2, 1893, Vol. 9, Herbert Papers.

pired he has been, as it were, the legislative representative and head of the Navy Department—a sort of American parliamentary secretary. He will now manage the Department from the inside instead of from the outside, that is all. His success in Congress has been marked, but it has been so quietly achieved that the country at large has hardly heard of it. Except that the public eye has not much noted him, he has won a cabinet place quite after the English fashion, by a steady course of eminently useful parliamentary service. He has come forward by that process of self-selection which is the most stimulating and significant feature of free institutions under parliamentary forms of government.[71]

It was with such confident public affirmation that Hilary Herbert moved to work in a new vineyard on behalf of the navy and the nation.

---

[71] Woodrow Wilson, "Mr. Cleveland's Cabinet," *Review of Reviews* 7 (April, 1893): p. 290.

VII. Herbert at the Helm: The Navy Department

> Previous Secretaries of the Navy, being obvious heads of the Department, have gotten the credit for many things planned, proposed and accomplished by Mr. Herbert. He is now Secretary of the Navy himself, and may realize both his plans and the reputation which those plans ought to bring him.
>
> —Woodrow Wilson, "Mr. Cleveland's Cabinet," *Review of Reviews*

I

THE new secretary of the navy found the Cleveland cabinet to be a congenial group. Hilary Herbert's personal relations with the president were exceptionally cordial. The colonel found that Cleveland was always willing to listen patiently to suggestions even though he did not always accept the advice they contained. Even when the president was plain-spoken and blunt, the Alabamian found that quality refreshing; Cleveland's directness prevented misinterpretation. In the margin of one of the president's more terse letters to him Herbert later penned, "Whenever he wrote or spoke, no one ever misunderstood him."[1]

President Cleveland gave Herbert a wide latitude in the conduct of all business relating to the navy. In his four years as head of the department, Herbert received only two suggestions from the chief executive concerning the assignments of officers, even though both the president and the secretary were frequently subjected to intense political and social pressure to reward various naval officers with more advantageous posts of duty.[2]

---

1 Cleveland to Herbert, April 5, 1895, Herbert Papers. See also Herbert, "Reminiscences," p. 325.

2 Herbert, "Grover Cleveland and His Cabinet at Work," *Century Magazine* 85 (March, 1913): pp. 740-744. For a typical example of Cleveland's support of his secretary of the navy, see *New York Times,* November 3, 1895.

Although Cleveland obviously had the greatest confidence in Hilary Herbert's ability to manage the Navy Department, it would be a mistake to attribute to the colonel a large personal influence within the administration. The Alabamian was not among Cleveland's closest political advisers or friends. In most important decisions the president turned to the Secretary of State Walter Q. Gresham, Secretary of War Daniel Lamont, or the head of the Treasury Department, the brilliant John G. Carlisle. On Gresham's death, Richard Olney succeeded him in the State Department and joined the circle of the president's closest advisers. A survey of the Cleveland papers shows that Hilary Herbert's letters to the president primarily concerned routine government business. Except in the field of foreign affairs in which the relationship between the Navy and State departments was necessarily close, there is no indication that Cleveland ever asked or received any advice from the secretary of the navy on matters such as the tariff, the financial situation, or the Pullman Strike. On occasion, of course, Herbert spoke out in support of various administration policies, but he was never considered to be a principal spokesman for Cleveland Democracy.[3]

In one sense it was a boon that Hilary Herbert could remain isolated from the problems which bred the rancorous discord that beset the Cleveland administration. Freed from a major role in the controversies of these years, the colonel was able to turn his full attention to the work that he knew best: the building of the new American navy. In taking up the naval portfolio in 1893, Herbert followed several illustrious and capable predecessors, secretaries Hunt, Chandler, Whitney, and Tracy. In large measure Herbert's administration was a perpetuation and enlargement of policies these men had already effected and over which the colonel himself had exercised no small influence in his eight years on the House Navy Committee. The knowledgeable naval historian, Charles O. Paullin, has remarked of these years, 1881-1897, that "it would be diffi-

---

[3] For a discussion of the relative influence of the members of the Cleveland Cabinet within the administration, see Sister Anne Marie Fitzsimmons, "The Political Career of Daniel S. Lamont" (Ph.D. dissertation, Catholic University, 1965), pp. 127-128. One can speculate that it was probably Herbert's lack of influence over national policies other than naval affairs in the Cleveland years that has prevented any scholar from giving him a full biographical treatment until this time.

FIG. 7. President Cleveland's Cabinet, 1893. Courtesy of Library of Congress.

cult to find another period of equal length since the founding
of the department when the navy was better managed. . . ."
Paullin wrote of Herbert specifically, "At the time of his appointment he was one of the best qualified men in the party
for the Navy Secretaryship, for he had taken a more prominent
part in obtaining the legislation for the rebuilding of the navy
than any other Democrat in the House."[4]

It was generally recognized in Washington that it took at
least a year for a civilian secretary to master thoroughly the
intricacies of the administration of the Navy Department. Most
short-term secretaries never even tried. It was very difficult for
most civilian administrators to become adjusted to naval customs, tradition, and eccentricities and to understand the complicated technology involved in ship and weapons construction.
Hilary Herbert, however, came to his new desk ready to make
executive decisions on the first day. During his years in Congress he had gained, as Leonard D. White has pointed out, "an

---

4 Paullin, *Paullin's History*, pp. 364-365, 367.

unsurpassed working knowledge of the navy."⁵ It is no exaggeration to say that Herbert was one of the best qualified civilians ever to head a military department in our nation's history.

The Alabamian attacked his new duties with the same display of energy that the personnel of the Navy Department had come to expect of him through their intimate acquaintance in the past eight years. The *Illustrated American* described him in 1894 as "one of the most industrious members of the Cabinet" and also remarked that he was one of the "most accessible." The secretary of the navy, the journal conjectured, apparently was able to dispatch his work very rapidly because he had come to the position with prior experience and competence. Herbert usually spent an hour at home each weekday morning, often with his private secretary, attending to personal correspondence. He arrived at the department by ten o'clock and often remained until six or seven in the evening. The morning hours were usually devoted to appointments, and afternoons were reserved for departmental business and conferences with the bureau chiefs. Herbert's personal office staff was very small: a private secretary; a stenographer; one naval aide; and the intractable seventy-five-year-old receptionist Jesse Harris, who fended off swarms of favor seekers with the skill of a practiced swordsman.⁶

The secretary was customarily inclined to stay fairly close to his desk. He did, however, use a month or two each summer. to visit and inspect the navy yards at Norfolk, Boston, Brooklyn, Philadelphia, and Portsmouth, New Hampshire. Herbert usually traveled on the dispatch boat *Dolphin* during each of these trips. In the summer of 1894, he pleased navy constituents on the West Coast when he journeyed across country to visit the yards at Puget Sound and at Mare Island, San Francisco. During his tours Herbert was able to add considerably to his knowledge of naval construction and was always delighted to receive practical suggestions from the men in the yards as to how their work could be facilitated. He always facetiously contended that the great naval slogan "Don't Give Up the Ship!" had nothing to do with action in battle but,

---

5 White, *The Republican Era,* pp. 154-157.

6 "The Ways of Cabinet Officers: Secretary Herbert," *Illustrated American* 16 (August 4, 1894): pp. 152-153.

rather, referred to the trouble the secretary had in getting a
vessel away from the navy yard once it had gone there for
repairs.[7]

Actually Herbert made his first inspection of a yard only a
week after he assumed his duties when he traveled to New
York and visited the Brooklyn Yard, the largest of the construction and repair facilities. The colonel's real purpose for traveling to New York City, however, was to attend a dinner at the
Hamilton Club offered in honor of his predecessor, Benjamin
F. Tracy. Herbert had not forgotten that bipartisanship was
absolutely essential for continued naval expansion. The colonel
graciously announced to the press that he planned to continue
the policies of secretaries Whitney and Tracy and that, more
especially, he would continue the system of civil service employment in the navy yards that Tracy had instituted. At the
Hamilton Club dinner, Herbert sat by Secretary Tracy's side.
During his remarks the colonel lauded Tracy's administration
as "masterful, original and progressive." Tracy in turn heaped
praise on the Alabamian, calling him "capable, honest, energetic, and patriotic" and assuring the audience that there was
no danger that the Navy Department would retrogress during
the Herbert years.[8] To the uninitiated, the affair might have
appeared to be just another testimonial dinner. The event,
however, was of dramatic significance. A pact for four more
years had been informally sealed. In naval affairs, at least, the
détente between Republicans and Democrats was to continue;
the navy would not suffer as a result of partisanship.

About a month after taking office, Secretary Herbert also
had the pleasure of presiding over an American-sponsored international naval review. Congress had authorized the pageant
in 1890, and Secretary Tracy had completed most of the plans
before leaving office. Modern warships from nine other nations
joined the American fleet for the extravaganza in the New
York harbor. The events, attracting thousands of spectators and
wide press coverage, greatly enhanced the prestige of the New
Navy among both Democrats and Republicans at home and
within the international community abroad.[9]

---

[7] *New York Times,* October 8, 1893; Herbert, "Reminiscences," pp. 334-340.

[8] *New York Times,* March 15, March 17, 1893.

[9] U.S. Navy Department, *Annual Report,* 1893: p. 49; Herbert, "The Lesson
of the Naval Review," *North American Review* 156 (June, 1893): pp. 641-647.

Throughout his four years in the administration, Herbert continued to enjoy a varied social life of dinners, parties, and the theater, although his own budget for entertainment was limited by his lack of independent financial resources. His daughter Leila served in her mother's place as Cabinet lady. She frequently entertained and often accompanied her father to official functions. Her youthful charm and eligibility made her a center of attention wherever they went; and in June, 1893, her proud father allowed her to christen the battleship *Massachusetts* at its launching in Philadelphia. Herbert did not neglect his own romantic interests. In 1896 he informed William L. Wilson, who was then postmaster general, that he had "at last found a woman he could love"; but a match with the unnamed captivator for some reason never materialized.[10]

One of Herbert's first duties in office was to assist the president in choosing an assistant secretary of the navy. The position of assistant secretary had been abolished after the Civil War but had finally been reinstituted in 1890-1891 because of the greatly expanded work of the department. There was evidently no doubt in Herbert's mind as to the man he wanted for the job. He strongly urged President Cleveland to offer the post to his old colleague from the House Committee on Naval Affairs, William McAdoo. McAdoo, the son of Irish immigrants, had come to the United States as a child. For many years he lived in Jersey City and in 1883 was elected to Congress. Leaving the House in 1891, he opened private law practice in New York City. Naval circles applauded the announcement of McAdoo's selection as another indication that President Cleveland was genuinely committed to a large navy policy. Hilary Herbert gave his new lieutenant a wide range of responsibility. During the four years McAdoo had general supervision over the repair and construction activities in the navy yards, naval boards of survey and investigation, the Navy Department Library, the Naval War Records Office, the Naval War College, the Office of Naval Intelligence, and the Marine Corps and Naval Militia.[11] In 1894 in an effort further to aug-

---

10 Festus P. Summers, ed., *The Cabinet Diary of William L. Wilson, 1896-1897* (Chapel Hill, University of North Carolina Press, 1957), pp. 24-27. See also *New York Times,* January 6, 1894; and New York *Sun,* June 11, 1893, Vol. 7, Herbert Papers.

11 Paullin, *Paullin's History,* pp. 368-369; *Harper's Weekly,* editorial, "Mr.

FIG. 8.   The International Naval Review in New York Harbor, 1893. Courtesy
of U.S. Navy Department.

ment civilian control over the department, Herbert appointed
his son-in-law Benjamin Micou to the vacant position of chief
clerk in the Navy Department. The appointment was made
with President Cleveland's personal approval in the hope that
Herbert's close relationship with Micou would also give the
secretary a closer view of the management of the bureaus.[12]

During Herbert's administration the work of the Navy Department continued to be divided among eight bureaus. The
most influential of the bureau chiefs was Rear Admiral Francis
M. Ramsay, head of the Bureau of Navigation. As Herbert's
closest associate and adviser, Admiral Ramsay took charge of
the department when both Herbert and assistant secretary
McAdoo were absent. As Chief of Navigation, Ramsay was the
most powerful officer in the service, maintaining a firm grip on
all matters related to personnel and to the operations of the
fleet. The next four bureaus were those that concerned in one
way or another the manufacture of ships. The Bureau of Construction and Repair, headed by the competent Rear Admiral
Philip Hichborn, was charged with the design, construction,
and fitting and repair of the hulls of all vessels belonging to
the fleet. The Bureau of Steam Engineering, charged with the
design, building, and repair of machinery, was under the super-

Cleveland's Nominations," **37** (March, 1893): pp. 285-286; *New York Daily
Tribune,* March 16, 1893, Vol. 9, Herbert Papers. McAdoo was not related to
William Gibbes McAdoo, who served as secretary of the treasury in the adminis-
tration of Woodrow Wilson.

12 *New York Times,* November 28, 1893; Herbert, "Reminiscences," p. 366.

vision of Rear Admiral George W. Melville, a brilliant engineer who personally designed the machinery for a number of the ships of the New Navy. The Bureau of Equipment, which secured and installed all equipment to go in naval craft, was headed by Commodore French E. Chadwick. Commodore William T. Sampson, as chief of ordnance, supervised the building and fitting of all armament for the ships of the fleet. The three lesser bureaus were those of Supplies and Accounts, Yards and Docks, and Medicine and Surgery. Another important office that was attached to the department was the Office of Naval Intelligence, which collected and classified information concerning foreign navies, coast defenses, and resources.[13]

Although Hilary Herbert had never been impressed with the bureau system as an institution, he found the eight chiefs to be quite capable and impressive men personally. During his years on the House Navy Committee, the colonel had developed a frank partiality toward naval officers, who generally were, as he phrased it, "a very superior class of men." In contrast to most army officers, Herbert observed, the naval elite traveled widely throughout the world in the course of duty and, consequently, acquired a broader knowledge about world affairs and the cultures of other peoples. On many occasions the secretary readily accepted the recommendations of the bureau chiefs. He had a special regard for the opinions of Admiral Ramsay, who was in effect his "chief of staff" and whom the colonel considered one of the most "upright and just-minded" men he had ever known. Herbert was not reluctant in the least, however, to disregard the chiefs' advice. Throughout his administration he was aware of a continued rivalry between three of the chiefs: Hichborn of Construction and Repair, Melville of Steam Engineering, and Sampson of Ordnance. Herbert was not inclined to follow the precedent of submitting matters of dispute between the chiefs to boards of officers for arbitration. Too often, the secretary observed, the decisions of the boards were based on friendships and influence rather than the merits of the cases at issue. Not unreasonably, Herbert concluded that such decisions were the responsibility of the

---

13 W. H. Beehler, "The United States Navy," in: T. A. Brassey, ed., *The Naval Annual*, 1899 (Portsmouth, England, J. Griffin and Company, 1899), pp. 93-96; Paullin, *Paullin's History*, pp. 373-375, 385; U.S. Navy Dept., *Annual Report*, 1896: pp. 56-57.

civilian secretary who was less moved by considerations of rank
and influence. Throughout his administration, the colonel sat
as judge and final arbiter of disputes between the bureaus.
When differences arose, each chief involved was invited to submit his case in writing. Before making a final determination,
Herbert also allowed each officer to explain his views verbally.
in the presence of all others involved.[14] The secretary's firm
guidance brought an order among the squabbling chiefs that
the department had rarely known.

II

The most pressing and time consuming business which occupied Secretary Herbert in his early days in office consisted
of interminable patronage problems. A deluge of office seekers
streamed into the Navy Department. So great was the press of
the crowd that the new secretary was able to transact routine
departmental business only in snatches. Moreover, Hilary Herbert had very little patronage as secretary of the navy. Of the
300 clerks assigned to the various parts of the department,
at least half were on civil service and could not be summarily
removed by the secretary. Especially troublesome were the
droves of southern women who beseiged the colonel. He recalled that

> it seemed to me as if all the loveliest and most eloquent women
> in the South, those at least who had been impoverished by the
> results of the war, had all at once made up their minds that I,
> a wounded ex-Confederate was the person to whom they could
> apply for office with a certainty of success, and my heart was
> never at any time in my life so wrung by piteous appeals.

Herbert was simply unable to accommodate most of his sup-
plicants. Of the 150 clerks who were under his personal control, only the most inefficient were replaced. His four years at
the Navy Department left him even more convinced that the
civil service system was the best way to fill government jobs.
Even though he gave his own appointments careful consideration, before leaving the department he reached the conclusion
that the clerks placed by the merit system were at least twenty-

---

14 Herbert, "Reminiscences," pp. 321-324.

FIG. 9. Launching the U.S.S. *Nashville*, 1895. Secretary Herbert is in the top
hat. Courtesy of U.S. Navy Department.

five per cent more efficient than those he had personally
chosen.[15]

The biggest patronage squabble, however, concerned the
navy yards rather than the Navy Department proper. For years
political interference had undermined the efficiency and effec-
tiveness of the yards. An investigation in 1876 had revealed
that in some yards it was customary to pad the payrolls with
hundreds of extra "employees" (few of whom actually worked)
around important local and national elections. During the
Grant administration, in fact, employees had been foisted off
on the yards even over the protests of the commandants who
insisted that they did not want or need any more workers.
Congressmen with yards in or near their districts kept unre-
lenting pressure on the secretary of the navy to keep patronage
open for them; and for many years a number of powerful legislators exercised almost arbitrary control over certain
yards.[16]

It was not until 1891 that a sweeping reform was made in
the navy yards, when Secretary Benjamin R. Tracy launched
"the most comprehensive administrative reform in naval history." In a series of directives to yard commandants, Tracy
wiped out the old patronage policies and instituted an em-

15 Herbert, "Reminiscences," p. 20.
16 Paullin, *Paullin's History*, pp. 351-352.

ployment system based on merit rather than political affiliation. All yard foremen were hired solely on the basis of competitive examinations, and other skilled workers were given preliminary examinations and a two-week trial period before they were hired. Tracy directed the boards of registration which supervised the application procedure to avoid any reference to political party.[17]

When Hilary Herbert took over the Navy Department, he found that Tracy's new system was working reasonably well; it was undoubtedly a vast improvement over the old patronage mills. The superintendent of one yard estimated that the reform had already reduced operating costs by at least twenty-five per cent. Secretary Herbert was the first Cabinet member in the Cleveland administration to make a statement on civil service. Concluding that he would only set a bad precedent for his successors if he started chipping away at the system, Herbert announced that politics would have no place in the navy yards during his tenure in office. Herbert's announcement that he would continue the Tracy system brought cries of anguish from spoils-hungry Democrats throughout the country. Democratic partisans charged that Tracy had stacked the yards with Republicans before changing the rules and that the new system had been unfairly administered in favor of Republicans. The New York *World* found it ironic that Herbert was now being abused by the Democratic bosses for upholding the very system for which greedy Republican party hacks had bitterly condemned Secretary Tracy. The *Brooklyn Daily Eagle* ran a large cartoon which showed Herbert and Uncle Sam standing arm in arm behind a navy yard gate which was secured with a padlock labeled "Civil Service," while outside the yard a motley assortment of angry spoilsmen were trying unsuccessfully to break in.[18]

Some of the Democratic bosses never forgave Herbert. In August, 1893, Boss Richard Croker of Tammany Hall who had expected "a clean sweep in all working departments," expressed his outrage and disgust that Herbert allowed him to choose only a stray clerk now and then. When Max Popper, the head

---

17 Herrick, *The American Naval Revolution,* pp. 134-136.

18 Paullin, *Paullin's History,* pp. 408-409; Herbert, "Reminiscences," p. 319; New York *World,* April 1, 1893; New York *Evening Post,* March 31, 1893; *Brooklyn Daily Eagle,* March 19, 1893; all newspapers in Vol. 9, Herbert Papers.

of the party in California, came to see Herbert about patronage at the San Francisco yard, he was politely told by the secretary that the navy "was not in business to do politics or look after patronage for the party." Infuriated, Popper left Washington openly declaring that Herbert was too traitorous to be called a Democrat. When the secretary journeyed to California in the summer of 1894 to visit the Mare Island yard, Popper snubbed the colonel by refusing to greet or have anything to do with him.[19]

Herbert made only one change in the system during his four years that indirectly aided members of his own party. In September of 1893 he issued a departmental order specifying that registrants' names would be kept on the application rolls of the yards for only a year at a time. The provision that applicants had to re-register each year did give Democrats an equal opportunity to move to the top of the lists. The new provision also prevented unnecessary delays in searching for applicants who had registered years earlier and then moved or taken other employment.[20]

The continued hostility of the Democratic bosses did not deter the colonel. In his first annual report in 1893, he bluntly suggested that although senators and representatives had in the past recommended men of character to the yards, the legislators usually had no knowledge of the individuals' abilities to build ships. Incompetence was often the result, Herbert explained, when a man was hired simply to please his friends. In his last report in 1896 Herbert happily reported that President Cleveland had extended the regular civil service classification to cover almost all the laborers in the navy yards. When the Civil Service Commission took over administrative procedures of the system, it found the rules already in effect in the yards so satisfactory that it simply adopted the Navy Department regulations as its own. When John D. Long succeeded Herbert as secretary of the navy under President McKinley, Long kept the civil service system intact; politics had been virtually removed from the navy yards.[21]

---

19 *Brooklyn Daily Eagle,* August 27, 1893; *San Francisco Chronicle,* June 15, 1894, both in Vol. 9, Herbert Papers.

20 *New York Times,* September 10, 1893.

21 U.S. Navy Dept., *Annual Report,* 1893: pp. 51-52 and *Annual Report,* 1896: pp. 45-48; Departmental Order No. 12, "Departmental Orders," Records of the

Fɪɢ. 10.   U.S.S. *Dolphin*, a dispatch boat, frequently conveyed the secretary of the navy to official functions. Courtesy of U.S. Navy Department.

Another decision facing Secretary Herbert as he began his term in the Navy Department concerned the fate of the Naval War College. The colonel had grown no more appreciative of the fledgling institution than he had been in his congressional years. The supporters of the school felt the cold chill of imminent disaster when Grover Cleveland had announced his choice for the naval portfolio. Even before the selection was made, Captain Alfred T. Mahan had written to Herbert begging him to continue the appropriation for the college at the second session of the 52nd Congress. Mahan argued that "despite the dead up-hill drag and a condition of half-suspended animation for so much of the time, the College had obtained wide recognition, abroad as well as at home."[22] By the summer of 1893, the sky looked even darker for the school. Rear Admiral Ramsay, who was rapidly emerging as the most powerful officer in the administration, had opposed the college from the start and would be only too happy to get Secretary Herbert's permission to wield the departmental axe against the young institution.[23]

Navy Department, National Archives, Record Group 80 (hereafter the abbreviation NA RG 80 will be used to cite the general collection of naval records). See also John D. Long, *The New American Navy* (New York, The Outlook Company, 1903) 1: pp. 55-56 and *Thirteenth Annual Report of the United States Civil Service Commission* (Washington, Government Printing Office, 1897), pp. 151-171.

[22] Mahan to Herbert, January 31, 1893, in Files of the Committee on Naval Affairs, House of Representatives, 52nd Cong., Legislative Records, NA.

[23] John A. S. Grenville and George Berkeley Young, *Politics, Strategy, and American Diplomacy: Studies in Foreign Policy, 1873-1917* (New Haven and London, Yale University Press, 1966), pp. 27-29.

The ominous portents of disaster for the college loomed even larger when Mahan, the leading light of the school, was ordered to sea to assume the command of the U. S. S. *Chicago*. Although Mahan had requested that he be allowed to continue shore duty to concentrate on his writing, Admiral Ramsay insisted that he go to sea; and Secretary Herbert acquiesced in the assignment. Mahan's volatile friend Theodore Roosevelt wrote to the captain:

> In common with all the rest of the world, I saw your orders to sea with the deepest regret and disgust. One is tempted to wonder at such short-sightedness and I can only believe that Secretary Herbert who is to me distinguished by his common sense is simply misinformed as to the scope and importance of the magnificent work upon which you are engaged.

Roosevelt had virtually given up hope for the War College already. He had earlier confided to his friend Mahan:

> I fear all hope for the War College (which is nothing without you) is gone; our prize idiots have thrown away a chance to give us an absolutely unique position in naval affairs. . . .

Admiral Ramsay, Roosevelt exploded, was a "blind, narrow, mean, jealous pedant"; and the young politician angrily concluded that "if I can ever do him a bad turn I most certainly will—and I'll see that [Henry Cabot] Lodge does."[24]

Nevertheless, before Herbert made his final decision about the college, he determined in the summer of 1893 to visit the school personally. On board the *Dolphin* during the trip to Newport, the commander of the vessel, Lieutenant B. H. Buckingham, contrived to give the secretary copies of Mahan's two-volume work, *The Influence of Sea Power Upon the French Revolution*. The colonel, who had previously lacked the time to read extensively in Mahan's writings, was delighted with the book. The profound impression that the book made, along with a most enjoyable visit at the War College, caused Herbert to alter his views. The secretary returned to Washington and informed a crestfallen Ramsay that he had changed his mind. Commodore French E. Chadwick, chief of the Bureau of Equipment, rushed off a note to Mahan, telling him that

---

24 Mahan to Roosevelt, March 18, 1893; Roosevelt to Mahan, May 1, May 18, 1893, in Special Correspondence, Alfred T. Mahan Papers, Library of Congress.

"the War College is safe—the Sec. read your last book (on Sea Power) and that convinced him." A relieved and delighted Mahan informed his friend Stephen B. Luce of the news and exclaimed, "But to think that Hilary A. Herbert should be the saviour of the College against Ramsay . . . and the other enemies."[25]

In October, 1893, the secretary himself told Mahan of his change of heart in a gracious personal letter. He wrote:

> Permit me to thank you for your kind letter, and to tell you of my change of opinion as to the War College, after inspecting the War College buildings personally, and carefully reading the two articles by you upon the subject, and also your two volumes upon "The Influence of Sea Power on the French Revolution." In my opinion you deserve all the encomiums of the British and American press for this great work. . . . You have conferred great honor, not only upon the American Navy, but also upon your country.

Herbert added that he found especially useful Mahan's observations on the "comparatively little effect" of commerce-destroyers and that he planned to use some of Mahan's arguments in his request for battleships in his annual report.[26] True to his word Secretary Herbert remained a warm supporter of the War College. In his annual report for 1894 he recounted his past opposition to the school but then added that he was now convinced that its work was so invaluable that the college should be established on a permanent basis. In August of 1896, the secretary traveled to Newport and delivered an address at the War College entitled "The Sea and Sea Power As a Factor in the History of the United States" in which he argued that the importance of the Union naval blockade during the Civil War had never been adequately recognized as one of the chief reasons for the eventual Union triumph. In his last annual report as secretary, Herbert again commended the

---

25 Grenville and Young, *Politics, Strategy,* pp. 27-29; F. E. Chadwick to Mahan, August 10, 1893, in Special Correspondence, Mahan Papers; Mahan to Luce, August 24, 1893, in Gleaves, ed., *Life and Letters of Stephen B. Luce,* pp. 322-323. For further substantiation of Secretary Herbert's fascinating conversion, see "Historical Notes Concerning the U.S. Naval War College," typescript of a lecture by Rear Admiral S. B. Luce, August 20, 1906, Presidents' Files, Naval War College Archives.

26 Herbert to Mahan, October 4, 1893, in Special Correspondence, Mahan Papers.

FIG. 11. Captain Alfred T. Mahan, seated left, with his officers aboard the U.S.S. *Chicago*. Courtesy of U.S. Navy Department.

work of the college and cited especially the importance of the strategic studies on seapower that A. T. Mahan had developed there.[27]

Early in 1894, Secretary Herbert again revealed his respect for A. T. Mahan when a bitter intra-service squabble erupted between Mahan, who was then in command of the *Chicago*, and Rear Admiral Henry Erben, the commanding officer of the European Station. The unfortunate episode was the result primarily of professional jealousy and of the prejudice which Erben shared with Admiral Ramsay and others of the old school that Mahan was a worthless "pen and ink sailor."[28] In December, 1893, Admiral Erben routinely inspected Mahan's vessel. The admiral's report of his inspection of the *Chicago* was not so routine, however; the document was a bombshell that stunned the entire service. Although Erben rated Mahan "excellent" on general conduct and sobriety and "good" on health, in the categories involving professional ability and atten-

27 U.S. Navy Dept., *Annual Report*, 1894: pp. 28-30 and *Annual Report*, 1896: pp. 53-55; *New York Times*, August 10, 1896; Herbert, "The Sea and Sea Power As a Factor in the History of the United States," *Proceedings of the United States Naval Institute* 12 (1896): pp. 561-576.

28 W. D. Puleston, *Mahan: The Life and Work of Captain Alfred Thayer Mahan, U.S.N.* (New Haven, Yale University Press, 1939), p. 151.

tion to duty he gave the captain only a grade of "tolerable."
Erben explained himself saying that:

> Mahan always appears to advantage to the service in all that
> does not appertain to ship life or matters, but in this particular
> he is lacking in interest. . . . His interests are entirely outside
> the service, for which, I am convinced he cares but little, and
> is therefore not a good naval officer.

No one was more shocked than Captain Mahan himself. He
replied directly to Secretary Herbert. He had not, the captain
asserted, neglected his duties at any time. He explained:

> A man may say, as I have, that details of administration,
> which make up so much of a Captain's duty, are to him un-
> interesting; it by no means follows that he does not interest
> himself in the proper discharge of them when a Captain. . . .
> The question is not what I feel but what I do; and the test of
> what I do is the results obtained. That is the question of the
> present condition and efficiency of the ship.

Mahan defended the condition of the *Chicago* and then offered
to put his personal reputation on the line as well as the record
of the ship before a full-scale board of inquiry. He added:

> At a time when distinguished officers of other nations are say-
> ing that my treatment of naval warfare is better than anything
> ever yet done, to have said that I am not a good naval officer
> gives an odd impression.[29]

Once again Theodore Roosevelt and Henry Cabot Lodge
sprang to Mahan's defense. Lodge went straight to Secretary
Herbert to discuss the matter. During the interview the colonel
told Lodge that he had concluded to endorse personally on
the Erben report that the charges were not of sufficient consequence to warrant further investigation or consideration. In
effect, Theodore Roosevelt informed Mahan's wife, by ending
the matter at his desk Secretary Herbert had virtually vindicated the captain's position and at the same time had wisely
avoided a newspaper scandal. In the middle of June, Herbert officially communicated his decision by letter to Captain
Mahan; and ten days later the secretary penned in his own hand

---

29 Erben Report, "Report on the Fitness of Officers," and Mahan to secretary
of the navy, January 25, 1894, in Mahan Papers.

a warm personal note to assure the captain that the matter would be dropped and forgotten. In closing Herbert graciously assured Mahan that the entire nation was proud of his work and of the international acclaim he had received.[30]

The first year of Herbert's administration was marred by two other unfortunate events. One involved the loss of the magnificent old fighting ship *Kearsarge* in February, 1894, on the Roncador Reef (about 200 miles north of Bluefields, Nicaragua). The *Kearsarge* was the vessel which had finally destroyed the formidable Confederate commerce-destroyer *Alabama*. Since that time *Kearsarge*, the most famous ship remaining in the old navy, had become virtually a national monument. Public dismay was not eased by the department's determination that the accident was primarily the result of carelessness and miscalculation. Herbert did not try to cover over the circumstances. In his second annual report he informed the president:

It was peculiarly unfortunate that this old ship, historic in battle, should go down upon a well-known reef in a time of profound peace when there was not a cloud in the sky. The prompt punishment, by sentence of court-martial of the officers responsible, does not repair the injury.

At Herbert's suggestion the Congress approved a departure from the tradition of naming battleships after states so that one of the ships being built for the New Navy might be given the name *Kearsarge*.[31]

Another episode was in a sense even more unfortunate because it cast a stigma on the reputation of the entire service. The events began in an unlikely way and at first involved only one officer and the secretary. By way of background, it is important to note that Hilary Herbert came to the Navy Department with the determination to be a strong secretary. During his years in the House he had sympathized with the difficulties that his predecessors at the department had found in dealing with a few of the officers of command rank who on occasion could be imperious and arrogant, almost to the point of in-

---

[30] Roosevelt to Mrs. A. T. Mahan, February 10, February 12, 1894; Herbert to Mahan, June 15, June 25, 1894, in Mahan Papers.

[31] U.S. Navy Dept., *Annual Report*, 1893: pp. 9-10. See also *New York Times*, February 9, March 21, April 5, 1894.

FIG. 12. Rear Admiral Francis M. Ramsey, Chief of Navigation, was the most powerful officer in the navy through most of the 1890's. Courtesy of U.S. Navy Department.

subordination to the civilian secretary. Herbert's testing (or so he thought at any rate) came scarcely two months after he had assumed his duties. In May of 1893 Herbert ordered the vessel *Atlanta,* under the command of Captain Francis J. Higginson, to proceed immediately to Nicaragua to protect American interests during revolutionary upheavals there. After a delay in coaling at New York, the ship took ten days to make the five-day trip to Kingston, Jamaica; and then Captain Higginson experienced another unexplained delay between Jamaica and Greytown, Nicaragua. It was well known in naval circles that tropical Greytown was a very undesirable post of duty during the summer. It was also common knowledge that the technique of delay had enabled naval officers in the past to defy temporarily at least their orders from the Navy Department. Long before the tardy Higginson reached his destination, the Navy Department and even several newspapers were buzzing with the talk that the *Atlanta's* skipper had openly challenged Secretary Herbert, circumventing the orders by deliberate delay.

The colonel's reaction was quite understandable. As soon as he was convinced that the reports were essentially correct, he fired off a telegram to Higginson, pre-emptorily dismissing him from duty and ordering him home.[32] In the aftermath of the episode, the *Marine Journal* carried a quotation:

> There are a great many dry bones in the navy which need an occasional rattling, and the determination of Secretary Herbert to rattle them will have a good effect throughout the service, and cause the officers from the highest to the lowest degree to realize that it is not wise to monkey with the landlubber from Alabama.[33]

When Captain John P. Bartlett replaced Captain Higginson as skipper of the *Atlanta*, everyone assumed that the affair had ended, pending at least a board of inquiry or court-martial for Higginson. The scandal had only just begun, however. On July 21 Captain Bartlett relinquished the *Atlanta* to the Norfolk Navy Yard for routine scraping, painting, and repairs. During the night a fire broke out aboard the vessel because someone had carelessly left hot ashes piled in a fire room. Although the fire itself caused only slight damage, the department ordered the customary investigation of the fire and inspection of the ship. A board of inquiry which convened early in August under Rear Admiral Thomas O. Selfridge was shocked and appalled at the conditions it discovered aboard the *Atlanta*. The evidence was indisputable that the vessel had been neglected and abused. Admiral Selfridge reported that the question of the fire which the board was orginally established to investigate was now secondary to the deplorable condition of the ship. The board's report called the *Atlanta's* condition "discreditable," one of the severest words in navy vocabulary.[34]

The *New York Times*, a paper known for the accuracy of its naval news and its support of the New Navy, described the *Atlanta* affair as a "veritable scandal" and pronounced the

---

[32] *Nation* 56 (May 25, June 1, 1893): pp. 378, 399-400; Higginson to secretary of the navy, May 12, 1893, in "Area File of the Naval Records Collection, 1775-1910," Roll 112, NA (cited hereafter as "Area File" followed by roll number). See also *Evergreen Star*, Evergreen, Alabama, June 8, 1893, and *Philadelphia Press*, June 22, 1893, Vol. 9, Herbert Papers.

[33] *Marine Journal*, June 10, 1893, Vol. 9, Herbert Papers.

[34] General Order No. 418 (September 7, 1893), "General Orders and Circulars," NA RG 80.

cruiser's condition "almost beyond belief." Such conditions
had evidently prevailed on the ship while it was under the
command of at least three different officers: Captains J. W.
Philips, Higginson, and Bartlett. Each of these men and their
subordinates, the paper observed, had successively covered up
for each other by submitting false reports that the *Atlanta* had
undergone and passed thorough inspection. The board of investigation found that the ship's collision doors were so rusted
that they had not been operable for months—yet reports had
continued to be submitted that they had been regularly tested
and were in working order. The only conclusion the *Times*
could reach was that the ship's officers had simply lied in their
official reports. The paper concluded by questioning the point
of even building a new navy if the officers were then going to
ruin it through abuse and neglect.[35]

Secretary Herbert faced a real dilemma in determining what
action to take in the *Atlanta* affair. He had no desire to try to
whitewash the malfeasance of the men responsible. Nevertheless, it was almost impossible to determine exactly where responsibility for the *Atlanta's* condition lay. The misuse of the
craft had extended over a number of months and through at
least three different commands. Most of the men involved had
already been transferred to other duty with squadrons in various parts of the world. To call so many men back for court-
martial would seriously disrupt the entire service and would
only intensify the scandal in the press. Even then, some of the
culprits would escape altogether.

Herbert finally decided that his emphasis should be on pre-
vention of such an episode in the future rather than upon punishment. In a lengthy general order the secretary published
for the entire fleet the full details of the *Atlanta* investigation.
He explained the difficulties which prevented the department
from taking further action and pointed out that a number of
the officers involved were "richly deserving" of court-martial.
Such conditions, Herbert sternly concluded, should never again
be allowed to exist on a ship of the United States Navy.[36]

An interesting sidelight is that the latter episode absolved
Captain Higginson from the original charge of deliberate delay

---

35 *New York Times*, September 3, 1893.
36 General Order No. 418, "General Orders and Circulars," NA RG 80;
Washington Post, September 8, 1893.

FIG. 13. U.S.S. *Atlanta*, the first vessel of the new American navy, was involved in a serious scandal in 1893. Courtesy of U.S. Navy Department.

in sailing for Greytown in May. The inspection at the Norfolk yard showed that the vessel was in terrible condition at the time and needed extensive repairs. Higginson was evidently fortunate to be able to get the ship to Greytown at all. Although the captain still obviously shared in the blame for the *Atlanta's* general condition, Herbert admitted that he had apparently been wrong in charging Higginson with calculated delay and promised that the original episode would not prejudice the captain's future assignments.[37]

Fortunately the *Atlanta* affair was the only major scandal to

---

37 *Boston Herald,* September 30, 1893, Vol. 9, Herbert Papers.

involve naval officers during Herbert's administration. During
the remainder of his tenure, the secretary was able to concentrate on the supervision of several significant developments in
ship construction. For example, his administration introduced
the sheathing of the steel hulls of vessels with copper. Herbert
ordered this process for two of the three gunboats contracted
in his first year at the department. The question of sheathing
had been under discussion for years. The process had been
avoided in the past because of added expense, but Herbert's
chief constructor Philip Hichborn favored giving sheathing a
trial. The introduction of the innovation for use in American
vessels was a significant advance. The copper coating prevented
erosion of a ship's hull by rust and also retarded fouling of
the bottom by buildup of barnacles and marine growth. The
improvement resulted in less frequent docking for scraping
and painting, and it materially reduced coal consumption
(which markedly increased as a ship's bottom fouled). The
money saved by the development was shown to offset easily
the original cost of the process.[38]

Another significant innovation of the Herbert years was the
introduction of electric power for use in the heavy gun turrets
of American ships. Experiments with electrically operated
mechanisms were first conducted in 1894. As a result of the
tests, Secretary Herbert ordered that the cruiser *Brooklyn* be
fitted with two electric turrets and two steam turrets to com-
pare further the relative merits of each. By the end of his administration, Herbert was convinced; he ordered the turrets of
the *Kearsarge* and *Kentucky,* then nearing completion, to be
changed from hydraulic to electric power. The wisdom of Herbert's decision was later shown by the universal introduction
of electrically controlled turrets on modern warships.[39]

By far, however, Herbert's most important reform was his
effort to centralize responsibility for the design and building
of vessels. Four different bureaus—Construction and Repair,
Steam Engineering, Ordnance, and Equipment—worked on
ship construction. It had been the desire of every secretary of
the navy since William E. Chandler to consolidate and co-

38 *New York Times,* May 29, 1893; W. R. Hinsdale to William McAdoo, June
24, 1893, in "General Correspondence," NA RG 80.
39 Chief Constructor, Bureau of Construction and Repair, to Herbert, October
18, 1915, memorandum in correspondence, Herbert Papers.

ordinate the work of these bureaus to save expense and delay. Hilary Herbert had unsuccessfully sought the same elusive goal when he was chairman of the House Committee on Naval Affairs. All efforts to consolidate the work, however, were thwarted by the powerful bureau chiefs who jealously resented any encroachment on their independence. Secretary Tracy had taken a first step in 1889 with the appointment of a construction board made up of the four chiefs involved, plus the chief of yards and docks. Tracy's board was some improvement, but Secretary Herbert determined to push on further.[40]

Especially disturbing to Secretary Herbert was the charge made by some naval experts that faulty construction marred several of the ships of the New Navy. The prestigious and knowledgeable *New York Times*, citing the gunboat *Machias* especially, had led the criticism that American vessels were top-heavy and unstable—"little short of unseaworthy," the *Times* had lamented. The officers of the Bureau of Construction and Repair readily acknowledged that structural problems did exist in several of the new ships, owing to changes made in the vessels by various bureau chiefs involved in the construction without the knowledge of the chief constructor. Circulars ordering the other chiefs to report all changes and additions to the Bureau of Construction and Repair were largely ignored. As a result of this abominable situation, some of the new ships were vastly over-armed. As the *Times* pointed out, the Bureau of Ordnance had a reputation for "crowding a gun in every nook of a ship where one could be placed." Because of the weight of the massive batteries, the vessels carried a firepower adequate for vessels twice their size but were top-heavy, instable, and unserviceable.[41]

On October 21, 1894, Secretary Herbert made a great stride forward when he issued General Order No. 433. He decreed that hereafter the Bureau of Construction and Repair was "charged with responsibility for the design, structural strength, and stability of vessels built for the Navy." This bureau was directly responsible for any change made in the design of a ship after the plans had been initially approved by the department. Any bureau chief who wanted to depart from the approved

---

[40] Paullin, *Paullin's History*, pp. 378-385.
[41] *New York Times*, October 31, 1891.

plan in any detail had to file his suggestion with the Bureau of Construction and Repair which had final authority unless overruled by the secretary himself. Although Herbert noted that it was not the intent of the order to subordinate any of the bureaus, the practical effect was to give one bureau the right to oversee all ship construction. With supervisory responsibility devolving on this one bureau, it would be easier for the department to determine the origin of mistakes in design and construction. The reform worked amazingly well and brought a degree of coordination into shipbuilding that the Navy Department had not known in years. In 1896 Herbert was able to report:

> Two years of practical experience under the provisions of this general order have demonstrated fully its wisdom, and the Department is now in a position to feel perfect confidence as to the ultimate results to be obtained from new designs, and can fix most definitely responsibility for any failure therein.[42]

In one other important area Herbert made a strong but, unfortunately, unsuccessful bid for reform in the navy. In his first annual report the secretary informed the Congress that reorganization of the personnel of the line of the navy through a reform of the promotion system was vitally needed. On taking office the colonel had discovered that stagnation in the line, owing to a top-heavy assortment of officers of command rank, was seriously threatening to impair the future efficiency of the service. By a law of 1882, Congress had reduced the total number of officers and had limited the number of men that could serve in each grade. The act limited the navy to 726 commissioned officers: six rear admirals, ten commodores, forty-five captains, eighty-five commanders, and an assortment of junior officers to complete the total. The bottleneck in the line which prevented the orderly progression of younger men through the ranks was known as the "hump," an inordinately large number of officers who had been enrolled and graduated by the Naval Academy during the time of the Civil War, 1861-1867. By the 1890's men from those seven classes entirely filled the ranks of commander, lieutenant commander, and the first 116 senior

---

42 U.S. Navy Dept., *Annual Report*, 1894: pp. 13-15 and *Annual Report*, 1896: p. 16; Paullin, *Paullin's History*, pp. 378-385. See also General Order No. 434, "General Orders and Circulars," NA RG 80.

lieutenant positions. With mechanical advancement through the ranks based primarily on date of commission rather than merit or ability, it was obvious that the large number of men in the "hump" would for years block the promotion of those in the lower grades. Herbert and Assistant Secretary McAdoo, who published a brilliant article on the need for reform in the *North American Review*, were especially alarmed that the command of the United States fleet was composed mostly of men already past their prime. In England the average age at which a naval officer reached command rank was thirty-seven years; in France—the highest abroad—the average age was forty-four years. In the United States Navy, however, an officer could not expect to attain the rank of commander until he was fifty-four years old.[43]

Testifying before a joint congressional committee on March 1, 1894, Secretary Herbert explained that the stagnation which was causing younger officers to spend practically their entire careers in subordinate ranks was especially "destructive to zeal and ambition." He expressed his deep fear that officers who had taken orders all their lives might not be able to think independently when command finally devolved on them at age fifty-five or sixty. By 1904, he pointed out, the men in the "hump" would completely fill the ranks from rear admiral down through half of lieutenant. Such circumstances, he mused, might well lead to ludicrous situations in which the admiral of a fleet might have only three more years of service than the first lieutenant on his flagship. Herbert concluded:

> I consider it an absolute and urgent necessity to provide for promotions to the common grades so that officers may reach those responsible positions while yet in their full vigor and sufficiently young to adapt themselves to their new duties and greater responsibilities. . . .[44]

---

[43] U.S. Navy Dept., *Annual Report*, 1893: pp. 41-43; Paullin, *Paullin's History*, pp. 418-420; William McAdoo, "Reorganization of the Personnel of the Navy," *North American Review* 159 (October, 1894): pp. 457-466.

[44] Report by Secretary Herbert to the Joint Congressional Committee to Study the Personnel of the Navy, March 1, 1894, in "General Correspondence," NA RG 80. See also Lieutenant W. L. Rodgers, "An Examination of the Testimony Taken by the Joint Committee of the Senate and House of Representatives in Regard to the Reorganization of the Navy," *Proceedings of the United States Naval Institute* 20 (1894): pp. 747-762.

Herbert offered the Congress several alternate plans to effect the desired reform, including provisions for an increase in the number of command positions and the opening by retirement each year of a specified number of command assignments. In his second and third annual reports, he pled with the Congress to take some action. Nevertheless, he was never able to overcome congressional indifference and the continued hostile influence of a number of powerful naval officers who felt threatened by the reform. It was not until after the Spanish-American War that Herbert's successor John D. Long was able to force through a reform to alleviate the stagnation in the line.[45]

In spite of Hilary Herbert's failure to win approval for his plan to reorganize the personnel of the navy, it is evident that —true to Benjamin F. Tracy's prediction—the Navy Department did not go backward under the colonel's leadership. Herbert's efforts appear less dramatic, perhaps, because he generally effected reforms in which he had already been interested before coming to the department and to which his predecessors there had also looked forward. His administration was one of rationalization and consolidation rather than startling innovation. When he gave up the naval portfolio in 1897, it is clear that the Navy Department was a much more viable and manageable arm of the executive branch than it had ever been before.

III

Herbert's years at the Navy Department were marked by two other bitter controversies. Fortunately, neither episode involved wrongdoing by any naval personnel but, rather, concerned the Carnegie and Bethlehem steel companies, both of which had contracted to manufacture armor plate for the United States Navy. It had been customary for the Congress to include in each appropriation for the New Navy a specification that all materials used in construction of the vessels be of domestic manufacture. Owing initially to a lack of facilities to produce heavy armor in the United States, for a number of years the work of ship construction was delayed until American plants could perfect a process. The Navy Department had made its

---

45 *New York Times,* May 5, May 22, December 16, 1894; McAdoo, "Reorganization of the Personnel," p. 463; U.S. Navy Dept., *Annual Report,* 1894: p. 27 and *Annual Report,* 1895: p. xxviii; Long, *The New American Navy* 1: pp. 81-87.

first contract on June 1, 1887, with the Bethlehem Steel Company for armor for four monitors and the second-class battleships *Maine* and *Texas*. Because of the approval of three more battleships and delays in the Bethlehem deliveries, on November 20, 1891, Secretary Tracy added a contract with the Carnegie Steel Company. Nevertheless, the development of American plants was pitifully slow. When Secretary Herbert took office, only 1949 tons of the 12,300 tons of armor specified in the two contracts had been delivered. In his first annual report, however, the secretary was happy to inform the Congress that both Bethlehem and Carnegie were beginning to overcome the inevitable setbacks that plagued all new industries. Two years later, the colonel reported that both companies had completed deliveries under their original contracts and were nearing the completion of two additional orders.[46]

On entering office Herbert was immediately faced with a technical problem concerning the manufacture of armor plates. In the course of development and experimentation, the American product had been greatly improved. Secretary Tracy had insisted on the addition of nickel into the process because extensive tests had shown that nickel-steel plates were less susceptible to cracking than plates made simply of steel. Tracy had also started extensive testing of the "Harvey process." This method of face-hardening the armor plates was developed by the Bethlehem works with the active assistance of the Bureau of Ordnance. The first important tests of Harveyized armor began at Annapolis in 1890 and had extended over the next two years. Impressive results indicated that the face-hardened plates caused the energy of a projectile to be dissipated principally in its own destruction rather than in the plate itself or in the frame of a ship. Nevertheless, when Herbert took office the armor-makers were clamoring against the Harvey process because of the extra trouble and expense it required. Convinced that American armor should be the best in the world, the new secretary ordered that in the future all new contracts for the navy would require Harveyized armor.[47] The decision

---

[46] U.S. Navy Dept., *Annual Report*, 1893: p. 15 and *Annual Report*, 1895: p. xvi.

[47] Herrick, *The American Naval Revolution*, p. 144; Paullin, *Paullin's History*, p. 401; U.S. Navy Dept., *Annual Report*, 1893: p. 28 and *Annual Report*, 1896: pp. 26-28; *New York Times*, March 19, 1893. See also R. B. Dashiell, "Report on

prompted one ordnance expert to write, "The ballistic acceptance test of armor plate for the United States Navy is more severe than that demanded in any other country." The wisdom of the American course, however, was demonstrated by the universal adoption of face-hardened armor by world naval powers in the next few years.[48]

The satisfactory relationship that had existed between the Navy Department and its armor suppliers was severely marred in September, 1893, when Secretary Herbert received a letter from James H. Smith, a Pittsburgh attorney, accusing the Carnegie Company of knowingly foisting defective armor plates off on the government. Smith represented four former employees of the company who, he alleged, possessed solid evidence of wholesale frauds at Carnegie's Homestead plant. These men, Smith explained, were willing to provide their information in return for a sufficient remuneration from the Navy Department. The charges placed the colonel in a genuine dilemma. He was reluctant to purchase information from informers but at the same time was even more reluctant to allow fraudulent practices to continue which might endanger the safety of American warships. With President Cleveland's permission, Herbert finally made an arrangement with the informants whereby they would receive twenty-five per cent of any damages assessed against the company in case malfeasance was discovered.[49]

The four Carnegie employees had gathered their information over a long period of time. Specifically, they charged that the company had failed to temper its armor plates evenly, had plugged and concealed blow holes, and had deceived naval inspectors by secretly reinforcing and strengthening the plates that the officers had selected for testing. Utilizing the information received, the department launched an extensive investigation, headed by the Chief of Ordnance William T. Sampson. The Sampson board was able to verify that a number of the charges were accurate; and the board recommended that the company be assessed a fine of fifteen per cent of the value of

---

the Test of a 14-Inch Nickel Steel Harveyized Armor Plate," *Proceedings of the United States Naval Institute* **19** (1893): pp. 117-120.

[48] Russel W. Davenport, "Gun Forgings and Armor Plate in the United States," *Proceedings of the United States Naval Institute* **19** (1893): pp. 485-486.

[49] *New York Times,* March 3, March 5, March 27, 1894.

all armor received by the government during the period that the frauds had occurred. President Cleveland then carefully examined the results of the investigation. He confided to Herbert, "I am convinced that a large portion of the armor supplied was not of the quality which would have been produced if all possible care and skill had been exercised in its construction." Nevertheless, Cleveland admitted, it was very difficult to determine what damages the company should pay. In an effort to be completely fair, the president reduced the fine to ten per cent of the price of the armor sold to the navy during the period of the frauds. By Cleveland's reckoning, the fine should amount to $140,489.[50]

Secretary Herbert dispatched a copy of the president's letter to H. C. Frick, the chairman of Carnegie Steel, and enclosed a covering letter explaining the department's regret that the incidents had occurred. The colonel readily agreed that the armor which the company had provided was "good and substantial," notwithstanding its defects and the fraud involved. The company had been fined, however, because it had represented the deliveries as being of premium quality (for which the department had paid extra) when, indeed, such was not the case. In closing, Herbert suggested that both the Navy Department and the company could learn from the episode. In the future, he assured Frick, the department would "redouble its watchfulness" and would also expect the "hearty cooperation" of the company in preventing such abuses from happening again. True to his word also, Herbert paid off the Pittsburgh informants and their lawyer with the sum of approximately $35,000.[51]

The armor controversy continued for at least another year. A board of investigation headed by Captain Sampson continued to amass evidence which only reinforced Herbert's conviction that deliberate fraud had been involved. The Pittsburgh informants issued a statement in April that the Navy Department was covering up for the company and that all abuses had not yet been revealed to the public. All the while, Andrew

---

50 *Ibid.*; Cleveland to Herbert, January 10, 1894, in Allan Nevins, ed., *Letters of Grover Cleveland, 1850-1908* (Boston and New York, Houghton Mifflin Company, 1933), pp. 343-344.

51 Herbert to H. C. Frick, January 12, 1894, and Herbert to James H. Smith *et al.*, January 20, 1894, in "Confidential Letters," NA RG 80.

Carnegie and H. C. Frick continued to wail that the company had been the innocent victim of unscrupulous employees and that the government should refund the fine under the circumstances. An extensive investigation by the House Committee on Naval Affairs resulted in a report of 980 pages in which the committee stated that "manifold frauds" bordering on criminality had been perpetrated at Homestead. Nevertheless, Secretary Herbert was tired of the controversy and felt that the company had made sufficient retribution. In January, 1895, he wrote to James McPherson, chairman of the Senate Committee on Naval Affairs, and told him that the Navy Department considered the issue settled. Taking Herbert's hint, the Congress also chose not to press the matter any longer.[52]

Unfortunately, the end of the Carnegie episode did not mean the end of Hilary Herbert's troubles with the armor manufacturers. By the summer of 1895 when Herbert was ready to contract for new armor deliveries, he had become deeply disturbed at what appeared to him to be collusion between the Bethlehem and Carnegie companies to maintain exorbitantly high prices. It was apparent to him that the two companies (which were the only manufacturers of heavy armor plate in the country) were dividing the Navy Department contracts almost equally between them. The prices of both companies were almost identical and had remained close to the figure first set by Secretary Whitney and the Bethlehem Company in 1887. According to law navy contracts were supposed to go to the lowest bidder. It was obvious, however, that prices were prearranged at approximately $600 per ton. The two companies had the government at their mercy. During the summer Herbert approached the management of each of the firms and demanded that prices be lowered. Now that their plants were firmly established, he argued, the cost of producing armor had fallen markedly. Yet, the prices they charged the government had not been lowered correspondingly. After lengthy

---

52 *New York Times,* May 5, May 17, July 14, December 25, 1894; *House of Representatives Reports,* 53rd Cong., 2nd Sess., No. 1468, p. 17; Report from W. T. Sampson to Secretary of the Navy, June 4, 1894, "General Correspondence," NA RG 80; Herbert to James McPherson, January 14, 1895, "Confidential Letters," NA RG 80. For a spirited defense of the Carnegie Company see Burton J. Hendrick, *The Life of Andrew Carnegie* (Garden City, N.Y., Doubleday, Doran & Co., Inc., 1932) 2: pp. 401-405.

negotiations the secretary secured a promise of reductions of at least fifty dollars per ton from both companies.[53] At Herbert's urging, the Congress also began to interest itself in armor prices. During appropriations debates in 1895 the Senate voted to limit the price that the government would pay for armor to $350 per ton. The House, however, opposed the limitation; and when a compromise figure of $425 was rejected, the chambers deadlocked. As a way out of the dilemma, by the Naval Appropriations Act of June 10, 1896, the Congress directed the secretary of the navy to launch a thorough inquiry and submit a full report showing the actual cost of armor manufacture and suggesting a fair price the government should pay.[54]

In beginning the study, Herbert knew that the records of the two companies contained the only absolutely accurate information as to costs of manufacturing and price-fixing. Writing to Robert P. Linderman, the president at Bethlehem, and John G. A. Leishman, the vice chairman at Carnegie, Herbert requested that the two men submit to him the records that could provide the necessary information for his report. As the colonel had feared, the response from the two companies was cold indeed. Linderman did come to Washington to confer with Herbert but refused to let the secretary see any important records. Leishman did not even bother to make a trip but sent Herbert a letter stating that the absence in Europe of several key Carnegie officials prevented the company from considering the secretary's request for a number of months. The colonel informed Leishman, however, that the mandate from Congress would not allow him to delay the investigation. He wrote:

> If I am not to have such help as the officials of your company can render me, I must resort to such means as are at my command, and it may be that reason of the imperfect methods thus necessarily adopted, the conclusions at which the Department arrives will be unjust to your company which I should very much regret.[55]

53 Herrick, *The American Naval Revolution*, p. 182; Herbert "Reminiscences," pp. 342-347.

54 Herbert, "Reminiscences," pp. 342-347; Walter F. LaFeber, "The Latin American Policy of the Second Cleveland Administration" (Ph.D. dissertation, University of Wisconsin, 1959), p. 132.

55 Herbert to Robert P. Linderman, June 13, July 18, and Herbert to John G. A. Leishman, June 13, June 25, 1896, "Confidential Letters," NA RG 80.

Realizing that he would get no aid from the two corporations, Herbert set out to utilize every other possible source of
information. Actually, he was not operating as much in the dark
as one might imagine. He received comprehensive reports and
estimates of costs from the naval officers who had been stationed
at the two plants to observe and inspect armor deliveries. He
secured from the auditor general of the State of Pennsylvania
copies of the tax returns made by the two companies from
1889 to 1895. Ascertaining that both corporations had imported material portions of their plants, he secured reports
from the secretary of the treasury concerning exactly what had
been imported and the duties paid between 1887 and 1893.
He also considered figures showing the stock gains of the two
companies.[56]

The most interesting aspect of the secretary's investigation
was his personal trip to Europe to determine for the sake of
comparison the cost of armor plants and manufacture abroad.
The colonel laid secret preparations for the trip so as not to
alert Carnegie and Bethlehem of his purpose. He sent letters
marked "strictly confidential" to Lieutenant Commander W. S.
Cowles, the American naval attaché at the London embassy, and
to Lieutenant Commander Raymond P. Rodgers, the attaché
in Paris. Herbert related to the two men the details of the
armor investigation. The combination between Carnegie and
Bethlehem, he wrote, was so evident that neither company had
even bothered to deny it. Moreover, he explained, prices now
seemed to indicate that the companies were probably also in
combination with European manufacturers as a part of a "world
wide trust." As secretly and discreetly as possible the two men
were to begin making inquiries, compiling data on the cost of
armor plants, and making arrangements for Herbert's visit. In
closing, the secretary again impressed on them that "absolute
secrecy" was imperative.[57]

In spite of the careful planning, Herbert's worst fears and
suspicions were realized when the Carnegie Company got word

---

56 *House of Representatives Documents*, 54th Cong., 2nd Sess., No. 151, pp. 5-6.
See also Herbert to Robert P. Linderman, December 7, December 22, 1896, and
Herbert to John G. Carlisle, December 17, 1896, in "Confidential Letters," NA
RG 80.

57 Herbert to W. S. Cowles, June 18, 1896, and Herbert to Raymond P. Rodgers,
June 18, 1896, "Confidential Letters," NA RG 80.

of his mission and baldly dispatched an agent to Europe on the same ship with the secretary! Moreover, the agent evidently got to the European manufacturers first. At every plant the colonel visited in Britain and France, he received ridiculously high estimates of the cost of armor manufacture. Thwarted in this direction and almost at his wits' end, he turned to his French counterpart, the minister of marine in Paris. The minister confirmed Herbert's suspicions about an international trust of armor makers and then obligingly supplied him with estimates of the Guerigny Works, a plant then under construction for the French government. Herbert also obtained an estimate in England by employing a friend there to secure figures by representing himself as an agent of another government.[58]

Having crossed swords with his robber baron opponents, Secretary Herbert returned home to complete his report. When the Congress reconvened in January of 1897, he submitted his findings in the form of a document that filled just under 100 printed pages. In a masterful review of his study he outlined in detail his difficulties with the Carnegie and Bethlehem managements. Herbert then explained how he had arrived at the figures he presented, appending his estimates from plants in Britain and France and the reports from the naval inspectors at the Carnegie and Bethlehem factories. The colonel, insisting that he was trying to be fair in every way, went so far as to publish in his report the full texts of letters from the two corporations in defense of their prices. He stated his own belief that the manufacturers should be "liberally treated" because they had to contend with rigid government specifications and inspections in making their product. He also reminded the Congress that the two companies had developed their plants at the government's request and, therefore, ought to receive a fair return on their initial investment.

Finally, the secretary presented his conclusion that a fair price for the armor the navy was receiving was approximately $400 per ton as opposed to the current price of approximately $563. Even at $400 a ton the two companies would be making a liberal profit of about fifty per cent since their total outlay

---

58 *New York Times,* August 6, October 4, 1896; Herbert, "Reminiscences," pp. 342-347; R. P. Rodgers to Herbert, November 24, December 20, 1896, Herbert Papers.

for manufacturing and maintenance was no more than $270 per ton. Herbert admitted that his figures were not infallible but added that the two companies needed only to open their books to dispute them. If the Congress accepted his recommendations only to have the two companies reject them, the colonel concluded, then the Congress should immediately empower the secretary of the navy to buy or erect an armor plant for the government. It would be better for the government to make its own armor than to remain locked in the costly clutches of a combine.[59]

The report on armor plate was one of Herbert's last major official duties. Unfortunately, the controversy was far from settled when he left office. Cries of anguish arose from Bethlehem and Carnegie at Herbert's figure of $400 per ton. Nevertheless, the Congress under the leadership of Senator William E. Chandler felt that the secretary had been too generous. When the Congress cut the maximum that the navy could pay for armor plates to $300 per ton the two companies balked and refused even to submit bids. For a time, Herbert's successor, Secretary John D. Long, could make no contracts at all. After months of squabbling and several reversals of policy, the Congress finally empowered the secretary of the navy to purchase armor plates at whatever price he deemed reasonable; accepting Herbert's original suggestion, the legislators also gave the secretary $4,000,000 to build or buy a government factory if he could not negotiate satisfactory contracts. Under this sensible arrangement Secretary Long was able to contract for the purchase of Harveyized armor at just over $400 per ton. Interestingly enough, the price Long obtained was approximately what Hilary Herbert said it should have been in the first place.[60]

---

59 *House of Representatives Documents,* 54th Cong., 2nd Sess., No. 151, *passim.*

60 Long, *The New American Navy* 1: pp. 50-52; *New York Times,* February 6, February 10, April 8, April 9, April 14, 1897; Richardson, *William E. Chandler,* pp. 502-602; Herbert, "Reminiscences," pp. 342-347.

VIII. Battleship Diplomacy: The Navy and American World Power

> If America is to profit by the lessons of the past,
> she will always have on hand a navy which can,
> at the moment when it is needed, take care of
> itself and of all the commerce which may at any
> time be or desire to be under our flag. This does
> not mean that we need a maritime force as large
> as that of Great Britain, or even of France, but
> it does mean that our Navy should always be so
> formidable that no power could ever deem it
> wise, even for a moment, to offend against the
> rights of our flag upon the seas.
>
> —Hilary Abner Herbert, "Our
> Navy and Our Naval Policy,"
> *Munsey's Magazine*

I

AS Professor Charles O. Paullin has pointed out, during the years 1881-1897 the building of the new American navy was the most important work undertaken by the Navy Department. Throughout the Cleveland years, Hilary Herbert continued to goad fellow Democrats further and further along the road toward a large navy policy. The task was not easy, however. Many men in the party of Jefferson and Jackson remained instinctively suspicious of a large military establishment. Shortly after Hilary Herbert took office, the *St. Louis Republic* vociferously denounced the secretary's calls for a larger fleet. Ridiculing the idea that a strong military was a deterrent to war, the *Republic* warned that the liberties of the people might be jeopardized if the military increases continued unabated. Secretary Herbert's expansive views, the *Republic* asserted, were heresy to true Democratic doctrine and were in actuality closer to the opinions of the old Federalists and the present Republicans. The editor concluded that the Democrats were aware that the Alabamian had given up "rebel Democracy" but did not realize when he entered the Navy Department that they were getting "a Southern man with Massachusetts Principles."[1] Nevertheless, Hilary Herbert's own appetite for a larger fleet became more voracious than ever before. Although his policy might still appropriately be described as one of gradual expansion, he intensified his efforts to equip the nation's fighting arm with a powerful battleship fleet.

When he took over the naval portfolio, Herbert's rather dramatic statements on behalf of a battleship strategy appeared to some observers as a marked contrast to the cautious approach he had taken in the House of Representatives. In August of 1893, for example, he told a newspaper correspondent that the country needed at least ten large battleships. Indeed, Herbert's earlier record of caution and conservatism has caused two fine scholars, professors Walter LaFeber and Walter R. Herrick, Jr., to perpetuate the myth that Herbert became an exponent of the capital ship theory only after moving into the Navy Department and reading some of A. T. Mahan's writings.[2] There is clear evidence that the Alabamian was moving toward a recognition of the importance of the battleship as early as 1890, long before he read Mahan. In the House debate on naval appropriations in 1890, for example, Herbert's disagreement with Charles Boutelle was simply one of tactics rather than strategy. Boutelle asked for three battleships; Herbert wanted to approve only two. The colonel's opposition was not to battleships as such but rather to the headlong approval of new expenditures for a naval program that was already moving forward as fast as American yards could possibly produce the ships. Indeed, in response to members of his own party who did oppose a capital ship strategy, the colonel forcefully argued that a limited number of battleships were indispensable for American security. When his own amendment calling for two capital ships failed, Herbert mustered enough Democratic support to approve Bou-

---

1 *St. Louis Republic*, June 1, 1893, Vol. 9, Herbert Papers. See also Herbert, "The Lesson of the Naval Review," pp. 641-647 and Paullin, *Paullin's History*, p. 364.

2 Walter LaFeber, *The New Empire: An Interpretation of American Expansion, 1860-1898* (Ithaca, N.Y., Cornell University Press, 1963), p. 230; Herrick, *The American Naval Revolution*, p. 156; *Philadelphia Weekly Item*, August 10, 1893, Vol. 9, Herbert Papers.

telle's initial request for three. In his report on the naval appropriations bill for 1892, Herbert took pains to point out that it was only because the work of construction had fallen so far behind appropriations that his committee was not recommending any new battleships. Nevertheless, he alerted the Congress that in the near future the nation would need the larger vessels.[3] In his last report as chairman of the Committee on Naval Affairs, the colonel again lamented the delays in construction, owing primarily to the failure of the armor makers to keep up deliveries. Once more the committee saw no reason to recommend approval of a ship for which no material was then available. At the same time, however, Herbert stated his belief that battleships were the key component of the "fighting strength of a modern navy." The construction of seven or eight such ships, he pointed out, would move the United States from the rank of seventh to fifth among world naval powers.[4]

On taking office, Hilary Herbert immediately set about plans for future naval increase. It was obvious that he now would have less direct influence over naval appropriations than in the past eight years. As secretary of the navy he could only recommend legislation to the Congress and could only indirectly make his opinions heard in the debates on Capitol Hill. Conversely, he was tied more closely to the chief executive than ever before. His loyalty to President Cleveland would have to come before his personal feelings about the naval program. Fortunately, Herbert was able to maintain excellent relations with his old comrades in Congress. He had a cordial working relationship with Amos J. Cummings, Democrat of New York who had succeeded him as chairman of the Committee on Naval Affairs, and with Charles Boutelle, who took the chairmanship in 1895.[5]

By the time that Herbert was ready for his first annual report in November, 1893, armor deliveries had reached the place that large-scale construction could resume. In preparing his recommendations, however, the secretary ran into trouble from an unexpected quarter. With the country in the throes of financial panic, President Cleveland was extremely reluctant to en-

---

[3] *Congressional Record*, 51st Cong., 1st Sess., pp. 3256-3262, 3395-3397; *House of Representatives Reports*, 52nd Cong., 1st Sess., No. 621.

[4] Washington *Evening News*, February 27, 1893, Vol. 8, Herbert Papers.

[5] "The Ways of Cabinet Officers," pp. 152-153; *Commerce Gazette*, Pittsburgh, Pennsylvania, March 23, 1893, Vol. 9, Herbert Papers.

Fig. 14.   The *Atlanta, Boston,* and *Chicago,* the first three ships of the New American Navy, are shown here with the *Yorktown.* Courtesy of U.S. Navy Department.

courage any large government expenditure. Accordingly, the colonel agreed to incorporate into his report only a very modest recommendation. Since the last annual statement from the Navy Department, he reported, five additional vessels of the New Navy had been launched: the battleships *Indiana, Massachusetts,* and *Oregon;* the armored cruiser *Minneapolis;* and the ram *Katahdin.* A table showed the condition of the steel fleet in Herbert's first year.[6] Herbert reported that only eight of the wooden cruisers of the old navy were still in active service, and six of these would soon disappear as a result of the ten per cent rule. Among the modern navies of the world, the United States presently ranked seventh.

Turning to his recommendations for naval increase, the secretary vigorously attacked the old conception of reliance on commerce-destroyers and harbor defense vessels. He wrote:

> But unarmored cruisers are not, properly speaking, fighting vessels. They can destroy merchant ships, they can fight vessels of their own class, but they can not meet armored vessels with any reasonable hope of success. . . .
> The military value of a commerce-destroying fleet is easily overrated.

The nation, the Secretary confessed, then had only four vessels that could properly be called first-class. Without a battleship

---

[6] See table 2.

fleet, Herbert warned, the United States could never cope with other world naval powers. For coast defense he advocated building a large force of small, fast torpedo boats. Specifically, Herbert asked the Congress to approve one battleship and six torpedo boats in the next appropriations bill.[7]

Unfortunately, the colonel's modest program was still too ambitious for the president. In submitting the departmental reports to Congress, although Cleveland commended the navy report, he undercut Herbert by suggesting that the large number of unfinished ships and the "depleted condition" of the Treasury caused him to doubt the propriety of beginning any new ships that year.[8] For a while, naval advocates held out the faint hope that the Congress would approve Herbert's modest proposal in spite of the president's reluctance. On this issue, however, the legislators bowed to Cleveland's wishes. Herbert received approval for only three torpedo boats.[9]

The following year Herbert reported that five new ships were complete and had undergone trials: the protected cruisers *Columbia, Minneapolis,* and *Olympia* and the cruisers *Marblehead* and *Montgomery.* Addressing himself directly to the problem of the depression which had thwarted his last proposal for naval increase, Herbert warned the Congress that the failure to authorize any new ships would undoubtedly lead to the shutting down of most of the country's shipyards. The economy would suffer even more, he asserted, if the thousands of skilled workmen in the navy yards and the yards of private contractors and their suppliers were thrown out of work. If Congress suddently halted the navy program, the domestic shipbuilding industry might be virtually wiped out overnight. Herbert concluded by asking for three battleships and twelve torpedo boats.[10]

Evidently, President Cleveland was swayed by Herbert's powerful argument; in his annual message on December 3, he fully endorsed the Navy Department proposal. The Congress was equally impressed. Although the legislators departed from the secretary's specific recommendation (as was often the case),

[7] U.S. Navy Dept., *Annual Report,* 1893.

[8] Richardson, ed., *Messages and Papers of the Presidents* 9: p. 451.

[9] U.S. Navy Dept., *Navy Yearbook,* 1911: pp. 206-207; *New York Herald,* December 6, 1893, Vol. 9, Herbert Papers.

[10] U.S. Navy Dept., *Annual Report,* 1894.

TABLE 2
CONDITION OF THE NEW AMERICAN NAVY IN 1893*

Type of vessel	Number authorized	Number building	Number in service	Total
Armored				
First-class battleships	...	4	...	4
Second-class battleships	...	2	...	2
Armored cruisers	...	1	1	2
Coast defense vessels	...	4	2	6
Harbor defense ram	...	1	...	1
Total		12	3	15
Unarmored				
Protected cruisers	...	5	8	13
Cruisers	...	2	1	3
Gunboats	3	...	6	9
Dynamite gun vessel	...	...	1	1
Total	3	7	16	26
Grand total	3	19	19	41

* Taken from Hilary Herbert's first annual report. See Navy Dept., *Annual Report,* 1893.

they did approve a considerable naval increase. The Navy Act of March 2, 1895, approved two large battleships, six light-draft gunboats, and three torpedo boats.[11]

In the election of 1894, the Republican party won control of both the House and the Senate. Herbert's old friend Charles Boutelle once again took charge of the House Committee on Naval Affairs. Secretary Herbert soon found himself in the extraordinarily unique situation (especially for a member of the Cleveland administration) of having the Congress grant him a larger appropriation than he requested. In his annual statement in 1895, Herbert reported that the second-class battleships *Maine* and *Texas* and the monitor *Amphitrite* had been completed and commissioned. With these vessels now out of the way, he asked the Congress for two new battleships and at least twelve new torpedo boats.[12]

In the background as Herbert made his report were the Cuban revolution of 1895, disturbances in Turkey, and the Venezuelan boundary crisis with Great Britain. Charles Bou-

---

11 Richardson, ed., *Messages and Papers of the Presidents* **9**: p. 540; U.S. Navy Dept., *Navy Yearbook*, 1911: pp. 209-229.
12 U.S. Navy Dept., *Annual Report*, 1895.

telle and the House Republicans were determined to give Herbert more than he asked for. Boutelle reported out a bill with four battleships and fifteen torpedo boats. When Democratic naval enthusiasts led by Amos Cummings also rallied behind the measure, the bill sailed through the House of Representatives. The Senate, however, was not quite as enthusiastic and cut the number of battleships to three. The final measure also approved three large torpedo boats, up to ten smaller torpedo boats depending on cost, and two submarine torpedo craft.[13]

By the time for Herbert's final report on the state of the fleet, it was evident that much of his work in the Congress and the Navy Department was coming to fruition. He proudly reported that since the last year the following new vessels had been completed: the battleships *Indiana, Massachusetts,* and *Oregon;* the low-freeboard defense monitors *Monadnock* and *Terror;* the armored ram *Katahdin;* and the *Ericsson,* a small torpedo boat. Among the world navies the United States now ranked in sixth place—behind England, France, Russia, Italy, and Germany, but in front of Spain. Moreover, Herbert reported that the department had let contracts on June 10, 1896, for three new battleships, the *Illinois, Alabama,* and *Wisconsin.* Additionally, tests were underway on an experimental submarine torpedo craft. On June 30, 1896, according to the document, the United States Navy had forty vessels afloat with a total displacement of 122,000 tons in comparison with the total of thirty vessels at 62,000 tons in commission in June, 1893. Having reviewed the state of the fleet, the secretary recommended that the Congress authorize three light-draft battleships (so that they could enter the shallow Atlantic and Gulf ports) and twelve additional torpedo boats.[14] Herbert was not as successful with his recommendations this year, however. Evidently the Republicans in Congress decided that any further significant increase should redound to the credit of the McKinley administration which was shortly to come into office. Accordingly, the legislators authorized only three torpedo boats.[15]

---

13 U.S. Navy Dept., *Navy Yearbook,* 1911: pp. 231-253; LaFeber, "The Latin American Policy of the Second Cleveland Administration," pp. 129-132.

14 U.S. Navy Dept., *Annual Report,* 1896.

15 U.S. Navy Dept., *Navy Yearbook,* 1911: pp. 255-275.

II

It is not mere coincidence that the story of the rise of the New American Navy is set in the same period in which most historians place the rise of America to world power. There can be no doubt that Captain A. T. Mahan had a profound effect upon the men of this time when he told them that the sea was a highway rather than a barrier, that seapower and world power were intimately related. The nation that controlled the sea, the captain explained, could control the course of history.[16]

Although Mahan is usually given his due in discussions of the revolution in attitude that marked America's rise to world power, surprisingly few American diplomatic historians have shown an adequate recognition of the fascinating connection between naval and diplomatic affairs.[17] The files of the Navy Department in Washington (which have thus far been mined primarily by military historians) are a treasury of numerous documents relating to foreign affairs. The navy's role was crucial in American diplomacy throughout the nineteenth century and even into the twentieth century with the coming of the age of air power. Whenever persuasion failed and American diplomats had to appeal to force or the threat of force and whenever American life and property were threatened in foreign revolutionary upheavals, the United States Navy became involved.

Of course, the men of the late nineteenth century knew that naval prowess was not the sole criterion of world power. Mahan himself listed a number of important factors which bore directly on seapower and, thus, national power: (1) geography, physical configuration, and extent of territory; (2) climate and natural resources; (3) size of the population; (4) character of the people and governmental institutions.[18] Nevertheless, for the men of Mahan's time, naval power was the most concrete and most

---

16 For Mahan, seapower was not simply naval power but also included peaceful maritime commerce. For an excellent analysis and compilation of Mahan's thought, see William E. Livezey, *Mahan on Sea Power* (Norman, University of Oklahoma Press, 1947).

17 An example of what can be done is Charles Oscar Paullin's *Diplomatic Negotiations of American Naval Officers, 1778-1883* (Baltimore, Johns Hopkins Press, 1912). A recent study is Kenneth J. Hagan, *American Gunboat Diplomacy and the Old Navy, 1877-1889* (Westport, Conn., Greenwood Press, 1973).

18 Livezey, *Mahan on Sea Power,* p. 42.

easily measured component of international prowess. Who of them would deny that tiny England, the mistress of the seas, was the world's most powerful nation? In England each year the populace eagerly awaited the publication of T. A. Brassey's *Naval Annual* with its detailed comparisons of the fleets of every major nation. In the United States the Navy Department faithfully published annual tables and charts showing the rank of the American fleet among the world navies.

The records of the Navy Department in the Cleveland years clearly evidence an ever-increasing awareness on the part of Secretary Herbert and his subordinates that the United States had an enlarged role to play in international affairs. There was constant interchange and shuffling of reports back and forth between the State and Navy departments. Hilary Herbert was gratified on one occasion when Secretary of State Gresham told him that the reports from Herbert's naval officers were sometimes superior to those from the foreign service personnel.[19] In 1893 the colonel pointed out succinctly, "A nation's navy is the right arm of its diplomacy."[20] Assistant Secretary McAdoo spoke at length of the navy's part in foreign relations in attempting to explain the need for well qualified officers:

> In this connection, it must not be forgotten that command in the navy, which is often exercised in far-distant ports, and which frequently deals with delicate and intricate questions of diplomacy, is very different from the ordinary exercise of authority in an army on land in one's own country; and that, from the very nature of things, the captain of a warship exercises kingly authority as compared with military command on land, subject only to the President of the United States, speaking through the Secretary of the Navy. To wield wisely and ably these necessarily autocratic powers, to assume the responsibilities incidental to them, and to accomplish with skill and wisdom the difficult tasks begotten by entangling and delicate diplomatic situations remote at times even from telegraphic communication, require what is happily termed the habit of command.[21]

Secretary Herbert's first annual report in 1893 clearly re-

<hr />

19 Herbert, "Grover Cleveland and His Cabinet at Work," p. 740; Herbert, "Reminiscences," p. 326.
20 Herbert, "The Lesson of the Naval Review," p. 643.
21 McAdoo, "Reorganization of the Personnel," pp. 459-460.

vealed his expanding concept of the role of the navy in America's diplomatic and commercial relations. He wrote:

> The increase of our population, and the expansion of our trade under more favorable commercial regulations than at present, which may be expected to result from future legislation, are certain to beget American interests which will look to naval protection in all parts of the world.

The nation now had, Herbert pointed out, "multifarious interests along the whole South and Central American coasts" which demanded "the presence of an American ship of war to a greater extent than ever before." This situation, the secretary conjectured, was not a temporary phenomenon but rather one that would "steadily increase." He added that the need for a naval force in Asiatic waters was now "universally recognized." Turning to the question of the relations of the United States to Europe, he wrote:

> We cannot but have most intimate relations, in every phase of national existence, with the great governments of the Old World, whose subjects are now in phenomenal numbers becoming citizens of our country. As we receive these we assume the responsibility of protecting them, in many cases against their former governments. With the growth of our population and our wonderful development, it is beyond doubt that the energies of our people will be more and more directed to foreign trade and to the extension of our interests in all directions, while the increasing immigration of subjects of foreign powers in both Europe and the Orient is all the time complicating our relations toward other governments. It seems certain, therefore, that the future is to bring with it an increase of international questions, to a settlement of which, in a manner which will be at once peaceful and honorable, naval strength will be absolutely essential. We must make and keep our Navy in such a condition of efficiency as to give weight and power to whatever policy it may be thought wise on the part of our Government to assume. The Navy is to maintain honorable peace, begotten by an assured strength to protect rights, enforce just claims, beget security against foreign aggression, and compel respect for any policy of our people which may affect foreign nations.[22]

Even the division of the American fleet during the Herbert

---

[22] U.S. Navy Dept., *Annual Report,* 1893.

administration revealed the possibilities for worldwide influence that fell to the navy. American vessels were assigned to one of six stations: the North Atlantic (the home squadron); the South Atlantic (Carribbean and eastern coasts of Central and South America); the North Pacific (primarily around Alaska and the Bering Sea); the South Pacific (west coast of Central and South America, Hawaii, and Samoa); the Asiatic (principally the coasts of China, Korea, and Japan); and the European (eastern Atlantic, Mediterranean, and western coast of Africa). Herbert never let his officers forget their intimate ties to the nation's diplomacy. When Paymaster J. C. Sullivan made public statements to the press criticizing American policies in the Bering Sea, the secretary issued a general order severely reprimanding him: "Every naval officer is an agent of the Government in executing its foreign policy, and the officer who criticizes that policy forgets his duty."[23]

Occasionally, naval officers became overly zealous in the performance of diplomatic functions. In late 1895 the cruiser *San Francisco,* under the command of Rear Admiral Thomas O. Selfridge, was sent to Turkey with orders to protect American life and property in disturbances and persecution there. When Admiral Selfridge learned of the burning of an American missionary station at Marash, he dispatched a terse note to the Vali of Aleppo, in whose province the outrage had occurred, and threatened to hold him accountable for the attack. Selfridge's misplaced gallantry, however, only exacerbated relations with the Sultan, who resented the warning and was incensed at Selfridge's attempt to deal directly with one of his vassals. Fortunately, the American minister was able to smooth over the breech. Secretary of State Richard Olney wrote to Herbert to suggest that in the future it would be far better to confine such discussions to regular diplomatic channels. Olney explained that independent local action in a country where power was centralized at the capital anyway only further complicated dealing with a ruler like the Sultan. The colonel promply warned Admiral Selfridge that in the future he should leave diplomatic protests to the diplomats.[24]

---

23 U.S. Navy Dept., *Annual Report,* 1894: p. 23; General Order No. 411, "General Orders and Circulars," NA, RG 80.

24 Herbert to Rear Admiral T. O. Selfridge, February 1, 1896, "Confidential Correspondence," NA, RG 80; *New York Times,* July 18, 1896. The Selfridge

On another occasion naval officers came disastrously near to causing the Cleveland administration genuine embarrassment and, perhaps, to precipitating an international crisis. The episodes were the result of a long chain of events concerning the Hawaiian policy of the administration. Early in 1893 a revolution in Hawaii, organized principally by American sugar planters, dethroned the ambitious Queen Liliuokalani. Aided and abetted by the American minister and American troops in the first place, the new provisional government immediately entreated the United States for annexation. An agreeable President Harrison in the waning days of his administration submitted an annexation pact to the Senate. When Grover Cleveland, a convinced anti-imperialist, entered the White House, he withdrew the treaty for further study. After lengthy deliberations with the administration on an unfavorable report by special agent James H. Blount as to the attitude of the native Hawaiians concerning the scheme, President Cleveland and his Cabinet came down in firm opposition to annexation. At the same time, however, the administration had no desire to push Hawaii out on its own where it might be snatched up by some greedy imperialist power. In brief, the Cleveland administration wanted to hold the islands in American limbo. The islands, by this conception, were not to belong officially to the United States, but it was to be understood that American interests would be paramount. On March 3, 1893, Secretary of State Gresham called in the Japanese minister and a number of European envoys to warn them specifically that although President Cleveland was hestitant about annexation, he would tolerate no foreign interference in Hawaii.[25]

One of the greatest difficulties experienced by the administration was communicating this rather ambivalent policy to American naval commanders in Honolulu. In August, 1893, Secretary Herbert instructed Rear Admiral J. S. Skerrett to give no aid of any kind, "physical or moral," to either of the groups struggling to control the government at Honolulu. Nevertheless, in his reports to the department Admiral Skerrett gave the impres-

---

incident is extensively documented in *Papers Relating to the Foreign Relations of the United States, 1895,* Pt. 2: pp. 1245-1459.

25 Grenville and Young, *Politics, Strategy,* p. 109; Allan Nevins, *Grover Cleveland: A Study in Courage* (New York, Dodd, Mead, and Company, 1933), pp. 549-562.

sion that his sympathies were tending strongly toward the Provisional Government. In July he had expressed the hope that several Royalist conspirators against the regime would be convicted and severely punished. In September he observed that the Provisional Government still showed "the same courageous disposition to control and to display their power to direct and lead these people in the right way." Finally, Secretary Herbert wrote to Skerrett in the bluntest terms, "I think I have observed from your correspondence an unconscious leaning on your part towards the new government in the Hawaiian Islands. . . ." He reminded the admiral that "the position the Government wishes you to occupy is that of complete neutrality." The United States, the colonel concluded, "does not intend to be the partisan either of the Queen or of the present government, and you are not to favor the one or the other by act, word, or deed."[26]

In September, 1893, Admiral Skerrett made a blunder that again complicated the Hawaiian situation. The insensitive skipper casually related the incident in one of his own dispatches without comprehending at all the *faux pas* he had made. Skerrett wrote:

> In conversation recently with H. M. B. Minister, he asked me if I had any instructions about giving protection to other than United States Citizens: I replied that my own instructions were to give protection to none but United States Citizens and their property. He remarked, that I will have to request my Government to send a ship here to give protection to Her Majesty's Legation should it be needed. So I dare say we will have English ships sent here.[27]

A report of the conversation at the State Department by Sir Julian Pauncefote, the British ambassador, accompanied by word that British war vessels would return to the area, brought a pained response from Assistant Secretary of State Alvey A. Adee. The State Department had been trying to minimize British influence in the islands. An embarrassed Secretary Herbert confessed to Adee that the British report was absolutely

---

[26] Skerrett to secretary of the navy, July 25, September 12, 1893, "Area File," Role 305; Herbert to Skerrett, October 3, 1893, "Confidential Letters," NA, RG 80.

[27] Skerrett to secretary of the navy, September 12, 1893, "Area File," Roll 305.

correct; Admiral Skerrett had unknowingly reported his blunder himself. Immediately, Herbert dispatched a stern rebuke to Skerrett and ordered him "to afford British subjects and property such protection as has always been accorded by vessels of American fleets to the subjects of Her Britannic Majesty and their property under like circumstances in the absence of British vessels." Nevertheless, the damage had been done; British ships returned to Pearl Harbor.[28]

Less than a month later, Herbert ordered Admiral Skerrett home and assigned to the station a more astute observer, Rear Admiral John Irwin. Within a few months, however, the department replaced Irwin with Rear Admiral John G. Walker. Walker had served as the all-but-omnipotent chief of the Bureau of Navigation from 1881-1889 and was still reputed to be, except for Admiral Ramsay, the most powerful officer in the service. Secretary Herbert issued to the admiral essentially the same instructions his predecessors had received. Walker was specifically cautioned to render "no aid or support, moral or physical" to either the Provisional Government or the Royalists. Any American citizen, according to Herbert's instructions, who participated willfully in revolutionary activity forfeited his right to Walker's protection. The secretary concluded by directing Walker to inform him immediately if a foreign power at any time tried to interpose itself into Hawaiian politics.[29]

In spite of Herbert's concise instructions, it became rapidly evident that, compared to Walker, Admiral Skerrett had been a diplomat's delight. A barely submerged hostility developed between Walker and the able American minister, Albert S. Willis. Fortunately, the lines of communication between secretaries Herbert and Gresham in Washington remained clear. In May, 1894, Gresham wrote to Willis in Honolulu:

> The Secretary of the Navy received a letter from Admiral Walker by the same post that brought yours. The Admiral's

---

28 Herbert to Adee, September 27, 1893, in "Confidential Letters," NA, RG 80; Herbert to Skerrett, September 27, 1893, "Ciphers Sent," NA, RG 80; LaFeber, *The New Empire*, pp. 207-208. See also Adee to Sir Julian Pauncefote, September 27, 1893, "Notes to Foreign Legations in the United States from the Department of State: Great Britain," General Records of the Department of State, NA, RG 59.

29 Herbert to Walker, March 24, 1894, Cleveland Papers, Roll 84; *New York Times*, September 9, 1894.

communication deals mainly with the political situation in the islands, more especially at Honolulu. He does not seem to realize that you represent the Government in such matters. The Admiral evidently strongly sympathizes with the Provisional Government and favors annexation.[30]

The next month, Willis reported that Admiral Walker was making himself conspicuously cordial to Sanford B. Dole, the new president of the recently declared Hawaiian Republic. Willis noted that Walker's conduct and the rumors that he had been sent to spy on the British minister were very disconcerting to the English representatives. The admiral, however, was apparently enjoying the attention and had made no effort to deny any of the sensational tales that were sweeping the capital. Walker added fuel to the fire, Willis reported, when Captain Rooke of the British warship *Champion* called on the admiral to express his willingness to offer aid in the event of riots or disturbances. Walker bluntly told Rooke that the American force was quite adequate to cope with any trouble and that he would not accept English help. To cap it all off, Walker told the captain that he suspected the British minister, J. H. Wodehouse, of conspiring with the Royalists to return Queen Liliuokalani to the throne. The admiral's statements, Willis observed, "smacked somewhat of a protectorate, which I did not think the President desired at this time if at all."[31]

Willis continued to report Admiral Walker's indiscretions to the State Department. In spite of the sensitive political situation, the admiral carried out practice troop drills and landings that gave the impression of support for the Dole regime. The *Hawaii Holomua,* a Honolulu paper sympathetic to Royalist aspirations, accused Walker of trying "to intimidate the people by a display of his one or two hundred men." After the admiral had entertained President Dole and a number of government officials on his flagship, the *Philadelphia,* the *Holomua* said that Walker had "hobnobbed, and associated with the men who assisted and fostered the revolution."[32] Another Honolulu paper, the *Pacific Commercial Advertiser,* unveiled a sensational story

---

30 Gresham to Willis, May 12, 1894, Walter Quintin Gresham Papers, LC.

31 Willis to Gresham, June 23, 1894, Gresham Papers.

32 *Ibid.,* June 23, June 29, 1894; *Hawaii Holomua,* June 16, June 19, 1894, clippings in Box 8, Gresham Papers.

that it had received information from an "absolutely reliable authority" that President Cleveland had personally dispatched Admiral Walker to Hawaii to prevent any British military occupation of the islands in case of revolutionary disturbances. The president feared, the article went on, that English troops might never leave if they once landed. The story concluded:

> The fact that the United States and not Great Britain or Japan or any other nation was to have the first voice in the settlement was made known by Admiral Walker to the representatives of foreign powers, naval as well as diplomatic.[33]

With tempers growing short at the British legation in Honolulu and irritation increasing among the English naval officers, a potential international crisis of the first magnitude was brewing. Admiral Walker had become a disastrous political liability. On July 22 Secretary Gresham wrote to Willis to inform him that President Cleveland had carefully read the clippings and dispatches he had sent. The secretary of state continued:

> Admiral Walker has no written or verbal instructions to act in any diplomatic capacity at Honolulu. The President does not think he should remain longer in the islands, nor that it is necessary for our warships to remain at Honolulu and the Admiral will doubtless receive orders, by the same mail that brings this letter to you, to return at once to the United States on board the Philadelphia. Of course, if it becomes necessary, another ship will be sent to Honolulu.[34]

Secretary Herbert had already cabled Admiral Walker to begin immediate preparations to sail for home to take a new assignment as superintendent of the Naval Academy. Herbert offered the admiral only the terse explanation that his removal to a new post was "required by the public interests." With Admiral Walker out of the way and American vessels temporarily withdrawn as a conciliatory gesture, the intrigue in Honolulu returned to its normal levels; and Anglo-American relations were not disrupted. For obvious reasons the Cleveland administration never revealed to the public that it had come so close

---

33 *Pacific Commercial Advertiser,* June 18, 1894, clipping in Box 8, Gresham Papers. This article, sections of which are heavily marked with blue pencil, is evidently the one which sealed Walker's fate.

34 Gresham to Willis, July 22, 1894, Gresham Papers.

to trouble in Hawaii. Even many old hands in the Navy Department believed that Walker's removal was the outgrowth of a personal feud with Admiral Ramsay.[35] The danger, of course, was not so much of a war with England but of a dramatic incident that might inflame public opinion and create irresistible pressures for the immediate annexation of the island group. Whether in retrospect one considers Cleveland's anti-annexation stance right or wrong, it cannot be denied that the issue was a *political* matter and should not have been settled by the actions of naval officers. Fortunately, the Walker episode was an aberration rather than a typical occurrence; most naval officers continued to be competent servants of the nation's diplomacy.

Throughout the Cleveland years Hilary Herbert kept a steady eye trained even further westward across the Pacific in behalf of American interests. When the Sino-Japanese War of 1894-1895 erupted, Herbert immediately ordered the fleet to provide the customary protection to American life and property. Nevertheless, his primary concern throughout the war was not American commercial interests. The mission in which the secretary took an avid personal interest was that of intelligence gathering. The colonel lost no time in ordering American naval officers to submit detailed reports of any significant naval and military engagements they observed. Rear Admiral C. C. Carpenter, commander of the Asiatic Squadron, was told to "afford every facility" for intelligence officers to gather and report information.[36]

Hilary Herbert knew that the events taking place in the Far East were of inestimable value for the study of naval tactics and strategy. For the first time since the advent of modern steel navies, two nations which both had a number of the latest ships and guns were locked in mortal combat on the sea. All of the

---

[35] Herbert to Walker, July 9, July 11, 1894, and Herbert to Cleveland, October 21, 1894, Rolls 85 and 87, Cleveland Papers, LC. For a partial account of Walker's activities in Hawaii, see William A. Russ, Jr., *The Hawaiian Republic (1894-98) and Its Struggle to Win Annexation* (Selinsgrove, Pa., Susquehanna University Press, 1961), pp. 38-41. The Walker affair, however, has never been fully revealed before, probably because most of the relevant documents were retained in the personal papers of Secretary of State Gresham rather than in the more readily accessible State Department files.

[36] Herbert to Carpenter, September 24, 1894, in "Area File," Roll 355; Herbert to Carpenter, October 6, October 9, 1894, in "Ciphers Sent," NA, RG 80. For a number of the intelligence reports, see "Area File," Rolls 355 and 356.

ships in the Chinese fleet, which was generally believed to be superior, had been commissioned since 1881; and many of the vessels had been built in Germany and England. A number of the Japanese ships, the oldest of which dated only to 1878, had been constructed in England, France, and Holland. Around the world, naval leaders eagerly watched the unfolding preview of what future naval warfare would be like. The climax came on September 17, 1894, with the famous battle off the Yalu River in which the smaller but faster and better trained Japanese navy all but destroyed the Chinese fleet as a fighting force. Utilizing the intelligence reports of American officers, Secretary Herbert published in a national journal two articles that analyzed the lessons of the conflict that would surely affect future naval development. The value of protective armor, the vindication of the battleship, the danger of unnecessary woodwork in modern ships, the importance of drill and training in using heavy guns, and the value of torpedo boats were among the important lessons which Herbert felt the war demonstrated. Japanese officials were so impressed with one of the essays, "The Fight Off the Yalu River," that they translated it into their language for use in their country.[37]

The secretary showed an ever-increasing awareness of events in the Far East during his term. Because of sporadic disturbances in the area and later because of the threat of war with Spain which might necessitate action against the Philippines, Herbert took vigorous steps to reinforce the Asiatic squadron. When the colonel took office in 1893 only two vessels were assigned to duty in the Far East; by the end of his second year he increased the total to eight.[38] As a result of the Sino-Japanese War, Herbert warned that the nation now had a strong potential naval rival on its western flank. He wrote:

> The Queen of the Asiatic seas the world has been in the habit of looking upon as a small country, but it will now be remembered in every reckoning of the resources of nations that Japan's people, homogeneous and united, are quite equal

---

37 Herbert, "The Fight Off the Yalu River," *North American Review* 159 (November, 1894): pp. 513-528; Herbert, "Military Lessons of the Chino-Japanese War," *North American Review* 160 (June, 1895): pp. 685-698; Naoki Miyaoka to Herbert, January 27, 1895, Herbert Papers.

38 Long, *The New American Navy* 1: p. 168; *New York Times*, September 9, November 29, 1894.

in numbers to the population of England, Ireland, Wales, and Scotland, and that the United Kingdom is and has been for years the mistress of the seas. Americans must remember too, that only the waters of one ocean, a wide one, no doubt, but easily transversed by navies, separate their country from Asia.[39]

Events to the South also claimed the attention of the secretary of the navy from 1893 to 1897. Hardly a month went by during Herbert's term when an American warship was not anchored off at least one of the "banana republics" to protect American interests during revolutionary upheavals. The most dramatic episode, however, that involved the navy in Latin American relations was the Brazilian revolution of 1893-1894. The insurgents against the government of Floriano Peixoto included most of the Brazilian navy, a number of members of the Brazilian Congress, and a group of private citizens. Led by Admiral José de Mello, the rebel navy instituted a blockade in the harbor of Rio de Janeiro. The admiral's simple strategy was quite feasible. By preventing the landing of goods from foreign merchant vessels, Mello could cut off the proceeds at the Rio customs house; without the revenue, the Peixoto government could not survive. Throughout the struggle the United States professed to be neutral but, in fact, favored the pro-American Peixoto regime by refusing even to accord belligerent status to the insurgents. Washington's disfavor undoubtedly intensified when Admiral Mello declared in favor of a monarchical type of government.[40]

The United States had concluded a reciprocity treaty with Brazil only in 1891. The State Department was determined that growing American trading interests must be protected. Although Great Britain never officially recognized the belligerency of the insurgents, Secretary of State Gresham feared that the rebels were receiving clandestine aid from English elements who wanted to jockey the United States out of its favorable position in the Brazilian market.[41] Because the insurgents had never been accorded belligerent status, the State Department in-

---

[39] Herbert, "Military Lessons of the Chino-Japanese War," p. 608.

[40] Thomas L. Thompson to Walter Q. Gresham, September 6, 1893, *Foreign Relations, 1893*, pp. 45-46. See also Lawrence F. Hill, *Diplomatic Relations Between the United States and Brazil* (Durham, N.C., Duke University Press, 1932), pp. 273-378; LaFeber, *The New Empire*, pp. 210-211.

[41] LaFeber, *The New Empire*, pp. 213-215.

formed the American minister, Thomas L. Thompson, that the blockade in Rio harbor was illegal and that he should strongly protest any attempt on the part of the rebels to prevent the landing of American goods. The fleet dispatched by Secretary Herbert to safeguard American interests, consisting of the *Charleston, Newark, Detroit,* and later the *San Francisco,* was the strongest force in the harbor.[42]

The American naval commanders, who evidently had some empathy with the officers of the insurgent navy, did not share Minister Thompson's strong determination to keep commerce flowing, even by force of arms if necessary. Rear Admiral O. F. Stanton, commanding aboard the *Newark,* took it upon himself to decide that the insurgents were a *"de facto* force." When Stanton saluted Admiral Mello's flagship the *Aquidaban* and later paid a personal courtesy call to the insurgent chief, the Brazilian government lodged a strong protest at the State Department. To mollify the Peixoto regime, Secretary Herbert had no choice but to remove Stanton immediately, informing the admiral that he had "committed a grave error of judgment."[43]

As it turned out, Captain Henry F. Picking, who assumed command of the United States force, was no more ready to break the blockade forcibly than Stanton had been. With the State Department following a cautious wait-and-see policy, Secretary Herbert did not specifically order Captain Picking to use force. Picking, therefore, determined that it would be unneutral to interpose his ships between the insurgents and merchantmen that were trying to land goods. His position, Picking wrote Minister·Thompson, was one of "absolute neutrality"; he added, "I don't care, officially, one snap which side wins."[44] Thompson, who did care, was miffed at Picking's attitude, as was William T. Townes, the consul general at Rio, who bitterly condemned

---

42 Gresham to Thompson, November 1, 1893, *Foreign Relations, 1893,* p. 62; Thompson to Captain Henry F. Picking, November 2, 1893, in International Relations and Politics, "Subject File," NA, RG 45.

43 Herbert to Stanton, December 21, 1893, "Confidential Letters," NA, RG 80; Stanton to Herbert, October 25, December 6, 1893, "Area File," Roll 26; Gresham to Thompson, December 20, 1893, "Diplomatic Instructions of the Department of State: Brazil," General Records of the Department of State, NA, RG 59.

44 Picking to Thompson, December 17, 1893, in International Relations and Politics, "Subject File," NA, RG 45; Thompson to Gresham, December 21, 31, 1893, *Foreign Relations, 1893,* pp. 85, 93-94.

Picking's decision in a rude letter. While fearful American merchants refused to risk landing their goods without a promise of protection, the feud between Captain Picking and the diplomatic and consular officials reached ludicrous proportions. Picking informed Secretary Herbert that the consul general was "excessively dense" and later volunteered the opinion that William Townes was unfit for his position. The captain even went so far as to send a spy to the American Consulate who reported that the building was unbefitting the dignity of the United States and that Negroes used the urinals in the water-closet, a "dark place" which was "too dirty and disgusting for decent people to use."[45]

The childish dialogue at Rio was disrupted about January 10, 1894, when Secretary Gresham finally made up his mind to take firm action against the blockade. He wired the American minister that the United States naval commanders would be ordered to tolerate no further interference with the landing of goods. The change in policy coincided with the arrival at Rio of Rear Admiral A. E. K. Benham on the *San Francisco*. Following explicit orders from Secretary Herbert, Benham told the insurgent leaders that they had no right to establish a blockade and that American cargoes would be landed with whatever force was necessary. Benham made his threat good on January 27. When the rebel ship *Trajans Guanabara* fired a blank shell across the bow of an American steamer that was moving toward the wharf, the *Detroit* sent a shell into the insurgent ship. With the *Detroit* threatening to sink the *Guanabara*, the bewildered rebel commander offered to surrender. For all practical purposes the revolution ended that morning in Rio harbor. Naval commanders of other nations followed Benham's lead, and the blockade was ruined. In just over two months the Peixoto government was in full control of the country once more. The following summer the grateful Brazilian regime awarded President Cleveland a medal and celebrated the fourth of July as a national holiday in honor of the United States. The direct intervention of the American navy had snuffed out one revolutionary fire in Latin America. Dissident elements in Brazil undoubtedly retained bitter memories of this heavy-handed Yankee interven-

---

45 Picking to secretary of the navy, December 28, 1893, January 8, 1894, in "Area File," Rolls 26 and 27.

tion; but from the point of view of the Peixoto regime and the State Department, the fleet had served as an effective arm of American diplomacy.[46]

The most severe foreign policy crisis of the Cleveland years also concerned one of the Latin American nations. The occasion of the crisis was the famous Venezuelan boundary dispute in which President Cleveland and his new secretary of state Richard Olney threw down the gauntlet before Great Britain. Frustrated over the delay of the British in settling the boundary line between British Guiana and Venezuela, in December, 1895, Cleveland and Olney belligerently threatened that the United States itself might establish and defend the line with force if necessary. The reckless assertion, creating a war scare on both sides of the Atlantic, undoubtedly stunned the British. It also sent shock waves rebounding through the Navy Department. The abilities and prowess of the American fleet would be laid on the line should the situation degenerate into armed conflict.

Hilary Herbert had been among the Cabinet members consulted by Olney in the summer of 1895 before the secretary of state dispatched his original note to the British invoking the Monroe Doctrine and demanding immediate settlement of the dispute by arbitration. By his own account, Herbert added his "warm approval" to that of secretaries Carlisle, Harmon, and Lamont but also agreed with their initial misgivings about its "startling boldness." Unfortunately, Cleveland and Olney did not consult with the other members of the Cabinet in December before the president dropped the bombshell that threatened to push the nation over the precipice of war.[47]

According to Professors John A. S. Grenville and George B. Young the president actually "did not contemplate war." Cleveland had no idea that the situation might degenerate to the place that he might have to run the boundary line and try to

---

[46] Edwin F. Uhl, acting secretary of state, to Herbert, January 10, 1894; Gresham to Thompson, January 10, 1894; A. E. K. Benham to Admiral Saldanha da Gama, January 24, January 27, January 28, 1894; Commander W. H. Brownson to Benham, January 30, 1894; all the preceding letters are in "Area File," Roll 27. See also LaFeber, *The New Empire*, pp. 210-218; and Hill, *Diplomatic Relations Between the United States and Brazil*, pp. 272-281.

[47] Herbert, "Grover Cleveland and His Cabinet at Work," pp. 741-742; Nevins, *Grover Cleveland*, p. 641.

make the British accept it. The American public, however, aggressively snatched up Cleveland's warlike phrases with reckless abandon. At any rate the Navy Department had to prepare for the eventuality that hostilities might occur.[48]

During Secretary Herbert's administration the Naval War College was already functioning in the place of a general staff. It was almost impossible for the eight bureaus to get together on the preparation of war plans and strategic studies. In fact, between 1890 and 1915 almost every war plan conceived for the navy was drawn up by the professors of the War College. Sometimes the college worked alone, but often it had the assistance of the Office of Naval Intelligence. After President Cleveland issued his blunt challenge to Great Britain, Hilary Herbert ordered Captain Henry C. Taylor, the president of the War College, to prepare plans for use in the event of war against Great Britain. Taylor found that the United States was hopelessly unprepared. For example, the three vessels of the South Atlantic squadron were thousands of miles away in winter quarter at Montevideo, leaving the Atlantic coast and the Great Lakes pitifully vulnerable to attack. Taylor reasoned that the nation would be in an almost hopeless position if matched against the might of the British navy alone. America had no chance of success, he bluntly reported to the secretary, unless she could get aid from France, Germany, or Russia, each of which had strained relations with England at the time.[49]

Nevertheless, Captain Taylor did inaugurate plans that the navy might use in an area where it might gain strategic advantage—on the Great Lakes, against America's hostage neighbor Canada. In January, 1895, Taylor had Commander Charles B. Gridley to begin a survey of steamers and merchantmen on the Great Lakes with the idea of establishing squadrons of these vessels to control the lakes and attack Canada in the event of war. Gridley was sworn to absolute secrecy because of the public furor his preparations might have caused were they revealed. The results of Gridley's efforts were also discouraging. He found that practically all of the craft on the

---

[48] Grenville and Young, *Politics, Strategy*, p. 168.

[49] Herbert to Taylor, January 22, February 23, 1896, Presidents' Files, Naval War College Archives; Ronald Harvey Spector, "'Professors of War,' The Naval War College and the Modern American Navy" (Ph.D. dissertation, Yale University, 1967), pp. 189-191.

lakes were of wood, and only a few of them were suitable for combat.[50]

In light of Captain Taylor's plans, it is interesting that Secretary Herbert evidently had his mind on similar schemes when he prepared his annual report in November, 1895—anticipating Cleveland's Venezuela message by almost a month. In his report the previous year, the secretary had informed the Congress that the navy vitally needed a reserve supply of ordnance. Even before Cleveland's Venezuela decision with the possibility of hostilities with Britain, Hilary Herbert sounded the same theme with new urgency. If auxiliary vessels ever had to be called into wartime service, Herbert reported, the nation at present had no guns with which to fit them. He then had offered a fantastically prophetic example:

> Under treaty provisions neither the United States nor the English can keep more than one small naval vessel upon our Northern lakes. So far the two countries are matched. In case, however, a war should unfortunately break out between them, Great Britain could promptly furnish guns and mounts to her merchant marine on the lakes, and though their marine is far inferior to ours in strength, the British might master those waters and do incalculable damage to our lake cities. If we had a reserve of ordnance and ordnance stores, we could dominate those waters without question.[51]

Others in the navy were disturbed about the possibility of war. For example, on January 3, 1896, Rear Admiral L. A. Beardslee, the commander of the Pacific Station at Honolulu, wrote to Herbert. Beardslee called the secretary's attention to the "unduly weak condition" of his command "in the event of a sudden call upon them to afford protection to the cities on the Coast and the Sound, and to take valuable part in any war, especially with England." Beardslee requested immediate repairs on one of his ships and asked that the rest of the fleet be drawn closer together if possible.[52]

Fortunately, neither nation wanted the crisis to get out of hand. Negotiations which led to a settlement began in January and continued for many months. Nevertheless, the Navy Department continued to be jumpy. On January 29, Hilary Her-

---

50 Grenville and Young, *Politics, Strategy*, pp. 171-172.
51 U.S. Navy Dept., *Annual Report*, 1895: pp. xi-xii.
52 Beardslee to secretary of the navy, January 3, 1895, "Area File," Roll 313.

Fig. 15. Charles Boutelle of Maine, shown in his Civil War uniform, was the most knowledgeable Republican in the House of Representatives in matters concerning the navy. Courtesy of U.S. Navy Department.

Fig. 16. Captain Henry C. Taylor, president of the Naval War College in 1895, strongly advised the Cleveland administration against armed conflict with Great Britain over the Venezuelan boundary dispute. Courtesy of U.S. Navy Department.

bert sent a confidential dispatch to each squadron commander ordering him to keep the ships under his command "coaled and in readiness for service."[53] As late as March, the secretary summoned Captain Taylor to Washington to continue work on war plans. Not until April did the department evidently decide that the danger was past.[54]

Perhaps because the nation was never actually faced with the catastrophic consequences of war with Great Britain, in retrospect Hilary Herbert applauded Cleveland's belligerent

[53] Herbert to Beardslee, January 29, 1896, and similar dispatches on the same date to Admirals T. O. Selfridge, C. S. Norton, and F. V. McNair, in "Confidential Correspondence," NA, RG 80. It remains a mystery as to what intelligence Herbert received that caused him to rush off the orders on January 29 to keep the fleets in a high state of readiness. The dispatches from Ambassador Thomas F. Bayard in London throughout the month of January indicate that the British government continued to demonstrate a restrained, responsible attitude toward the Venezuelan crisis. See "Dispatches from United States Minister to Great Britain," January, 1896, General Records of the Department of State, NA, RG 59.

[54] Grenville and Young, *Politics, Strategy*, p. 172.

Venezuelan policy because of its salutary domestic effects. Never
able to forget the sectional implications of a policy, Herbert
observed that the Venezuelan crisis was the first event since
the Civil War to cause both northern and southern congressmen to unite unreservedly in a common cause. It was the
Venezuelan crisis, he always maintained, rather than the Spanish-American War that first caused northerners and southerners
to forget "fratricidal strife" and "stand for their country as
one man."[55]

The possibility of a war with Spain also occupied Hilary
Herbert's attention in his last two years in the Navy Department. In February, 1895, a bloody revolt erupted in Cuba.
Because of American economic interests and the proximity of
the island to the American mainland, continued hostilities
carried dangerous implications for the United States. Although
he pressed on Spanish officials the need for reform in Cuba,
President Cleveland was determined that the nation would not
get involved in the struggle. Although the president issued the
usual neutrality proclamation, he refused to recognize the
Cuban rebels as belligerents. In accordance with Cleveland's
wishes, Secretary Herbert ordered special precautions to prevent filibusterers from sailing for Cuba from American ports.
In an effort to avoid any friction with the Spanish squadron,
Herbert was careful to keep American warships out of Cuban
waters unless absolutely necessary. In July, 1896, the American
consul general at Havana, Fitzhugh Lee, petitioned Secretary
of State Olney to station a vessel with a full contingent of
marines at Key West as a "precautionary measure" against
trouble at Havana. Although Olney was not inclined personally to grant the request, he referred the matter to Herbert
for advice. The colonel's answer was unequivocal. The Spanish, he told Olney, already had sixteen vessels in Cuban waters,
a force more than sufficient to keep the peace in Havana. He
added, "To send a ship there, it seems to me, would be to
invite a conflict with the Spanish vessels."[56]

---

55 Herbert, "Grover Cleveland and His Cabinet at Work," p. 742.

56 Lee to Olney, July 8, 1896, "Dispatches from United States Consuls in
Havana," General Records of the Department of State, NA, RG 59; Olney to
Herbert, July 14, 1896, Herbert Papers; Herbert to Olney, July 15, 1896, "Con-
fidential Letters," NA, RG 80.

By December, however, with the outbreak of serious disturbances in Havana, Olney had other thoughts. At a Cabinet meeting on the morning of December 8, the secretary of state advocated sending a warship to Havana harbor. President Cleveland acquiesced in the suggestion and directed Secretary Herbert to send the cruiser *Newark*. The colonel, however, retained grave reservations about the wisdom of the decision. In the afternoon he returned to the White House and offered his objections to the president. With an uncanny prophetic insight, Herbert expressed his fear that some calamity might befall the ship at Havana. Were it to be destroyed even by accident, he asserted, the United States could surely not avoid war with Spain. Moreover, he again pointed out that the Spanish force was quite sufficient to handle any disturbance. Herbert's forceful objections carried the day; the *Newark* was not sent. Two days later Herbert dispatched explicit instructions to the U.S.S. *Raleigh* at Key West. In the event of riots at Havana, Herbert specified, the ship was to proceed to Cuba *only* if the American consul secured permission from the Spanish authorities for the vessel to visit the island. Even after that formality, the captain was to signal Spanish authorities in the city and receive permission once again before entering the harbor at Havana. Herbert was determined that if the nation went to war it would be by conscious national choice and not because of accident or the reckless action of one of his naval commanders.[57]

At the same time, the secretary was determined that war would not catch the United States unprepared. Early in 1896 the newspapers were already comparing the fleets of Spain and the United States.[58] Again Herbert looked to the Naval War College. In February, 1895, the very month that the Cuban insurrection erupted, Herbert ordered the college to include the "general strategic consideration of the Gulf of Mexico" in its problems for the June session. For the session the following January, the colonel ordered a "special study of the strategy of

---

[57] Summers, ed., *The Cabinet Diary of William L. Wilson*, p. 184; Herbert to Captain Merrill Miller, December 10, 1896, "Confidential Correspondence," NA, RG 80.

[58] See, for example, the *New York Times*, March 3, June 7, 1896, January 10, 1897.

the Gulf of Mexico and vicinity" and a study of the "strategy of the Caribbean Sea."[59]

In the spring of 1896, the college worked with Lieutenant W. W. Kimball of the Office of Naval Intelligence to prepare the first complete plan for a possible war with Spain. The Kimball plan envisaged a blockade of Cuba, attacks against the Spanish mainland by a flying squadron, and the seizure of the Philippine Islands. In August, Secretary Herbert went even further and ordered a high-level planning board to convene in Washington. Included in the council were the chiefs of navigation and ordnance, the commander of the North Atlantic Station, the president of the War College, and the chief of naval intelligence. The group junked much of the Kimball plan including the seizure of the Philippines. It substituted an ambitious joint operation of the army and navy against Cuba and Puerto Rico and projected the capture of the Canary Islands for use as a base of operations against the Spanish coast. When the board met again in March, 1897, it reversed itself in part and returned to the idea of taking the Philippines rather than the Canaries.[60] It is apparent, then, that, although the McKinley administration made a few additions and subtractions from the earlier plans, the basic scheme for America's successful war against Spain had been thought out and set down before Secretary Herbert left office.

When the war finally came, Hilary Herbert took an intense interest in the conflict. He was justly proud of the New Navy, which emerged as the darling of the affair. Of the six vessels under Admiral George Dewey that were actually engaged at Manila, all but the *Boston* had been approved while Herbert was chairman of the House Navy Committee. Of the vessels that destroyed the Spanish fleet off Santiago, all excepting the small converted yachts *Glouchester*, *Vixen*, and *Hist* had been authorized during Herbert's tenure on the committee. Secretary of the Navy John D. Long recorded in his journal that

---

[59] Special Circular No. 20 (February 18, 1895) and Special Circular No. 19 (November 15, 1895), "General Orders and Circulars," NA, RG 80.

[60] Spector, "Professors of War," pp. 191-192; Special Order No. 51 (August 19, 1896), "General Orders and Circulars," NA, RG 80; John A. S. Grenville, "Naval Preparations for War with Spain, 1896-1898," *Journal of American Studies* 2 (April, 1968): pp. 36-37. See the handwritten note by Herbert appended to "Plan of Operations Against Spain," December 17, 1896, in Classified Operational Archives, Naval History Division, Washington, D.C.

FIG. 17.   Hilary Herbert's legacy to the nation: the United States Navy, 1898.
Courtesy of U.S. Navy Department.

in large measure Hilary Herbert deserved the credit for the
fleet's preparedness.[61]

It was somewhat ironic that Hilary Herbert, a convinced
anti-imperialist, should have played so major a role in fashion-
ing the weapon with which the imperialists accomplished their
purpose. Although the colonel accepted the need for leasing
naval bases in distant lands, he never accepted the idea that
the nation needed colonial possessions. In October, 1898, two
months before the final settlement with Spain in which the
United States acquired the Philippines, Herbert delivered a
major address at the Quill Club in New York City. The colonel
addressed himself directly to the question of whether the
United States ought to have colonies. For a century of her
history, Herbert asserted, the nation was "a community of co-
equal states" with a few territories which, once they were
settled, looked forward toward full admission to the Union.
Nevertheless, he explained, with the annexation of Hawaii and
the prospect that Cuba, Puerto Rico, and the Philippines would
become colonies, the nation had unquestionably reached "a
parting of the ways." It was probably Herbert's racial fears

[61] Margaret Long, ed., *The Journal of John D. Long* (Rindge, N.H., Richard
R. Smith Publishers, Inc., 1956), p. 219.

that gave him' the greatest pause. Having lived in the South with a colored race which he considered alien, the colonel was reluctant to add any other non-white ingredients to the melting pot. He stated:

> No man in the company, I think, will dare to say, however ardent an expansionist he may be, that we can, without danger now or at any time in the immediate future, make states of these colonies. The masses of their people are not fitted to govern themselves, certainly not fitted to help govern us.

These areas with their inferior peoples, he conjectured, would probably never be competent to come into the Union as states. Moreover, Herbert expressed his belief that these tropical places would not serve as feasible outlets for excess population. Few Americans, he suggested, would ever want to make such climates their permanent homes. He saw no indication that American civilization would follow the flag to these colonies.

The colonel then turned to the bothersome strategic implications of a colonialist course. To have these colonies, he explained, meant that the United States would have to protect them. It meant an increase in expenditures for the Army. It meant also that the country would have to build a larger navy than had ever before been anticipated. He reasoned, "If we are to defend distant sea-girt possessions against all the world, we must have one of the great navies of the world." Nor did Herbert believe that American prosperity would be measurably enhanced by the addition of the Philippines themselves or the access which they gave to China. To place the American flag over a colonial area, he asserted, did not change its climate or make its people more efficient or industrious. All in all, Herbert concluded, the dangers and risks of owning such colonies far outweighed their benefit. He explained, "For myself, I should have preferred that our Government should go forward . . . in the ways of our fathers, a republican government throughout—from center to circumference."[62]

Long after Herbert's advice had been ignored, he remained convinced of his stand. In October, 1901, he confided to Grover

---

[62] Herbert, "Our Place Among the Nations," address at the Quill Club in New York City, October 17, 1898, in correspondence, Herbert Papers. See also the *New York Times*, October 19, 1898, and June 29, 1901.

Cleveland that he still believed the Philippine policy to be "a great mistake" but added that he supposed that nothing could be gained by agitating about it then.[63] It is unfortunate that Herbert had not been in a position to affect the colonial policy of the McKinley administration. As every student of foreign policy knows, the Philippines remained an embarrassing and vulnerable chink in America's armor until after the Second World War.

III

Near the end of his term in the Navy Department, Herbert spoke out one last time on national politics. In July, 1896, the abuse heaped on President Cleveland for four years came to a triumphant climax when the silverites captured the presidential nomination of the Democratic party for William Jennings Bryan. The platform adopted at the Democratic convention in Chicago was a direct slap at the monetary policies of the previous administration. Cleveland and most of the members of his Cabinet were undecided as to whether they should publicly bolt the party's choice. Hilary Herbert, however, had no hesitancy about his course. The Alabamian, undoubtedly remembering the bitter attacks made on him by many of the same farmer radicals in his home state, now seized the opportunity to strike back. Although he had previously throughout his political career equivocated about the currency issue (insisting that he was a "bimetallist"), Herbert finally chose to make a stand.

In effect, Herbert took the lead among the members of the Cleveland Cabinet. On July 15 the papers announced that the secretary of the navy had publicly refused to support William Jennings Bryan. A similar statement from Secretary of State Olney followed. President Cleveland appreciated Herbert's loyalty but was sorry that the Alabamian intensified the party feud by speaking out. As the president told Daniel Lamont, "We have a right to be quiet—indeed, I feel I have been invited to that course." Hilary Herbert saw it differently, however; to him the failure to repudiate Bryanism would mean

---

[63] Herbert to Cleveland, October 19, 1901, Cleveland Papers, Roll 98.

the loss of principle and self-respect.[64] In October, the colonel published an article in the *North American Review* in which he asserted that it was not the state of the monetary supply but rather the eternal agitation of the silver question that had "destroyed confidence in the future, frightened capital, crippled industries, and thrown labor out of employment." Throughout the presidential campaign the colonel did not really consider himself a defector from the Democratic party. His stand, he believed, was rooted in the sound principles of the old party of Tilden and Cleveland. It was the Bryanites who had left the Democracy.[65] The next year Herbert confided to his old friend Robert McKee:

> When our Democratic friends kicked the administration overboard at Chicago to make room for the populists, I was the first Cabinet officer to kick back and I am foolish enough not to regret it. I can't go over to the Republicans, and there's no place left for me except a law office.[66]

As his time in office neared its end, Herbert began to think about the future. So late in life, he was hesitant to begin the practice of law over again. He expressed his interest to the president in a vacancy on the United States Court of Claims. Cleveland was reluctant, however, to break up his Cabinet circle and was not sure that this particular judgeship was of sufficient stature for a Cabinet member to step down to take it. When Secretaries Olney and Harmon expressed their preference that the job go to a jurist who had been connected with the Justice Department, Herbert was angry and hurt. President Cleveland, embarrassed by the rift, simply removed the Cabinet from consideration and refused to entertain further suggestions from his inner council.[67]

When Hilary Herbert looked back over his four years as secretary of the navy, he could point with pride to a record of

---

[64] Nevins, *Grover Cleveland*, p. 705; Summers, ed., *The Cabinet Diary of William L. Wilson*, p. 119; Nevins, ed., *The Letters of Grover Cleveland*, p. 44; Herbert, "Reminiscences," pp. 293-296.

[65] Herbert, "Why American Industry Languishes," *North American Review* **163** (October, 1896): pp. 488-495.

[66] Herbert to McKee, July 30, 1897, McKee Papers, Alabama Archives.

[67] Summers, ed., *The Cabinet Diary of William L. Wilson*, pp. 157-159, 166; Herbert to William L. Wilson, October 27, 1898, Cleveland Papers, Roll 95; *New York Times*, November 15, November 19, 1896.

TABLE 3
VESSELS AUTHORIZED BY CONGRESS DURING HERBERT'S ADMINISTRATION AS SECRETARY OF THE NAVY, 1893-1897*

Ship	Tons Displacement	Contract Date of Completion
Battleships:		
Kearsarge	11,520	2 January, 1899
Kentucky	11,520	2 January, 1899
Alabama	11,520	26 September, 1899
Illinois	11,520	24 September, 1899
Wisconsin	11,520	19 September, 1899
Total (5)	57,600	
Gunboats:		
Annapolis	1000	20 February, 1897
Vicksburg	1000	15 February, 1897
Newport	1000	15 February, 1897
Wheeling	1000	26 February, 1897
Marietta	1000	26 February, 1897
Princeton	1000	20 February, 1897
Total (6)	6000	
Torpedo boats:		
No. 3	142	3 August, 1896
No. 4	142	3 August, 1896
No. 5	142	3 August, 1896
No. 6	182	19 August, 1896
No. 7	182	19 November, 1896
No. 8	182	19 January, 1897
No. 9	146	6 April, 1898
No. 10	146	6 April, 1898
No. 11	273	5 April, 1898
No. 12	117	6 October, 1897
No. 13	117	6 October, 1897
No. 14	103	6 October, 1897
No. 15	47	6 October, 1897
No. 16	47	6 October, 1897
No. 17	65	17 October, 1897
No. 18	65	17 October, 1897
Total (16)	2098	
Submarine torpedo boat	...	3 March, 1897
Grand Total	65,866	

* This table does not include the three torpedo boats authorized in the 2nd session of the 54th Congress, just as Hilary Herbert left office. Tables 3, 4, and 5 are taken from "Growth of the U.S. Navy," *Proceedings of the United States Naval Institute,* 23 (1896): pp. 821-823.

solid achievement. In spite of the most difficult financial conditions, Herbert was able to continue the expansion of the New Navy. His emphasis on torpedo boats and battleships was

TABLE 4
New Vessels Placed in Commission during Herbert's Administration,
4 March, 1893 to 4 March, 1897

Ship and Type	Tons Displacement	Date of Commission
Armored		
Indiana, sea-going coastline battleship	10,288	20 November, 1895
Massachusetts, sea-going coastline battleship	10,288	10 June, 1896
Oregon, sea-going coastline battleship	10,288	15 July, 1896
Maine, second-class battleship	6682	17 September, 1895
Texas, second-class battleship	6315	15 August, 1895
New York, armored cruiser	8200	1 August, 1893
Brooklyn, armored cruiser	9271	1 December, 1896
Amphitrite, low-freeboard coast defense monitor	3990	23 April, 1896
Monadnock, low-freeboard coast defense monitor	3990	20 February, 1896
Terror, low-freeboard coast defense monitor	3990	15 February, 1896
Katahdin, armored ram	2155	20 February, 1896
Total	75,457	
Unarmored		
Cincinnati, protected cruiser	3213	16 June, 1894
Raleigh, protected cruiser	3213	17 April, 1894
Columbia, protected cruiser	7375	23 April, 1894
Minneapolis, protected cruiser	7375	13 December, 1894
Olympia, protected cruiser	5870	5 February, 1895
Detroit, cruiser	2089	20 July, 1893
Marblehead, cruiser	2089	2 April, 1894
Montgomery, cruiser	2089	21 June, 1894
Castine, gunboat	1177	22 October, 1894
Machias, gunboat	1177	20 July, 1893
Total	35,667	
Puritan, low-freeboard coast defense monitor	6060	Will be commissioned 7 December, 1896*
Annapolis, gunboat	1000	Will be commissioned 20 February, 1897*

* Put into commission after the statistics on Herbert's administration compiled for the *Proceedings of the United States Naval Institute.*

an important step in the progression toward destroyers and superdreadnaughts. Although his administration in the Navy Department was not noted for pioneering achievement or flamboyant style, it was a significant period of consolidation, rationalization, and fulfillment. Herbert had the unique privilege of seeing the New Navy, over which he and others had toiled for so long, come into its own. Shortly after the time Herbert

TABLE 5
New Tonnage Authorized by Congress, New Tonnage Begun, and
New Tonnage Placed in Commission since March, 1881

March 4-	New Vessels Authorized	New Vessels Begun	New Vessels Commissioned
1881-1885	23,076	12,363	...
1885-1889	67,183	34,814	7,863
1889-1893	66,618	93,164	54,832
1893-1897	65,942	80,788	118,184

left office many authorities ranked the United States as fifth among the naval powers of the world. The fleet which he left was essentially that which won the Spanish-American War. Once again the statistics, as shown in the accompanying tables, speak for themselves.[68]

After leaving the Navy Department, the colonel continued to follow the fortunes of the fleet and to press continually for a more vigorous naval policy.[69] Somehow, however, in the long years that followed, historians charged with keeping the record of America's national achievement all but forgot about Herbert's monumental contribution to the building of the new fleet. Fortunately, a few people remembered. On the occasion of the colonel's death in March, 1919, the Montgomery *Advertiser* evaluated his contribution. Although the *Advertiser* might be excused for exaggeration on the grounds of partiality, this writer at least is convinced that the paper did not overstate the case. Herbert, the paper pointed out, took up the cause of the navy before it became a popular issue, especially among Democrats. The article concluded:

> He was among the first men of his time to visualize the enlarged field which America had come to occupy, and to see that its responsibilities as a world power carried with them the necessity for naval strength. In consequence the navy was in a condition of readiness at the outbreak of the Spanish-American war which its friends ten years before had no right to expect it would attain. More than any other one man, Colonel Herbert deserves the credit for the renewed growth of our seapower.[70]

[68] See tables 3, 4, and 5.
[69] See, for example, Herbert, "Our Navy and Our Naval Policy," *Munsey's Magazine* 17 (May, 1897): pp. 182-186; "A Plea for the Navy," *Forum* 24 (September, 1897): pp. 1-15; "The Fifty Million Appropriation and Its Lessons," *Forum* 25 (May, 1898): pp. 267-275.
[70] *Montgomery Advertiser,* March 7, 1919, Vol. 12, Herbert Papers.

IX. Elder Southern Statesman: Old Wine in New Flasks

> I was always conservative and day by day am becoming more so. I believe in old friends and old ways.
>
> —Hilary Abner Herbert,
> to an old friend

I

WITH the advent of the McKinley administration, Hilary Herbert, now sixty-three years old, returned to private life after twenty years of continuous public service in Washington. With the enthusiastic recommendations of the new secretary of the navy, John D. Long, and his assistant, Theodore Roosevelt, Herbert sought an appointment as a special counsel to the Justice Department; but Attorney General Philander C. Knox, professing uncertainty as to Herbert's legal abilities after his twenty-year absence from law practice, declined to make an appointment. Herbert, who had always lived on his salary both as a congressman and cabinet officer, was thus driven late in life to his own resources. With little choice in the matter if he were to survive, he established a law practice in partnership with his son-in-law Benjamin Micou, who was also out of a job since he had served as Herbert's chief clerk in the Navy Department. The *New York Times* reported the founding of the firm, the initial circular of which announced a specialty in prosecuting claims against the Navy Department. Editorial concern over the cryptic notice was unfounded, however, because there is no evidence that Herbert ever used information gained from his former political associations to the detriment of any government agency.[1] Undoubtedly Herbert was discouraged, perhaps even disgruntled, at having to start all over again so

---

[1] *New York Times*, May 11, 1897; Theodore Roosevelt to John D. Long, September 15, 1897, in Elting E. Morrison, *et al.*, eds., *The Letters of Theodore Roosevelt* (Cambridge, Harvard University Press, 1951) 1: p. 675.

late in life. He confided to his mother-in-law, "I am doing fairly well and hope to succeed here, but if I do it will be only by hard work and economy. It was a misfortune for me to have gone into public life—it will be hard on my children after I am gone."[2]

In spite of the colonel's initial pessimism, "Herbert and Micou" flourished and eventually cultivated such large clients as Seaboard Air Line Railroad and the United Iron Works of San Francisco. In 1900 Herbert bought a house in Washington which he insured for $18,000; and ten years later he retired comfortably from active participation in the law firm.[3]

During these later years Herbert, enjoying the role of an elder southern statesman, found time for many activities in which his attendance to public duties had formerly denied him participation. He held membership in numerous honorary, charitable, professional, and social organizations and was in constant demand as a speaker on the banquet circuit. In 1905 he played a prominent role, along with Mabel F. Boardman and John W. Foster, as one of the incorporators of the reorganized American National Red Cross; and it is under the charter secured from the United States Congress in that year that the organization still operates. In recognition of his distinguished career, Tulane University awarded Herbert an honorary doctorate, as did the University of Alabama, which had once expelled him as a student rebel.[4]

Veterans' affairs also occupied much of his time. In these later years, most of the bitterness of the Civil War had passed. With their numbers rapidly declining, the old Rebels and Yankees put away their former animosity and came together; and in an almost mystical sense, they enjoyed the common bond of the experience of the war and of having lived so long to tell about it. Herbert, for example, who was the commanding general of the District of Columbia Brigade of the United Confederate

---

2 Herbert to Susan Parker Smith, May 12, 1897, Washington M. Smith Papers.

3 *Washington Mirror,* September 17, 1904, Vol. 11, Herbert Papers; Insurance policy, District Title Insurance Company, issued to Herbert on April 30, 1900, in correspondence, Herbert Papers; Herbert, "Reminiscences, 1910-1911; 1918," Vol. 4, Herbert Papers.

4 Mabel F. Boardman to Mrs. Benjamin Micou, May 16, 1919, and December 23, 1919, Herbert Papers; Carey Vitallis Stabler, "The Career of Hilary Abner Herbert" (M.A. thesis, University of Alabama, 1932), pp. 87-88; Barringer, *University of Virginia* 1: p. 409.

Veterans, was also unanimously elected to honorary membership in the Second Corps Association of the Army of the Potomac. One of Herbert's most ambitious projects was the erection
of the Arlington Confederate Monument in the national cemetery near Washington in 1914. The monument was dedicated
at an impressive ceremony over which Herbert presided and
at which President Woodrow Wilson graciously consented to
speak.[5]

In private life Herbert also found more opportunity for
writing. In 1903, at the insistence of his daughter Ella, he wrote
his fascinating reminiscences which he called "Grandfather's
Talks About His Life Under Two Flags." Aside from a number
of articles, his major literary effort was the book, already discussed in detail, *The Abolition Crusade and Its Consequences,*
published in 1912. Herbert's purpose in writing was not only
to present to northerners a southern point of view but also to
remind southern authors not to forget "to inculcate in the
minds of the present and coming generations of Southerners
the admiration of, and veneration for, their fighting ancestors
which in my opinion is their just due."[6] Although he did not
agree with Herbert's thesis, the historian James Ford Rhodes
consented to provide his friend with an introduction to be
published with the book. According to the historian's biographer, Rhodes was motivated in part by the sense of alarm
which he shared with Herbert over Theodore Roosevelt's
demand in the campaign of 1912 for recall of judicial decisions;
and the Boston historian felt that Herbert's monograph did at
least warn against the dangerous methods of fanatics who had
no respect for the Constitution.[7]

As the years waned, Herbert seemed more and more to be a
man who had lived beyond his time. Although he had helped
midwife the American navy into the modern world and had in
many ways been an unapologetic "New South man," it was the
Old South which had captured his heart. As Professor Hugh
Charles Davis has perceived, Herbert always hoped that the

---

5 *Washington Post,* June 5, 1914. See also Gabriel Edmonston to Herbert,
January 5, 1917; Myron M. Parker to Herbert, March 21, 1914; Herbert Papers.
6 Herbert, "Jottings, March—April, 1912," Vol. 5, Herbert Papers; Herbert,
"Reminiscences," p. 1.
7 Herbert, *Abolition Crusade,* pp. vii-ix; James Ford Rhodes to Herbert, November 11, 1911, Herbert Papers; Cruden, *James Ford Rhodes,* pp. 120-121.

result of "Redemption" for the South would be "a return to the ideas and values of the pre-Garrison era."[8] Nor is it surprising that a man born on a South Carolina plantation almost three decades before the Civil War should feel somewhat anachronistic in the bustling years of the Progressive Era. He had outlived not only his wife Ella but also his son Hilary Abner Herbert, Jr., and his eldest daughter Leila, whose tragic suicide following evident brain damage as a result of a fall while horseback riding in 1897 undoubtedly scarred her father deeply.[9]

In the later years, death claimed many of the old friends and intimates whom Herbert had known in the Congress and the Cabinet. His relations with Grover Cleveland remained cordial until the former president's passing. Like Herbert, Cleveland remained as conservative as ever; and even as late as 1907, his letters to his friend revealed his bitterness at the Bryan capture of the Democratic party in 1896. The former president confessed that his greatest apprehension was that he might not live to see the party restored to "rational councils"; and although he predicted "impending ruin" if the party did not return to sound and conservative doctrines, Cleveland was not inclined to stir himself to speak in public as forcefully as he expressed himself to Herbert by mail.[10] In the last decade of his life, in fact, most of Herbert's interest in politics was confined to discussions by letter and in person with old friends. He had a warm appreciation for William Howard Taft, whom he believed to be a fellow conservative; and the southerner was overjoyed when in 1912 Taft wrested the Republican nomination away from a determined Theodore Roosevelt, who was to Herbert a "reckless popular leader whose influence on the masses would be such to endanger the republic."[11]

In a sense, the former secretary of the navy apparently rather enjoyed the role of an old-fashioned man. He formed opinions

8 Davis, "An Analysis of the Rationale of Representative Conservative Alabamians, 1874-1914" (Ph.D. dissertation, Vanderbilt University, 1964), pp. 295-296.

9 New York Times, December 22, 1897; Herbert, "Reminiscences, 1910-1911, 1918," Vol. 4, Herbert Papers.

10 Grover Cleveland to Herbert, April 27, 1907, Herbert Papers. See also Maurice S. Fortin, "Hilary Abner Herbert: Post-Reconstruction Southern Politician" (M.A. thesis, University of Maryland, 1965), p. 116.

11 Herbert to Charles Frances Adams, June 8, 1912, Herbert Papers; Herbert, "Jottings, March–April, 1912," Vol. 5, Herbert Papers.

about many things and was especially critical of newfangled notions. He lamented, for example, the declining literacy of modern children who did not learn Latin and Greek as thoroughly as had the children of his youth. Many schools, he complained, had dispensed altogether with the traditional spelling book, leaving children unable to divide words correctly into syllables. Increasingly for Herbert the "good old days" radiated a golden glow.[12]

II

Although the scope of his national contribution was much more narrow in the years after Herbert left the Navy Department, in the area of race relations his voice was heard a number of times, not only on a regional but also on a national level. It was the issue of the Negro's place in the South that had plagued Herbert and fellow southerners since the earliest days of Reconstruction. It was this problem which, as we have seen, left Hilary Herbert less than a free man himself, which prevented his seeking meaningful solutions to the other myriad problems which beset his region. The necessity of always keeping the racial reference point in focus doubtless forced him to adopt a narrow, defensive, and provincial posture that circumscribed his own intellect and abilities.

To say on the one hand that Herbert was an unapologetic racist and to contend on the other that he worked and spoke out for constructive solution to the southern racial crisis of the Progressive years is to admit to an ambivalence and lack of moral certainty which the young modern historian may be hard pressed to comprehend. Nevertheless, rather than succumb to the temptation to judge a historical figure by our own standards, the biographer must make an honest effort to measure him by the standards and criteria of his own time. In the context of the poisoned and stifling atmosphere created in the South by such notorious race-baiters and demagogues as Ben Tillman and Cole Blease, Tom Watson and Hoke Smith, James K. Vardaman and Theodore Bilbo, the calm and conservative voice of Hilary Herbert appears strangely like a fresh breeze of springtime.

---

12 See Davis, "Analysis of the Rationale of Representative Conservative Alabamians," p. 352; Herbert, Laurens school speech, in undated correspondence, Herbert Papers.

Herbert was a leader among those whom C. Vann Woodward has classed as "conservative" in their approach to race relations. This group, represented also by men such as Wade Hampton of South Carolina and Thomas Goode Jones of Alabama, steered a steady course between the insignificant number of "liberals" on the one side and the large number of fanatical Negrophobes on the other. While the conservatives championed white supremacy, they did not at the same time believe in unnecessary personal debasement of Negroes. Like Hilary Herbert, many of them were men of the old as well as the new South; they had known slavery times and, therefore, according to Edgar Gardner Murphy, felt "a sense of responsibility, deepened rather than destroyed by the burden of slavery. . . ." It was their sense of *noblesse* oblige concerning the Negro which Murphy saw as the "noble and fruitful gift of the old south to the new, a gift brought out of the conditions of an aristocracy, but responsive and operative under every challenge in the changing conditions of the later order."[13] One recent writer has said:

> Hilary Herbert was probably as close to an approximation of the "best" Southern white man one could expect to find. He was conservative, but realistic enough to comprehend that the crisis facing the South required extraordinary measures, particularly in education. His attitude toward the Negro race was paternalistic, but while his principles led him to be kindly disposed toward the black man, they in no wise altered his conviction that the Negro was inferior.[14]

Herbert's philosophy, however, is best expressed in his own words:

> We cannot afford to break down the partition wall between the races; we can do nothing that will tend to social equality, nothing that will look towards amalgamation. And yet we must do justice, we must educate and lift up the negro so as to make

---

13 Murphy, *Problems of the Present South* (New York, Macmillan Company, 1904), p. 21; Woodward, *The Strange Career of Jim Crow*, pp. 45-48; George M. Stephenson, *American History Since 1865* (New York and London, Harper & Brothers Publishers, 1939), p. 32.

14 Hines H. Hall, "The Montgomery Race Conference of 1900: Focal Point of Racial Attitudes at the Turn of the Century" (M.A. thesis, Auburn University, 1965), pp. 37-38. See also Claude H. Nolen, *The Negro's Image in the South: The Anatomy of White Supremacy* (Lexington, University of Kentucky Press, 1967), p. 170.

him a better citizen, and give him in our laws and in the courts all his rights.[15]

Although Herbert would give lip-service to his own idea of "justice" for the Negro, his ingrained prejudices tragically prevented his ever being able to conceive of anything approaching equality for blacks in America. Indeed, he envisaged the black man as forever lagging behind. He wrote on one occasion:

> Taken in the aggregate, the shortcomings of the Negro are numerous and regrettable, but not greater than was to be expected. The general advance of an inferior race will never equal that of one which is superior by nature and already centuries ahead. The laggard and thriftless among the inferior people will naturally be more, and it is from these classes that prison houses are filled.

Naïvely accepting the stereotyped justification for so much of the white violence of the Progressive years, Herbert argued that one major cause for inflammation of racial passions was the increasing frequency of rape, "the crime of the negro against white women." Although he personally denounced lynching, he readily accepted the malignant notion that it was a direct result of the "criminality of the negro," which was "three times greater than that of the white man."[16]

Nevertheless, the racial violence of these years weighed heavily on Herbert's mind and conscience. Although he had consistently preached white supremacy and had acquiesced in defrauding black voters throughout his own campaigns for Congress over a period of fourteen years, Herbert had never stooped to direct race-baiting or deliberate demagoguery to inflame white passions against the Negro as a person. In private, at least, he deplored the work of professional racists like Thomas Dixon, whose books *The Leopard's Spots, The Clansman,* and *The Traitor* exemplified the violent anti-Negro virus which infected the nation around the turn of the century.[17]

In his attempts to discover the reasons for this more virulent strain of racial hatred, Herbert inevitably turned to his own historical experience. The faults of the black man notwith-

---

15 Herbert, Laurens school speech, in undated correspondence, Herbert Papers.
16 Herbert, *Abolition Crusade,* pp. 230-238.
17 Herbert to William Watts Ball, April 23, 1912, Ball Papers, Duke University Library.

standing, he came to the conclusion that the root of the trouble, "the Negro problem," lay in the years immediately before and after the Civil War. In the years prior to the war, he asserted, fanatical abolitionists had preached the "monstrous idea that the only difference between the white and the black races was in color—that the negro was simply 'a white man in ebony.'" The agitation first brought the war and then Reconstruction, in which a new group of fanatics gave the Negro the vote and injected him into politics, the effect of which was "to array the two races in a bitter struggle against each other for political power and to create animosities between the younger members of both races that had never existed between master and slave. . . ."[18]

Herbert's assessment of the reasons for the southern racial crisis led him to advocate openly in these later years a malevolent solution which he had not supported in the time that he was directly involved in politics. If the Negro in politics were the cause of the current racial strife, he reasoned, then the remedy was quite simple—the black man should be eliminated from all political activity. In 1901 he confessed, "In my opinion the granting of universal suffrage to the Negro was the mistake of the nineteenth century."[19] In another article he wrote:

> It is not making any new or startling assertion to say that negro suffrage was a failure. It did not give Republican control at the South, except for a brief period, and it did not benefit, but injured the freedmen; it made unavoidable in the South the color line, and *impossible there two capable political parties, of which all men, North and South alike, now see the crying need.*[20]

It was Herbert's fervent hope that a meaningful politics would result with the end of Negro participation. Although he had beat the drums of white supremacy himself for many years, he was not foolish enough to believe that such distractions offered the solution to the region's pressing social, economic, and political problems. It was in his home state of Alabama that he made his most forceful plea. Although he had

---

18 Herbert, "Reminiscences," p. 291.

19 Herbert, "The Race Problem at the South," *Annals of the American Academy of Political and Social Science* 18 (July, 1901): p. 99.

20 Herbert, "Conditions of the Reconstruction Problem," p. 156.

remained in Washington after his retirement, the colonel's ties in Alabama continued to be strong. Speaking in June, 1901, to the Alabama State Bar Association, he accepted as inevitable that the Negro would be disfranchised by the state's constitutional convention (in which many members of his audience were participants). Indeed, he likened the policy of the federal government toward the new island possessions acquired as a result of the Spanish-American War to the policy of the South in disfranchising the Negro. He said:

> The Declaration of Independence does not apply to inferior races over whom we acquire dominion. The South contended that before the war, and is vindicated by Republican policy to-day. The Constitutional Convention in seeking to limit negro suffrage is doing precisely what the country is doing in its new island possessions, asserting the right of the superior race to govern savage tribes and mixed races.

The remainder of Herbert's address, however, gave evidence that he did not personally use the idea of a freer southern politics merely as a hypocritical justification for black disfranchisement. Herbert actually believed that such a result was possible. He astounded his audience and the reporter of the *New York Times,* who headed his article "Ex-Secretary Herbert as an Independent," by advocating that, once the blacks were effectively eliminated, every voter should cast his ballot for the best candidate and platform—regardless of party. Denouncing demagoguery and party manipulation, Herbert proclaimed:

> We need freer thought and freer action in the South and must give party managers to understand that they must put up good men whom we can approve, and can get our votes only on the man and the platform. It may happen that no party puts up a nominee on a platform to suit us, and it will be our duty to reject them all, and give partisans to understand that clauses put in to catch ignorant votes will lose intelligent votes.[21]

It was a virtuoso performance and, to say the least, a monumental flip-flop for a man who, except for his minor aberration in 1896, had been known for years as a high priest of Democratic unity.

---

[21] *New York Times,* June 21, 1901.

Although southerners might successfully disfranchise the Negro, there was no guarantee that the federal government under an activist and unpredictable president like Theodore Roosevelt might not act directly in some way to thwart southern schemes. The apprehensions of whites in the South increased when President Roosevelt lunched with Booker T. Washington, appointed a Negro to the customs collectorship of the port of Charleston, and closed the post office in Indianola, Mississippi, when the townspeople refused to accept their mail from a black postmistress.[22]

With Roosevelt's election in his own right to a full presidential term in 1904, Hilary Herbert began a personal campaign to influence the president's southern policy. Writing to Roosevelt a few days after the election, Herbert reminded the president that when he had become secretary of the navy in 1893, a certain young man named Roosevelt had written to congratulate him and to make suggestions. It was now his turn, Herbert wrote, to offer congratulations and advice. In his lengthy letter, he addressed himself to the numerous problems of "race antagonism" that had beset the South of late. Although he could offer no certain solution, the Alabamian assured the young chief executive that the answer did not lie in federal intervention, a strategy which had been tried once before and was now in part responsible for the present hostility. Action by the national government, he argued, would only intensify burning antagonisms. Roosevelt's brief reply to Herbert was conciliatory but noncommittal, confessing that "in the main my views are yours" but at the same time promising justice to the Negro.[23]

Evidently it was well known among southerners in Washington that Hilary Herbert was spearheading an effort to influence the administration's policies. Although Representative John Sharp Williams from Mississippi's Eighth Congressional District could have easily had access to the president, he apparently believed that Herbert's influence would be greater and, therefore, sent to the Alabamian a letter from a constituent

---

22 Seth M. Scheiner, "President Roosevelt and the Negro," *The Journal of Negro History* 57 (July, 1962): pp. 171-175.

23 Herbert to Theodore Roosevelt, November 12, 1904; Roosevelt to Herbert, November 12, 1904, Herbert Papers.

concerning race relations that he wanted Herbert to try to bring
to Roosevelt's attention in some way.[24]

Realizing that his own influence was not great enough, Herbert turned to his friend James Ford Rhodes, for whom Theodore Roosevelt's admiration was unmistakable. Rhodes and the
president were cordial friends, and the two had on occasion
discussed the "southern problem," usually with Rhodes taking
the side of the South while Roosevelt remained painfully suspicious of the goodness of southern intentions toward the black
man. Rhodes did not hesitate to express to Herbert his deep-
seated disagreements with the "liberal" trend of Roosevelt's
race policies although he still retained the greatest admiration
for the young chief executive. Nor did the Boston historian
need much encouragement from his southern friend to spur
him to present his opinions to the president. Rhodes stated his
own feeling quite succinctly to Herbert:

> It is unnecessary for me to repeat my views on the Southern
> question. They become more fixed the more I study the ques-
> tion of Reconstruction. If the negroes stop commiting rape on
> white women and lynchings therefore cease there will be no
> longer any Southern question at the North so far as it concerns
> practical action.

In response to Herbert's plea for help, Rhodes confided that he
and an unnamed friend of considerable influence (evidently
President Henry Smith Pritchett of the Massachusetts Institute
of Technology) had apprised the president of their views.[25]

Herbert was also instrumental in arranging the president's
famous visit to the South in the fall of 1905 at which time
Roosevelt's uneasy rapprochement with that region was finally
sealed. Undoubtedly, the colonel was gratified when Roosevelt,
speaking at Tuskegee, told the assembled blacks that southern
white men were their "best friends" and it was to this group
that the Negroes should look for aid. From this point on, it was
evident that the president, whether influenced by Herbert's

---

24 Williams to Herbert, December 10, 1904, Herbert Papers.

25 Herbert to Rhodes, November 25, 1904; Rhodes to Herbert, November 24,
1904, December 17, 1904, March 4, 1905, Herbert Papers; Theodore Roosevelt
to Rhodes, November 29, 1904, February 20, 1905, and Roosevelt to Henry Smith
Pritchett, December 14, 1904, in Morison, ed., The Letters of Theodore Roosevelt
4: pp. 1049-1051, 1066-1072, 1125. See also Cruden, James Ford Rhodes, pp. 112-
113.

lobbying, by northern intellectuals such as Rhodes and Pritchett, or by national public opinion, had abandoned any
thought of federal intervention to assure Negro rights.[26]

With the Taft years, there was obviously no danger whatever of any federal action on behalf of the Negro. Herbert no
doubt breathed more easily. He felt confident enough to assure
fellow southerners:

> Intelligent public opinion at the north is at this writing
> so thoroughly with us that there is now no longer any danger
> of interference with us from Washington, either legislative or
> executive, so long as we do not, by harsh or unjust treatment
> of the negro, now at our mercy, alienate the sympathies of the
> majority section of our union.[27]

Had Herbert's efforts ended here, his record would be a
sorry one indeed, even from the point of view of his own era,
since the historical evidence is perfectly clear that the position
of black Americans was steadily deteriorating throughout the
South in these years. Indeed, one may in retrospect suggest that
the attitudes and actions of the so-called "best class" of Southerners, like Herbert, who—even more than lynchers and virulent
platform demagogues—prevented progress toward racial justice
in Dixie. One can say for Herbert, however, that he was not
oblivious to the alarming rise of violent racism. While he could
never countenance outside interference, he did believe strongly
that responsible southerners could and should act to alleviate
the mounting racial difficulties. To that end he joined in the
work of the Southern Society for the Promotion of the Study
of Race Conditions in the South.

In spite of the organization's auspicious title, its existence
was short-lived; better known as the Montgomery Race Conference, the first annual meeting was the only one ever held.
Arising out of the controversy and politics surrounding the
Alabama Constitutional Convention of 1900, the conference,
scheduled for May of that year, was organized principally by

---

[26] James Weatherly to Herbert, December 31, 1904, Herbert Papers; "Visit of
the President to the South," *Confederate Veteran* 13 (November, 1905): p. 490;
Scheiner, "President Roosevelt and the Negro," pp. 179-182.

[27] Quoted in Dewey W. Grantham, Jr., "The Progressive Movement and the
Negro," *South Atlantic Quarterly* 54 (October, 1955): p. 475; Henry Litchfield
West, "President Taft and the South," *Forum* 41 (April, 1909): p. 294.

the Montgomery clergyman Edgar Gardner Murphy. Nearly all the leading figures in the various factions of the state Democratic party supported the endeavor. Even William Wallace Screws, the editor of the conservative *Montgomery Advertiser,* temporarily put aside his feud of long standing with the mildly Populist wing of the party, now led by Joseph F. Johnston. The program for the meeting was to consist of a number of addresses on such topics as Negro suffrage, social relations between the races, Negro education, and lynching. Among the prominent personalities invited to participate were: Congressman Bourke Cochran of New York, the only northerner on the program; J. L. M. Curry, ex-minister to Spain and agent for the Peabody and Slater educational funds; Dr. Hollis Burke Frissell, principal of Hampton Institute; Dr. Julius D. Dreher, president of Roanoke College in Salem, Virginia; and ex-Governor William A. MacCorkle of West Virginia. The promoters of the meeting successfully enhanced the prestige of the effort when Hilary Herbert accepted their invitation to become the permanent chairman of the conference. The *New York Times* commented on the announcement of the colonel's participation.

> He is a man of force and independence of mind, who is well acquainted with the course of events and opinion in the entire country, and while he enjoys the confidence of the people of the South, he will understand the relations of its action to the Nation, which is a matter not to be forgotten.[28]

When the Montgomery Conference opened on May 8, Herbert was the first major speaker; it was his address which set the tone for the meeting. In his customary bow to white supremacy, he asserted, "The negro is not the equal of the white man; science and history alike proclaim this truth. His skull is thicker and his brain is smaller than the white man's. . . ." In his regular fashion, he then trotted out his usual catalog of the horrors of Reconstruction, deprecated Negro participation in politics, and called up white fears of amalgamation were racial barriers to be lowered. Turning then to the real issue at hand, Herbert candidly outlined some of the most pressing problems facing the

---

28 *New York Times,* April 9, 1900; Hall, "The Montgomery Race Conference of 1900," pp. 21-27; John Joel Culley, "Muted Trumpets: Four Efforts to Better Southern Race Relations, 1900-1919" (Ph.D. dissertation, University of Virginia, 1967), pp. 28-57.

South, including lynching and the movement in some states to cease support for black education altogether. In soft and conciliatory tones, he called upon the participants in the meeting to lay aside partisan recrimination and vengeful racial antipathies and to seek "the adjustment of the relations between the two races in . . . a spirit of moderation, charity and justice. . . ."

Herbert deprecated such crack-brained schemes as deportation or the repeal of the Fifteenth Amendment and assured his audience that, like it or not, black and white were destined to live side by side in the South. In an effort to suggest a solution for one of the most pressing problems, he suggested that speedier judicial procedures be instituted in an effort to deter lynchings. Herbert's most powerful appeal, however, was on behalf of Negro education. It was an increase rather than a decrease in the expenditures for black schools that was needed. He asked:

> Is not negro criminology largely due to poverty, want of education, and home training? Is not the system of industrial education as taught at Tuskegee by that remarkable man, Booker Washington, a key to the situation? And are there not so many thousand instances of negroes becoming faithful and orderly citizens as to lead us to the conclusion that much of the evil we now see is the result of miseducation, and that in the establishment of more harmonious relations between the races and better training for the negro, we are to look for the solution of this problem.[29]

Although it amply demonstrated the tragic prejudice and bigotry that gripped the minds of even responsible southern leaders, Herbert's widely reported address had defined many of the political, social, and economic issues with which the assembled whites had to deal. The *Atlanta Constitution* called

---

29 Herbert, "The Problems that Present Themselves," speech at Montgomery Race Conference, May 8, 1900, in correspondence, Herbert Papers; *New York Times*, May 9, 1900. See also *Race Problems of the South: Report of the Proceedings of the First Annual Conference Held Under the Auspices of the Southern Society for the Promotion of the Study of Race Conditions and Problems in the South* (Richmond, B. F. Johnson Publishing Company, 1900) for the official report of the conference. Herbert's manuscript copy of his speech differs in several places from the official report, indicating that he may have wandered from his prepared text or that his speech was edited or partly rewritten for publication.

his address "brilliant" and a writer for one national magazine
characterized it as easily one of the most forceful and dynamic
speeches of the conference.[30] The results of the meeting generally, however, were depressing. The participants were too bound
by their own provincialism and prejudice to offer much in the
way of constructive solutions to the racial crisis. A modern
scholar has found little to admire in the work of the "mis-
named" association, the meeting of which turned out to be
little more than a procession of the faithful to the altar of white
supremacy.[31] Nevertheless, a number of Herbert's contemporaries were encouraged by the conference which was widely reported nationally. The *New York Times* had heralded the meeting, saying, "The main thing in the conference is that it will give
a chance for open talk chiefly by Southern men." The *Outlook*
had reported, "The mere fact that such a Conference was held
should be regarded by all who have at heart the interests of the
African race and of the country as an encouraging sign." The
Independent was more negative:

> The negro problem is purely one for southern whites. It is
> the question whether they shall, and how they shall, keep the
> negroes in the condition of serfdom, while at the same time the
> National Constitution endows them with the rights of citizen-
> ship. The Montgomery Conference is a good sign, even altho
> the predominant sentiment of speakers and hearers was against
> the conclusions of justice.[32]

The most interesting assessment of the meeting came from
Booker T. Washington, who, although he had quietly participated in the planning of the convention, had to view the proceedings from the gallery (since blacks were not allowed to
participate). While Washington strongly dissented from many
of the statements that were made, his opinion of the meeting
was on the whole favorable. Out of the nineteen formal speeches

---

30 *Atlanta Constitution,* May 9, 1900; Isabel C. Barrows, "The Montgomery
Conference," *Outlook* 65 (May 19, 1900): p. 161.

31 See Gilbert Osofsky, ed., *The Burden of Race: A Documentary History of
Negro-White Relations in America* (New York and Evanston, Harper & Row,
Publishers, 1967), p. 208.

32 *New York Times,* April 9, 1900; *Outlook,* Editorial, "The Montgomery Conference," 65 (May 19, 1900): pp. 153-155; *Independent,* Editorial, "The Eternal
Negro," 52 (May 17, 1900): pp. 1207-1208.

FIG. 18. The historian James Ford er T. Washington com- Hilary Herbert and was in- fluenced by his writings. Courtesy of Library of Con- gress.

FIG. 19. The Tuskegee educator Book- er T. Washington com- mended Herbert's actions in the Montgomery race conven- tion and the Georgia railroad strike of 1909. Courtesy of Library of Congress.

which he heard, he considered only four to be blatantly anti-negro. He wrote:

> I consider that this conference represents in a large measure the "Silent South." For years we have heard the voice of the North, the voice of the negro, the voice of the politician, and the voice of the mob; but the voice of the educated, cultivated white South has been too long silent.

Interestingly enough, the Tuskegee educator even had mild commendation for Hilary Herbert personally. During the closing session Herbert had spoken out in disagreement with a particularly malicious characterization of the Negro presented by Professor Paul B. Barringer, chairman of the faculty of the University of Virginia. Washington gave an account of the incident:

> When the proper time came, ex-Secretary Herbert, the chair-man of the meeting, and an ex-slaveholder, in the most courteous language, firmly dissented from many of Dr. Bar-ringer's discouraging views. This incident proved that the Southern white people who have known and lived with the

negro for three centuries could not pass over in silence a
speech in which the negro as a freeman was not given credit
for having even one redeeming quality.[33]

It was almost ten years later when Herbert's voice was heard
again in the South and nation on an even more important matter affecting racial relationships. The occasion concerned events
resulting from a bitter strike by the Brotherhood of Locomotive
Firemen and Engineers against the Georgia Railroad. The dispute was set off when a minor official of the railroad, as an
economy measure, removed ten white assistant hostlers (who
were members of the firemen's union) and replaced them with
Negroes at lower wages.

Negroes had served as firemen on southern railroads since
antebellum days when the position was a hot and dirty job,
known as "nigger work." By custom blacks continued to work
in this capacity alongside white engineers even after the turn
of the century; and, in fact, Negro firemen were the most important group of black workers on railroads in the nation at
this time. The Georgia Railroad had always found its black
firemen to be responsible, efficient, and loyal employees. Barred
from joining the white union, the Negroes were forced to work
for lower wages than whites received for the same job. Many
white engineers actually preferred to work with black firemen
since they were generally more responsive to orders than whites
and, unlike white firemen, had no chance of competing for
positions as engineers.[34]

When the white firemen went out on strike against the railroad on May 17, 1909, tension began to build up immediately.
It is evident that the union did have an economic grievance.

---

[33] Booker T. Washington, "The Montgomery Race Conference," *Century
Magazine* 60 (August, 1900): pp. 630-632. See also Hugh C. Bailey, *Edgar Gardner
Murphy: Gentle Progressive* (Coral Gables, University of Miami Press, 1968),
p. 37.

[34] Hugh B. Hammett, "Labor and Race: The Georgia Railroad Strike of
1909," *Labor History* 16 (Fall, 1975): pp. 24-43; another recent essay, emphasizing
local and racial affairs, is John Michael Matthews, "The Georgia 'Race Strike'
of 1909," *Journal of Southern History* 40 (November, 1974): pp. 613-630. See
also Lorenzo J. Greene and Carter G. Woodson, *The Negro Wage Earner* (Washington, Association for the Study of Negro Life and History, Inc., 1930), pp. 104-
106; Ray Marshall, "The Negro in Southern Unions," in Julius Jacobson, ed.,
The Negro and the American Labor Movement (Garden City, New York, Doubleday & Company, Inc., 1968), p. 135.

The spokesmen for the strikers argued that because of the cheaper Negro labor, the Georgia line had been able to keep the wages of white firemen at only forty-seven per cent of those of the engineers—the lowest pay scale in the entire region. Undoubtedly, the railroad had been trying to economize by using black labor. On the run between Atlanta and Augusta, a white fireman earned $2.77 but a Negro received only $1.75. On the average, black firemen made about fifty cents less per day than whites doing exactly the same work. When the railroad began to displace members of the union with blacks at lower wages, a labor dispute became inevitable.

Unfortunately, what began primarily as a labor dispute rapidly escalated into a racial crisis of the first magnitude. Although many union leaders disavowed any attempt to launch a crusade for white supremacy, it was perfectly evident from the start that some officials were eager to win public sympathy by injecting the race issue into the affair. The initial demand for wage and personnel adjustments quickly accelerated into a crusade to eliminate the black firemen from the line altogether. At first, the extreme racists found themselves in a confusing dilemma. The union had condemned the company's practice of keeping white wages down by the use of Negro labor. Yet, to raise the pay of the black firemen to that of the whites would seem to make the two groups equal—something the white firemen did not want to accept either. Therefore, the only solution seemed to be the total elimination of Negro firemen.[35]

When the railroad decided to stand behind its black employees, the situation along the line grew ugly. Negro firemen were assaulted by mobs, whipped, and run off from their jobs. Whites who replaced strikers were threatened with pistols. Even railroad guards and detectives were assaulted and in some cases arrested by local authorities along the line. In Augusta a mob of 250 tried to lynch a Negro fireman; at Macon jeering crowds numbering over 1,000 people delayed the trains. The citizens of Thompson warned railroad officials that no black firemen would be allowed to pass through their town. At Covington the people declared that they would rather not receive mail than have it delivered by trains with Negro firemen. When the company appealed to Governor Hoke Smith

---

[35] *Atlanta Constitution,* May 16, 17, 1909; *Atlanta Journal,* May 17, 1909.

to send state troops to protect railroad property, Smith, who
sympathized with the strikers, refused, declaring that he did
not want to take any "partisan action." A number of the more
responsible conservative newspapers, including the New Orleans
Times-Democrat and the *State* of Columbia, South Carolina,
condemned Smith's refusal to act. The *Nation* indignantly edi-
torialized:

> Unfortunately for the railway company, there is an anti-negro
> demagogue in the Governor's chair at Atlanta. Hoke Smith,
> leader in Negro disfranchisement, is the last man to meet this
> situation properly. His political ambitions have not been
> quenched by his failure to secure re-election, so he tells the
> railway that it cannot have the protection of troops because he
> has not enough militia to patrol 500 miles of road!

Politics and prejudice had created a crisis situation.[36]

With the union threatening to call out firemen on all lines
handling freight from the Georgia Railroad, a move which
would have tied up the entire Southeast, federal officials intervened. Brought together through the efforts of Martin A. Knapp,
the chairman of the Interstate Commerce Commission, and
Charles P. Neill, United States commissioner of labor, the railroad and the union agreed to submit the dispute to arbitration
under the Erdman Act. In the meantime, the original ten whites
were reinstated but all other Negro employees retained their
jobs, pending the outcome of the settlement.[37]

The strike attracted national attention not only because of
the attendant violence but also on account of its long-range
implications. The *Outlook* found the situation "full of menace"—for the South and the nation:

> This is the first time that an industrial contest has followed
> the lines of racial struggle to a serious degree. Heretofore the
> two problems in acute form have been kept distinct. In the
> North, where strife between organized labor and capital has
> been frequent, the comparative smallness of the negro popula-
> tion has kept it free from racial complications. In the South,

---

[36] *Atlanta Constitution*, May 20, 21, 22, 1909; *Atlanta Journal*, May 23, 1909;
Nation, Editorials **88** (May 27 and June 3, 1909): pp. 523, 547. See also Dewey
W. Grantham, Jr., *Hoke Smith and the Politics of the New South* (Baton Rouge,
Louisiana State University Press, 1958), pp. 176-177.

[37] *Atlanta Journal*, May 24, 1909; *Atlanta Constitution*, May 30, 1909.

on the other hand, where racial strife has been frequent, the comparatively unorganized condition of white labor and the comparatively unadvanced condition of negro labor have kept it free from finding expression in strikes and lockouts. Now, however, with the progress of organized labor in the South and the progress of the negro in industrial efficiency, there has arisen an occasion on which the labor problem and the race problem, each a spring of passion, have mingled.[38]

A writer for *Harper's Weekly* accurately summed up the ominous implications for the Negro:

> It is therefore not improbable that the strike may culminate in a demand for the complete elimination of negro firemen from the road's service; and it is even predicted that the movement will spread to every railroad in the South. As things are now, no negro is ever promoted to be an engineer. He can rise no higher than fireman and apparently the race is now threatened with the complete loss of this occupation.[39]

The *Nation* minced no words in its unsympathetic treatment of the strikers, "It is a race issue, pure and simple. To its great credit, the railway has manfully stood by its negro employees." Also the journal predicted:

> Triumph of the union's policy spells economic disaster for a section which continually complains that it cannot get trained workers from the negroes in sufficient number for its mines, mills, and shops.[40]

While tensions smoldered along the tracks of the Georgia Railroad, shortly after the middle of June a board of arbitration was selected. Hilary Herbert was chosen to represent the railroad. Commenting on Herbert's appointment, *Harper's Weekly* conjectured that "his record, his character, and his age incline us to believe that he will turn to his present task thoughtfully, conscientiously, and free from passion and low prejudice." Georgia Congressman Thomas W. Hardwick, selected by the union, was described simply as "active in politics." The third member of the board, chosen by the other two, was Chancellor

---

[38] *Outlook*, Editorial, "The Georgia Railroad Strike," **92** (June 5, 1905): p. 311.
[39] *Harper's Weekly*, Editorial, "The Georgia Race Strike," **53** (June 5, 1909): p. 5.
[40] *Nation*, Editorial **88** (May 27, 1909): p. 523.

David C. Barrow of the University of Georgia, hardly a man, the journal suggested, who could afford to ignore the distinctly moral questions involved in the arbitration.[41]

In the extensive hearings before the tribunal, the union spokesmen adopted two lines of attack. First they presented witnesses who declared that Negroes were "too incompetent and stupid to be safe firemen." The blacks were said to be offensive to the white engineers who worked with them and to the traveling public which was endangered by their incompetence. When the union tried as a second and more dramatic line of argument to present witnesses to testify of the outrage of white citizens who lived along the line of the railroad, the board ruled that it would consider the case only on the facts directly involved with railroad operation. Speaking for the board, Herbert declared that fifteen of the "outraged citizens" who came as witnesses were "incompetent to testify." For the railroad's part, company officials stoutly defended their black employees but selfishly refused to modify wage policies, asking, "If we can get what we want cheap, is it a crime to take it?"[42]

Hilary Herbert announced the decision of the board of arbitration on the morning of June 27. By a two to one vote, the tribunal flatly rejected union demands that the Negro firemen on the Georgia line be dismissed. As a concession to the union, Herbert explained that the company would thereafter have to pay blacks and whites the same wages for equal work, thus eliminating the strikers' economic grievance. Representative Hardwick, who wanted the blacks to be fired, dissented from the board's decision.

Because Chancellor Barrow had to continue to live in the midst of the Georgia mob, it was left to Herbert to defend the decision before the public. The Alabamian patiently explained that blacks and whites had worked on the railroad for years in harmony and had maintained such a fine safety record that there had been only one passenger fatality in seventy-eight years of the railroad's operation. He assured the public that there was

---

41 *Harper's Weekly*, Editorial, "The Georgia Strike Arbitration," 13 (July 3, 1909): p. 4. See also *Atlanta Constitution*, June 20, 1909, and *New York Times*, June 20, 1909.

42 Sterling D. Spero and Abram L. Harris, *The Black Worker: The Negro and the Labor Movement* (New York, Columbia University Press, 1931), p. 290; *Atlanta Journal*, June 24, 1909; *Atlanta Constitution*, June 23, 1909.

not the slightest evidence that black firemen were unsafe or dangerous to the traveling public. In fact, the commission had found that some white engineers routinely requested black firemen because of their efficiency. In attempting to undercut extremist criticism, Herbert proudly exhibited his own credentials as a loyal southerner and devotee of white supremacy. Nevertheless, he warned the Georgians that the South would be allowed to handle the race question itself only so long as it treated the Negro fairly and did not alienate northern opinion. He asked with devastating reasonableness, "If the negro is not competent to do the duties of fireman under the immediate supervision of a white engineer, what IS he fit for? What are we to do with the ten million negroes in the South?" closing his case with a slashing attack upon the union policy, Herbert asserted:

We will not be doing justice to the negro if we allow one labor union to come down from the North and exclude him from railroad work, then others to come and exclude him successively from carpentering and blacksmithing and sawmilling and mining, etc. until we finally shall have organizations interfering with even domestic service. We all approve labor unions when they confine themselves to their proper spheres. They have undoubtedly accomplished much good, but it is difficult to see how public opinion at the South can approve their course when they come down among us to stir up strife between the races. The white man of the South has nothing to fear from competition with the negroes, as we all believe. The negro is not anywhere his equal. When idleness and crime are justly complained of against the negro, it is strange that thoughtful men should aid in a movement to deprive him of work he is fit for.[43]

Although there was considerable discontent in Georgia over the outcome of the arbitration, the union grudgingly accepted the decision as a victory, promising its members that the provision for equal pay would eventually lead to the elimination of black workers (since it was impossible to conceive of a company hiring Negroes when it could get whites for the same pay). A number of conservative newspapers in the South praised the

---

[43] *Augusta Chronicle,* July 12, 1909, Vol. 11, Herbert Papers. See also *Atlanta Constitution,* June 27, 1909; *Atlanta Journal,* June 27, 1909; *New York Times,* June 28, 1909.

decision, including the *Augusta Chronicle* and the *Montgomery Advertiser*.[44] Nationally, the decision created something of a minor sensation. *Harper's Weekly* cried: "Good for Colonel Herbert and Chancellor Barrow! As arbitrators of the case . . . , they have responded, as we trusted they would, to the better sort of public opinion in the South. . . ." The *Nation* called the award a "gratifying triumph of common sense and common honesty." Editorially pleased, the *New York Times* pointed out: "This is not a question of the right of the negro to social or political equality. It is a question of the right to live, for the right to work is the right to subsistence."[45]

In reality, it is not surprising that Herbert voted in favor of the Negro firemen. Nor was he any less racist for having done so. Nevertheless, in Herbert's day, as in our own, there were different varieties of "racists," some violent and some paternalistic. Nor is it likely that Herbert's decision was made out of a fear of northern reaction had the blacks been dismissed. Rather, the episode put to the test Herbert's conservative rationale and his lifelong assumptions about the place of the Negro in the South. Although he was never willing to concede political and social equality to the black man, he was determined in his own way always to treat him with minimal justice. Moreover, Herbert could not have been oblivious to the reality that any other decision would have been a flagrant breach of the highly praised racial accommodation dating from Booker T. Washington's "Atlanta Compromise" of 1895.

The Negro firemen were the real winners in the dispute. Black men continued to fire the engines on the Georgia Railroad and on other southern lines. The *Colored American Magazine* heralded the decision:

> Even though it be but an act of simple justice the decision of the Georgia Railroad strike arbitrators is one of the most commendable and courageous decisions ever given by a Southern board.[46]

---

44 *Atlanta Journal,* June 28, 1909; *Atlanta Constitution,* June 28, 1909. See also the *Augusta Chronicle,* July 12, 1909 and the *Montgomery Advertiser,* July 12, 1909, both in Vol. 11, Herbert Papers.

45 *Harper's Weekly,* Editorial, "A Hope Fulfilled," 52 (July 10, 1909): p. 5; *Nation,* Editorial 89 (July 1, 1909): p. 1; *New York Times,* June 29, 1909.

46 Quoted in Greene and Woodson, *The Negro Wage Earner,* p. 107.

Most interesting of all is the praise that Herbert received from the most eminent southerner of his day. Writing to Herbert shortly after the decision, Booker T. Washington said:

It has been my purpose for sometime to write to thank you for the wise, generous and brave decision reached by you in determining the protests against the employment of black men in the Georgia Railroad. The Negro people everywhere feel under the greatest obligation to you for the position taken by you and Chancellor Barrow at that time. I think I can say that every one of them with whom I have talked feels that this decision rendered by Southern men will be as far reaching in effect as any single thing in helping forward the progress of the Negro people.[47]

Herbert never lost faith in the idea that responsible white southerners could solve the race problem themselves. He hoped that southern whites would develop "a growing spirit of altruism, begotten of responsibility," and, he asserted, "this promises much for the amelioration of race friction." He added:

The white man, with his pride of race, must more and more be made to feel that noblesse oblige. His sense of duty to others must measure up to his responsibilities and opportunities. He must accord the negro all his rights under the laws as they exist.[48]

Herbert's hopes, of course, were not realized in his own time or even for decades after. The historical record offers ample evidence that many whites in the South were hardly willing to recognize the Negro as a person, much less accord him that dignity commensurate with such a status. Although men like Herbert did offer some stabilizing influence in the race-wracked Progressive era, their tragedy is that they would not—or could not—conceive of policies that might better reconcile American ideals with southern practices.

III

In the half-decade before his death, Hilary Herbert's voice was heard one last time, now weakened by advancing age, but,

---

[47] Booker T. Washington to Herbert, August 12, 1909, Herbert Papers.
[48] Herbert, *The Abolition Crusade,* pp. 234, 243.

nevertheless, still clear and powerful. The issue in this case involved preparedness and the entry of the United States into the First World War. Consistent with the policies that he had supported since the 1880's, Herbert argued for a strong and credible military establishment. Although he never called directly for American entry into the conflict, he persuasively argued that the United States must be militarily strong if she were to be respected abroad and have any influence on the outcome of the struggle in Europe. He contended: "If we are to play our part in this great drama we must be able to command respect, because we are united as a people and as a nation armed to command the peace. . . ." He rejected the idea that big armaments necessarily led to war:

> Had Great Britain, France, and Russia, with their superior resources, been as well prepared as was Germany, the probabilities are that, instead of a world war, we should now see already negotiated treaties looking to the peace of the world. It was lack of preparedness that brought the present war in Europe.[49]

The ex-secretary of the navy had little use for the pacifism of William Jennings Bryan. In assailing the pacifist attitude, Herbert recalled a childhood incident:

> This reminds the writer of an experience in his early boyhood. A boy of eight started to school with the admonition from his pious mother to be good and not to fight. The rule had worked well when the boy was among his sisters at home, but at school he was with boys, and as soon as they "got the curves" the poor little fellow got kicked and cuffed, even by the undersized would-be-bullies, until at last, with the approbation of his father, the little chap, after many tough battles, established his reputation as a fighter. After that he enjoyed peace.
>
> That good mother of seventy-odd years ago, like the pacifist of today, had omitted to consider the other boys.[50]

With the coming of American participation in the war, however, Herbert's thoughts turned to the preparations for a peace settlement. In a lengthy letter to the *New York Times*, he condemned the idea, championed chiefly by Theodore Roosevelt, that the nation should not arbitrate any dispute involving

---

49 Herbert, "Bryan is Wrong on Preparedness, Says Herbert," *New York Times Magazine*, November 21, 1915, pp. 7-8.

50 Herbert, "The Gravest Crisis in Human History," *Manufacturers Record* 69 (January 20, 1916): pp. 43-44.

FIG. 20. Destroyer U.S.S. *Herbert,* commissioned after the former secretary's death in 1919, continued service until after World War II. Courtesy of U.S. Navy Department.

"national honor." Recalling again his experiences in the Old South, he argued that the purpose of the "gentlemen's code of honor" was to bring about the peaceful and dignified settlement of disagreements. It was precisely because honor was involved that friends and intermediaries—mediators—were needed; without them, violence would be inevitable. Herbert scolded:

> Why nations should be more punctilious than were the gentlemen whose ideas of chivalry have been so often ridiculed by some of those who are insisting today that questions of honor shall be exempted from arbitration treaties is difficult to see.
>
> There is nothing peculiar about the honor of men or of nations. Honor requires strict justice—nothing more, nothing less.[51]

Herbert finally came to the conclusion that Woodrow Wilson was right, that the League of Nations was the only hope for world peace. He wrote:

> If the time has not come when peoples can trust each other enough to make just one honest effort to substitute . . . concert of action for peace for the old system of competition that since civilization began has kept the world always at war or arming for war, then the future holds out no hope.[52]

---

51 *New York Times,* January 21, 1917.
52 New York *World,* [January 6, 1919], Vol. 12, Herbert Papers.

Herbert was never able to elaborate fully his opinions on the League of Nations. In the midst of preparation for a speech on the subject to be given in Montgomery, he finally lost the race with time. In his eighty-fifth year, death claimed him at last. To the very end, his mind was clear and his perception undimmed. Perhaps knowing somehow of the events to come, a few days before his death he penned some lines reaffirming his devout religious commitment.[53] The secretary of the navy, Josephus Daniels, telegraphed that Herbert's death was a "personal loss" and added:

> When the history of the navy comes to be written his vision and his large contribution to it will be one of its brightest pages. . . . I have this day ordered one of our newest and finest destroyers to be named "Herbert" in some recognition of his service in Congress as chairman of the Naval Affairs Committee and as secretary of the navy.[54]

The last rites were fitting and impressive. Hundreds of mourners viewed the body as it lay in state in the capitol in Montgomery. Flanked by a military guard of honor, the casket was surrounded by flowers and draped with both the American and Confederate flags. Nearby stood a wreath from President Woodrow Wilson. After funeral services at which Governor Thomas E. Kilby of Alabama served as an honorary pallbearer, Herbert's body was laid to rest next to that of his wife Ella in the sprawling Oakwood Cemetery in a plot not far from the graves of the Confederate dead.

Governor Kilby, perhaps, described Herbert most accurately as "a gentleman to the manner born, kindly but firm in his dealings with men. . . ."[55] Herbert was a man in whom the old and new uniquely came together. He was both modern and old-fashioned. Although he was a herald of the New South, to borrow a phrase from Edgar Gardner Murphy, he possessed "much of the fine genius of the old aristocracy." The South had not only lost a statesman; the nation had lost a loyal and valued citizen. Both were the better for his living. Both were the poorer at his parting.

---

53 Boston *Evening Transcript*, March 6, 1919, Vol. 12, Herbert Papers; Herbert, "Retrospect," (1919) Vol. 12, Herbert Papers.

54 New York *Herald*, March 7, 1919, Vol. 12, Herbert Papers.

55 Unidentified newspaper clipping, Vol. 12, Herbert Papers.

Bibliography

MANUSCRIPTS

Hilary Abner Herbert Papers, University of North Carolina Library, Chapel Hill. The principal source for this study, this is a small but exceptionally rich collection. It consists of approximately 700 items of correspondence and twelve volumes. Volumes one through six contain Herbert's unpublished writings, including his memoirs, "Grandfather's Talks about his Life Under Two Flags"; his "Short History of the 8th Alabama Regiment"; and other jottings and reminiscences. Volumes seven through twelve are scrapbooks of photographs and newspaper clippings concerning almost every aspect of Herbert's public career. The newspaper clippings were drawn from papers all across the country and were included in the scrapbooks even when the opinions expressed were not especially favorable to Herbert.

Hilary Abner Herbert Collection, Alabama Department of Archives and History, Montgomery. This is a very small collection containing only a few letters by Herbert and his family, a copy of his reminiscences, and a political scrapbook that he compiled on the presidential election of 1896.

Edward Porter Alexander Papers, University of North Carolina Library, Chapel Hill. The papers of this former Confederate general contain several letters from Herbert dealing with incidents in the Civil War, including a copy of the "Short History of the 8th Alabama Regiment" in Herbert's handwriting.

William Watts Ball Papers, Duke University Library, Durham, North Carolina. Ball was the editor of *The State* newspaper of Columbia, South Carolina. His papers contain several friendly letters from Herbert.

Grover Cleveland Papers, Library of Congress. Most of the Herbert letters in this collection deal with routine government business.

Walter Quintin Gresham Papers, Library of Congress. This collection of Secretary of State Gresham's letters is invaluable for following the diplomatic episodes in which naval officers were involved during Herbert's tenure at the Navy Department.

Thomas Goode Jones Papers, Alabama Department of Archives and History. Several Herbert letters relating to state politics and personal concerns are included. Jones was twice governor of Alabama in the early 1890's.

George Nolan Lewis Letters. This small collection of Civil War letters concerning Alabamians involved in the conflict is in the possession of Mrs. Myra Crenshaw, Chairman of the Butler County [Alabama] Historical Society.

Robert McKee Papers, Alabama Department of Archives and History. The papers of this Alabama newspaperman contain a number of letters from Herbert about political and personal subjects.

Alfred Thayer Mahan Papers, Library of Congress. A number of letters between Mahan and Secretary Herbert are in this small but invaluable collection.

Washington M. Smith Papers, Duke University Library. Smith was Hilary Herbert's father-in-law. Most of the Herbert letters in this collection deal with family matters and provide fascinating insights into the colonel's character.

GOVERNMENT ARCHIVES (Unpublished)

United States, Records of the Department of the Navy. National Archives, Washington, D.C.

——, Records in the Classified Operational Archives. Naval History Division, Department of the Navy, Washington, D.C.

——, Records of the Naval War College, Newport, Rhode Island.

——, Records of the Department of State. Washington, D.C.

——, Committee Records of the House of Representatives. Washington, D.C.

——, Fifth Census of the United States (1830), South Carolina, III, Newberry District. South Carolina Historical Commission, Columbia.

——, Sixth Census of the United States (1840), South Carolina, IV, Laurens District. South Carolina Historical Commission.

——, Seventh Census of the United States (1850), Alabama, Butler County. Alabama Department of Archives and History.

——, Eighth Census of the United States (1860), Alabama, Butler County. Alabama Department of Archives and History.

PUBLISHED ARCHIVAL AND OTHER GOVERNMENT RECORDS

Congressional Directory. Washington, D.C.

Congressional Record. Washington, D.C.

House of Representatives Executive Documents. Washington, D.C.

House of Representatives Miscellaneous Documents. Washington, D.C.

Papers Relating to the Foreign Relations of the United States. Washington, D.C.

Richardson, James D., ed., *A Compilation of the Messages and Papers of the Presidents.* 10 vols. Washington, D.C., Published by Authority of Congress, 1898-1899.

Rowell, Chester H., ed., *A Historical and Legal Digest of All the Contested Election Cases in the House of Representatives of the United States from the First to the Fifty-Sixth Congress, 1789-1901.* Washington, D.C., Government Printing Office, 1901.

Senate Executive Documents. Washington, D.C.

Senate Reports. Washington, D.C.

Thirteenth Annual Report of the United States Civil Service Commission. Washington, D.C.: Government Printing Office, 1897.

U.S. Navy Department, *Annual Reports of the Secretary of the Navy.* Washington, D.C.

——, *Navy Yearbook.* Washington, D.C.

The War of the Rebellion: A Compilation of the Official Records of the Union and Confederate Armies. 70 vols. in 128 parts. Washington, D.C.: Government Printing Office, 1880-1901.

NEWSPAPERS AND MAGAZINES

Newspapers

Atlanta Constitution.

Atlanta Journal.

Covington Times, Andalusia, Alabama.

Daily Confederation, Montgomery, Alabama.

Daily Register, Mobile, Alabama.

Evening Journal, Montgomery, Alabama.

Greenville Advocate, Greenville, Alabama.

Montgomery [Daily] Advertiser.

New York Times.

South Alabamian, Greenville, Alabama.

Southern Messenger, Greenville, Alabama.

Standard Gauge, Brewton, Alabama.
Troy Enquirer, Troy, Alabama.
Troy Messenger, Troy, Alabama.
Washington Post.
Weekly Advertiser, Montgomery, Alabama. This was a weekly condensation of its larger parent paper. It was primarily distributed to rural areas.

Contemporary Magazines

Harper's Weekly
Illustrated American
Independent
Outlook
Nation
Review of Reviews

WRITINGS BY HERBERT

Books

HERBERT, HILARY ABNER. 1912. *The Abolition Crusade and Its Consequences: Four Periods of American History* (New York, Charles Scribner's Sons).
———— 1890. *Why the Solid South? or, Reconstruction and Its Results* (Baltimore, R. H. Woodward & Company).

Articles and Pamphlets

———— 1887. *An Address Delivered before the Society of Alumni of the University of Virginia on Commencement Day, June 29, 1887.* Pamphlet. Lynchburg, J. P. Bell & Co.
———— 1893. "Alabama in Federal Politics." In *Memorial Record of Alabama* (Madison, Wis., Brant & Fuller) 2: pp. 17-106.
———— "Bryan is Wrong on Preparedness, Says Herbert." *New York Times Magazine,* November 21, 1915: pp. 7-8.
———— 1901. "The Conditions of the Reconstruction Problem." *The Atlantic Monthly* 87: pp. 145-157.
———— "Ex-Secretary of the Navy Urges Preparedness." *New York Times Magazine,* December 12, 1915: p. 7.
———— 1898. "The Fifty Million Appropriation and Its Lessons." *Forum* 25: pp. 267-275.
———— 1894. "The Fight Off the Yalu River." *North American Review* 159: pp. 513-528.
———— 1916. "The Gravest Crisis in Human History." *Manufacturers Record* 69: pp. 43-44.
———— 1913. "Grover Cleveland and His Cabinet at Work." *Century Magazine* 85: pp. 740-744.
———— 1914. *History of the Arlington Confederate Monument* (Pamphlet; Washington, D.C., United Daughters of the Confederacy).
———— 1894. "The House of Representatives and the House of Commons." *North American Review* 158: pp. 257-269.
———— 1913. "How We Redeemed Alabama." *Century Magazine* 85: pp. 854-862.
———— 1893. "The Lesson of the Naval Review." *North American Review* 156: pp. 641-647.
———— 1911. "Losses and Battles of the Civil War and What They Mean." In

The Photographic History of the Civil War (New York, Review of Reviews)
10: pp. 120-138.

—— 1895. "Military Lessons of the Chino-Japanese War." *North American Review* 160: pp. 685-698.

—— 1897. "Our Navy and Our Naval Policy." *Munsey's Magazine* 17: pp. 182-186.

—— 1888. "The Navy." In *The National Democratic Party: Its History, Principles, Achievements, and Aims*, ed. by William L. Wilson (Baltimore, H. L. Harvey & Co.) pp. 515-571.

—— 1897. "A Plea for the Navy." *Forum* 24: pp. 1-15.

—— 1901. "The Race Problem at the South." *Annals of the American Academy of Political and Social Science* 18: pp. 95-101.

—— 1892. "Reciprocity and the Farmer." *North American Review* 154: pp. 414-423.

—— 1896. "The Sea and Sea Power as a Factor in the History of the United States." *Proceedings of the United States Naval Institute* 22: pp. 561-576.

—— 1896. "Why American Industry Languishes." *North American Review* 163: pp. 488-495.

UNIVERSITY RECORDS

University of Alabama:
Palmer, Thomas W., ed. 1901. *A Register of the Officers and Students of the University of Alabama, 1831-1909* (Tuscaloosa, University of Alabama).
University of Virginia:
Catalogue of the University of Virginia: Session of 1854-55 (Richmond, H. K. Ellyson, 1855).
Catalogue of the University of Virginia: Session of 1855-56 (Richmond, H. K. Ellyson, 1856).
"Matriculation Books, 1826-1879." Office of the Registrar, University of Virginia.
"Minutes of the Faculty, 1848-56." VII, Manuscript Division, University of Virginia Library.

THESES AND DISSERTATIONS

BRANDT, WALTHER I. 1920. "Steel and the New Navy, 1882-1895." Ph.D. dissertation, University of Wisconsin.

CULLEY, JOHN JOEL. 1967. "Muted Trumpets: Four Efforts to Better Southern Race Relations, 1900-1919." Ph.D. dissertation, University of Virginia.

DAVIS, HUGH CHARLES. 1964. "An Analysis of the Rationale of Representative Conservative Alabamians, 1874-1914." Ph.D. dissertation, Vanderbilt University.

FITZSIMMONS, SISTER ANNE MARIE. 1965. "The Political Career of Daniel S. Lamont." Ph.D. dissertation, Catholic University.

FORTIN, MAURICE S. 1965. "Hilary Abner Herbert: Post-Reconstruction Southern Politician." M.A. thesis, University of Maryland.

HALL, HINES H. 1965. "The Montgomery Race Conference of 1900: Focal Point of Racial Attitudes at the Turn of the Century." M.A. thesis, Auburn University.

HAMMETT, HUGH B. 1967. "Hilary Abner Herbert: The Early Years, 1834-1865." M.A. thesis, University of Virginia. This paper was distributed in December, 1967, to the membership of the Butler County [Alabama] Historical Society.

LaFeber, Walter Fredrick. 1959. "The Latin American Policy of the Second Cleveland Administration." Ph.D. dissertation, University of Wisconsin.

Richardson, Louise McCullough. 1928. "The Development of Education in Laurens County." M.A. thesis, University of South Carolina.

Spector, Ronald Harvey. 1967. "'Professors of War,' The Naval War College and the Modern American Navy." Ph.D. dissertation, Yale University.

Stabler, Carey Vitallis. 1932. "The Career of Hilary Abner Herbert." M.A. thesis, University of Alabama.

Articles

Barrows, Isabel C. 1900. "The Montgomery Conference." *Outlook* 65: pp. 160-162.

Beale, Howard K. 1940. "On Rewriting Reconstruction History." *American Historical Review* 45: pp. 807-827.

Beehler, William H. 1899. "The United States Navy." In *The Naval Annual,* ed. by T. A. Brassey (Portsmouth, Eng., J. Griffin and Company), pp. 90-122.

———— 1906. "Needs of the Navy." In: *Selected Articles on the Enlargement of the United States Navy,* ed. by Clara E. Fanning. (Minneapolis, The H. W. Wilson Company), pp. 16-24.

Brodie, Fawn. 1962. "Who Won the Civil War, Anyway?" *New York Times Book Review* 67 (August 5): pp. 1, 22-23.

Brown, William Garrott. 1910. "The South in National Politics." *South Atlantic Quarterly* 9: pp. 103-115.

Chadwick, F. E. 1894. "Navy Department Organization." *Proceedings of the United States Naval Institute* 20: pp. 493-525.

Chesnutt, Charles W. 1903. "The Disfranchisement of the Negro." In: *The Negro Problem,* ed. by Booker T. Washington (New York, James Pott & Company), pp. 77-124.

Dashiell, R. B. 1893. "Report on the Test of a 14-Inch Nickel Steel Harveyized Armor Plate." *Proceedings of the United States Naval Institute* 19: pp. 117-120.

Davenport, Russell W. 1893. "Gun Forgings and Armor Plate in the United States." *Proceedings of the United States Naval Institute* 19: pp. 485-486.

Davis, Hugh C. 1967. "Hilary A. Herbert: Bourbon Apologist." *Alabama Review* 20: pp. 216-225.

Garner, James W. 1910. "New Politics for the South." *Annals of the American Academy of Political and Social Science* 35: pp. 172-183.

Grantham, Dewey W., Jr. 1955. "The Progressive Movement and the Negro." *South Atlantic Quarterly* 54: pp. 461-477.

———— 1961. "The Southern Bourbons Revisited." *South Atlantic Quarterly* 60: pp. 286-295.

Grenville, John A. S. 1968. "American Naval Preparations for War with Spain, 1896-1898." *Journal of American Studies* 2: pp. 33-47.

"Growth of the U.S. Navy." *Proceedings of the United States Naval Institute* 22 (1896): pp. 821-823.

Hammett, Hugh B. 1975. "Labor and Race: The Georgia Railroad Strike of 1909." *Labor History* 16: pp. 24-43.

———— 1974. "Reconstruction History Before Dunning." *Alabama Review* 27: pp. 185-196.

Johnson, Guion Griffis. 1949. "The Ideology of White Supremacy, 1876-1890." In: *Essays in Southern History,* ed. by Fletcher M. Green (Chapel Hill, University of North Carolina Press), pp. 124-156.

McADOO, WILLIAM. 1894. "Reorganization of the Personnel of the Navy." *North American Review* 159: pp. 457-466.

McINTOSH, CHARLES F. 1927. "Four Generations of Herberts of Lower Norfolk Co., Va." *The Researcher: A Magazine of History and Genealogical Exchange* 1: pp. 249-252.

MARSHALL, RAY. 1968. "The Negro in Southern Unions." In: *The Negro and the American Labor Movement*, ed. by Jules Jacobson (Garden City, N.Y., Doubleday & Company, Inc.), pp. 128-154.

MATTHEWS, JOHN MICHAEL. 1974. "The Georgia 'Race Strike' of 1909." *Journal of Southern History* 40: pp. 613-630.

MORGAN, JOHN TYLER. 1891. "The Danger of the Farmers' Alliance." *Forum* 12: pp. 399-409.

O'LAUGHLIN, JOHN CALLAN. 1906. "The American Fighting Fleet: Its Strategic Disposition." In: *Selected Articles on the Enlargement of the United States Navy*, ed. by Clara E. Fanning (Minneapolis, The H. W. Wilson Company), pp. 24-37.

OWEN, THOMAS McADORY. 1898. "A Bibliography of Alabama." In: *Annual Report of the American Historical Association for the Year 1897* (Washington, D.C., Government Printing Office), pp. 777-1248.

PLESUR, MILTON. 1968. "Rumblings Beneath the Surface: America's Outward Thrust, 1865-1890." In: *The Gilded Age: A Reappraisal*, ed. by H. Wayne Morgan (Syracuse, N.Y., Syracuse University Press), pp. 140-168.

RHODES, ROBERT S. 1955. "The Registration of Voters and the Election of Delegates to the Reconstruction Convention in Alabama." *Alabama Review* 8: pp. 119-142.

RODGERS, W. L. 1894. "An Examination of the Testimony Taken by the Joint Committee of the Senate and House of Representatives in Regard to the Reorganization of the Navy." *Proceedings of the United States Naval Institute* 20: pp. 747-762.

ROGERS, WILLIAM WARREN. 1960. "The Negro Alliance in Alabama." *Journal of Negro History* 45: pp. 38-44.

———1962. "The Farmers' Alliance in Alabama." *Alabama Review* 15: pp. 5-18.

ROYALL, DORA CALHOUN. 1927. "Descendants of Lt. Thomas Herbert of Virginia and South Carolina." *The Researcher: A Magazine of History and Genealogical Exchange* 2: pp. 48-57. The author was Herbert's niece.

——— 1927. "Sketch of Col. Hilary Abner Herbert." *The Researcher: A Magazine of History and Genealogical Exchange* 2: pp. 45-47.

SCHEINER, SETH M. 1962. "President Roosevelt and the Negro." *Journal of Negro History* 47: pp. 169-182.

SEAGER, ROBERT. 1953. "Ten Years Before Mahan: The Unofficial Case for the New Navy, 1880-1890." *Mississippi Valley Historical Review* 40: pp. 491-512.

SMITH, EMMA FRANCES LEE. 1919. "Personal Recollections of a Noble Man." *Confederate Veteran* 27: pp. 246-248.

SUMMERSELL, CHARLES G. 1957. "Kolb and the Populist Revolt as Viewed by Newspapers." *Alabama Historical Quarterly* 19: pp. 375-394.

"Visit of the President to the South." *Confederate Veteran* 13 (November, 1905): pp. 488-490.

WASHINGTON, BOOKER T. 1900. "The Montgomery Race Conference." *Century Magazine* 60: pp. 630-632.

"The Ways of Cabinet Officers: Secretary Herbert." *Illustrated American* 16 (August 4, 1894): pp. 152-153.

WEST, HENRY LITCHFIELD. 1909. "President Taft and the South." *Forum* 41: pp. 289-296.

WHARTON, VERNON L. 1965. "Reconstruction." In: *Writing Southern History,* ed. by Arthur S. Link and Rembert W. Patrick (Baton Rouge, Louisiana State University Press), pp. 295-315.

WILLIAMSON, EDWARD C. 1964. "The Alabama Election of 1874." *Alabama Review* 17: pp. 210-218.

WILSON, WOODROW. 1893. "Mr. Cleveland's Cabinet." *Review of Reviews* 7: pp. 286-297.

WOOLFOLK, SARAH VA. 1962. "Carpetbaggers in Alabama: Tradition Versus Truth." *Alabama Review* 15: pp. 133-144.

—— 1964. "Five Men Called Scalawags." *Alabama Review* 17: pp. 45-55.

ZINN, HOWARD. 1965. "Abolitionists, Freedom-Riders and the Tactics of Agitation." In *The Antislavery Vangard: New Essays on the Abolitionists*, ed. by Martin Duberman (Princeton, Princeton University Press), pp. 417-451.

BOOKS

ALEXANDER, DEALVA STANWOOD. 1916. *History and Procedure of the House of Representatives* (Boston and New York, Houghton Mifflin Company).

BAILEY, HUGH C. 1968. *Edgar Gardner Murphy: Gentle Progressive* (Coral Gables, University of Miami Press).

BARNES, JAMES A. 1931. *John G. Carlisle: Financial Statesman* (New York, Dodd, Mead & Company).

BARRINGER, PAUL B., GAINES M. GARNETT, and ROSEWELL PAGE, eds. 1904. *University of Virginia: Its History, Influence, Equipment, and Characteristics* (2 v., New York, Lewis Publishing Company).

BOND, HORACE MANN. 1939. *Negro Education in Alabama: A Study in Cotton and Steel* (Washington, D.C., Associated Publishers, Inc.).

BOYD, MINNE CLARE. 1931. *Alabama in the Fifties: A Social Study* (New York, Columbia University Press).

BROWN, WILLIAM GARROTT. 1905. *A History of Alabama* (New York and New Orleans, University Publishing Company).

BRUCE, PHILIP ALEXANDER. 1905. *The Rise of the New South* (Philadelphia, George Barrie & Sons).

—— 1921. *History of the University of Virginia, 1819-1919* (5 v., New York, Macmillan Company).

BUCK, PAUL H. 1937. *The Road to Reunion, 1865-1900* (Boston and Toronto, Little, Brown and Company).

CASH, WILBUR J. 1941. *The Mind of the South* (New York, Alfred A. Knopf).

CLARK, JOHN B. 1921. *Populism in Alabama* (Auburn, Ala., Auburn Printing Company).

COOPER, WILLIAM J., JR. 1968. *The Conservative Regime in South Carolina, 1877-1890* (Baltimore, Johns Hopkins Press).

COULTER, ELLIS MERTON. 1928. *College Life in the Old South* (New York, Macmillan Company).

CRUDEN, ROBERT. 1961. *James Ford Rhodes: The Man, the Historian and his Work* (Western Reserve University, Press of Western Reserve University).

DARRAH, WILLIAM CULP. 1951. *Powell of the Colorado* (Princeton, Princeton University Press).

DAVIES, WALLACE EVAN. 1955. *Patriotism on Parade: The Story of Veterans' and Hereditary Organizations in America, 1783-1900* (Cambridge, Harvard University Press).

DAVIS, GEORGE T. 1940. *A Navy Second to None: The Development of Modern American Naval Policy* (New York, Harcourt, Brace and Company).

DEARING, MARY R. 1952. *Veterans in Politics: The Story of the G.A.R.* (Baton Rouge, Louisiana State University Press).

DEGLER, CARL N. 1970. *Out of Our Past: The Forces that Shaped Modern America* (rev. ed. New York and Evanston, Harper & Row).

DENMAN, CLARENCE P. 1933. *The Secession Movement in Alabama* (Montgomery, Alabama State Department of Archives and History).

DESANTIS, VINCENT P. 1959. *Republicans Face the Southern Question: The New Departure Years, 1877-1897* (Baltimore, Johns Hopkins Press).

DORMAN, LEWY. 1935. *Party Politics in Alabama from 1850 through 1860* (Wetumpka, Ala., Wetumpka Printing Company).

DuBOSE, JOHN WITHERSPOON. 1940. *Alabama's Tragic Decade: Ten Years of Alabama, 1865-1874*, ed. by James K. Greer (Birmingham, Webb Book Company).

DUNNING, WILLIAM ARCHIBALD. 1907. *Reconstruction: Political and Economic, 1865-1877* (New York and London, Harper & Brothers).

DULLES, FOSTER RHEA. 1956. *The Imperial Years* (New York, Thomas Y. Crowell).

ELKINS, STANLEY M. 1959. *Slavery: A Problem in American Institutional and Intellectual Life* (Chicago, University of Chicago Press).

FLEMING, WALTER L. 1905. *Civil War and Reconstruction in Alabama* (New York, Columbia University Press).

———, ed. 1906-1907. *Documentary History of Reconstruction: Political, Military, Social, Religious, Educational & Industrial 1865 to the Present Time* (2 v., Cleveland, Ohio, Arthur H. Clark Company).

——— 1919. *The Sequel of Appomattox* (New Haven, Yale University Press).

FOGEL, ROBERT WILLIAM, and STANLEY L. ENGERMAN. 1974. *Time on the Cross: Volume One, The Economics of American Negro Slavery; Volume Two, Evidence and Methods* (Boston, Little, Brown).

FORD, HENRY JONES. 1919. *The Cleveland Era: A Chronicle of the New Order in Politics* (New Haven, Yale University Press).

FULLER, HERBERT BRUCE. 1909. *The Speakers of the House* (Boston, Little, Brown, and Company).

GARRATY, JOHN A. 1968. *The New Commonwealth, 1877-1890* (New York, Harper & Row).

GASTON, PAUL M. 1970. *The New South Creed: A Study in Southern Mythmaking* (New York, Alfred A. Knopf).

GATES, MERRILL E., ed. 1906. *Men of Mark in America* (2 v., Washington, D.C., Men of Mark Publishing Company).

GENOVESE, EUGENE D. 1974. *Roll, Jordan, Roll: The World the Slaves Made* (New York, Pantheon).

GLEAVES, ALBERT. 1925. *Life and Letters of Rear Admiral Stephen B. Luce, U.S. Navy* (New York and London, G. P. Putnam's Sons).

GOING, ALLEN JOHNSTON. 1951. *Bourbon Democracy in Alabama, 1874-1890* (University, Alabama, University of Alabama Press).

GRANTHAM, DEWEY W., JR., 1958. *Hoke Smith and the Politics of the New South* (Baton Rouge, Louisiana State University Press).

GREENE, LORENZO J., and CARTER G. WOODSON. 1930. *The Negro Wage Earner* (Washington, D.C., Association for the Study of Negro Life and History).

GRENVILLE, JOHN A. S., and GEORGE BERKELEY YOUNG. 1966. *Politics, Strategy, and American Diplomacy: Studies in Foreign Policy, 1873-1917* (New Haven and London, Yale University Press).

GRESHAM, MATILDA. 1919. *Life of Walter Quintin Gresham* (2 v., Chicago, Rand McNally & Company).

HACKNEY, SHELDON. *Populism to Progressivism in Alabama* (Princeton, N.J., Princeton University Press).

HAGAN, KENNETH. 1973. *American Gunboat Diplomacy and The Old Navy, 1877-1889* (Westport, Conn., Greenwood Press).

HAMILTON, GAIL [pseudonym for Mary Abigail Dodge]. 1895. *Biography of James G. Blaine* (Norwich, Conn., Henry Bill Publishing Company).

HARDY, JOHN. 1879. *Selma: Her Institutions, and Her Men* (Selma, Ala., Times Book and Job Office).

HENDRICK, BURTON J. 1932. *The Life of Andrew Carnegie* (2 v., Garden City, N.Y., Doubleday, Doran & Co.).

HENRY, H. M. 1914. *The Police Control of the Slave in South Carolina* (Emory, Va.).

HERRICK, WALTER R., JR. 1966. *The American Naval Revolution* (Baton Rouge, Louisiana State University Press).

HERSKOVITS, MELVILLE J. 1941. *The Myth of the Negro Past* (New York, Harper & Brothers).

HILL, LAWRENCE F. 1932. *Diplomatic Relations Between the United States and Brazil* (Durham, Duke University Press).

HIRSCH, MARK D. 1948. *William C. Whitney: Modern Warwick* (New York, Dodd, Mead & Company).

HIRSHSON, STANLEY P. 1962. *Farewell to the Bloody Shirt: Northern Republicans & the Southern Negro, 1877-1893* (Bloomington, Ind., Indiana University Press).

HUNT, THOMAS. 1922. *The Life of William H. Hunt* (Brattleboro, Vt., E. L. Hildreth & Co.).

JAMES, HENRY. 1923. *Richard Olney and His Public Service* (Boston and New York, Houghton Mifflin Company).

JOHNSON, ROBERT ERWIN. 1967. *Rear Admiral John Rodgers, 1812-1882* (Annapolis, United States Naval Institute).

KARSTEN, PETER. 1972. *The Naval Aristocracy: The Golden Age of Annapolis and the Emergence of Modern American Navalism* (New York, Free Press).

KNIGHT, EDGAR W. 1919. *The Academy Movement in the South* (Chapel Hill, University of North Carolina).

LAFEBER, WALTER. 1963. *The New Empire: An Interpretation of American Expansion, 1860-1898* (Ithaca, N.Y., Cornell University Press).

LITTLE, GEORGE. 1924. *Memoirs of George Little* (Tuscaloosa, Ala., Weatherford Printing Company).

LITTLE, JOHN BUCKNER. 1885. *The History of Butler County from 1815 to 1885* (Cincinnati, Elm Street Printing Company).

LIVEZEY, WILLIAM E. 1947. *Mahan on Seapower* (Norman, University of Oklahoma Press).

LONG, JOHN D. 1903. *The New American Navy* (2 v., New York, Outlook Company).

LONG, MARGARET, ed. 1956. *The Journal of John D. Long* (Rindge, N.H., Richard R. Smith Publisher).

LYNCH, DENIS TILDEN. 1932. *Grover Cleveland: A Man Four-Square* (New York, Horace Liveright).

MCCALL, SAMUEL W. 1911. *The Business of Congress* (New York, Columbia University Press).

MCELROY, ROBERT. 1923. *Grover Cleveland: The Man and the Statesman* (2 v., New York and London, Harper & Brothers).

MCMILLAN, MALCOLM COOK. 1955. *Constitutional Development in Alabama, 1798-1901: A Study in Politics, the Negro, and Sectionalism* (Chapel Hill, University of North Carolina Press).

MAHAN, A. T. 1894. *The Influence of Sea Power Upon History, 1660-1783* (Boston, Little, Brown, and Company; originally published 1890).

———— 1894. The *Influence of Sea Power Upon the French Revolution and Empire, 1783-1812* (2 v., Boston, Little, Brown, and Company).

—— 1898. *The Interest of America in Sea Power, Present and Future* (Boston, Little, Brown, and Company).

—— 1907. *From Sail to Steam: Recollections of Naval Life* (New York and London, Harper & Brothers, Publishers).

MANNING, JOSEPH COLUMBUS. 1928. *The Fadeout of Populism* (New York, T. A. Hebbons).

MANNING, THOMAS G. 1967. *Government in Science: The U.S. Geological Survey, 1867-1894* (Lexington, University of Kentucky Press).

MERRILL, HORACE SAMUEL. 1957. *Bourbon Leader: Grover Cleveland and the Democratic Party* (Boston and Toronto, Little, Brown, and Company).

MOORE, ALBERT B. 1927. *History of Alabama and Her People* (3 v., Chicago, American Historical Society).

MORGAN, H. WAYNE. 1969. *From Hayes to McKinley: National Politics, 1877-1896* (Syracuse, N.Y., Syracuse University Press).

MORISON, ELTING E., *et al.*, eds. 1951-1954. *The Letters of Theodore Roosevelt* (8 v., Cambridge, Harvard University Press).

MURPHY, EDGAR GARDNER. 1904. *Problems of the Present South* (New York, Macmillan Company).

MUZZEY, DAVID SAVILLE. 1934. *James G. Blaine: A Political Idol of Other Days* (New York, Dodd, Mead & Company).

NESSER, R. W. 1909. *Statistical and Chronological History of the United States Navy, 1775-1907* (2 v., New York, Macmillan Company).

NEVINS, ALLAN. 1933. *Grover Cleveland: A Study in Courage* (New York, Dodd, Mead & Company).

——, ed. 1933. *Letters of Grover Cleveland, 1850-1908* (Boston and New York, Houghton Mifflin Company).

NEWBY, I. A., ed. 1968. *The Development of Segregationist Thought* (Homewood, Ill., Dorsey Press).

NOLEN, CLAUDE H. 1967. *The Negro's Image in the South: The Anatomy of White Supremacy* (Lexington, University of Kentucky Press).

OSOFSKY, GILBERT, ed. 1967. *The Burden of Race: A Documentary History of Negro-White Relations in America* (New York and Evanston, Harper & Row).

OWEN, THOMAS M. 1921. *History of Alabama and Dictionary of Alabama Biography* (4 v., Chicago, S. J. Clarke Publishing Company).

PARKER, GEORGE F. 1909. *Recollections of Grover Cleveland* (New York, Century Co.).

PAULLIN, CHARLES OSCAR. 1968. *Paullin's History of Naval Administration, 1775-1911: A Collection of Articles from the U.S. Naval Institute Proceedings* (Annapolis, U.S. Naval Institute).

PECK, HARRY THURSTON. 1907. *Twenty Years of the Republic, 1885-1905* (New York, Dodd, Mead & Company).

PHILLIPS, ULRICH B. 1936. *American Negro Slavery* (New York and London, D. Appleton-Century Company; originally published 1918).

PLETCHER, DAVID M. 1962. *The Awkward Years: American Foreign Relations Under Garfield and Arthur* (Columbia, University of Missouri Press).

POTTER, E. B., and FREDLAND, J. R., eds. 1955. *The United States and World Sea Power* (Englewood Cliffs, N.J., Prentice-Hall, Inc.).

PRESSLY, THOMAS J. 1965. *Americans Interpret Their Civil War* (New York, Free Press; originally published 1954).

PRINGLE, HENRY G. 1931. *Theodore Roosevelt: A Biography* (New York, Harcourt, Brace and Company).

PULESTON, W. D. 1939. *Mahan: The Life and Work of Captain Alfred Thayer Mahan, U.S.N.* (New Haven, Yale University Press).

Race Problems of the South: Report of the Proceedings of the First Annual Conference Held Under the Auspices of the Southern Society for the Promotion of the Study of Race Conditions and Problems in the South (Richmond, B. F. Johnson Publishing Company, 1900).

RHODES, JAMES FORD. 1896-1906. *History of the United States from the Compromise of 1850 to the Final Restoration of Home Rule at the South in 1877* (7 v., New York, Macmillan Company).

—— 1913. *Lectures on the American Civil War* (London and New York, Macmillan Company).

—— 1923. *The McKinley and Roosevelt Administrations, 1897-1909* (New York, Macmillan Company).

—— 1928. *History of the United States from Hayes to McKinley, 1877-1896* (New York, Macmillan Company).

RICHARDSON, LEON BURR. 1940. *William E. Chandler: Republican* (New York, Dodd, Mead & Company).

ROGERS, WILLIAM WARREN. 1970. *The One-Gallused Rebellion: Agrarianism in Alabama, 1865-1896* (Baton Rouge, Louisiana State University Press).

ROLL, CHARLES. 1948. *Colonel Dick Thompson: The Persistent Whig* (Indianapolis, Indiana Historical Bureau).

ROTHMAN, DAVID J. 1966. *Politics and Power: The United States Senate, 1869-1901* (Cambridge, Harvard University Press).

RUSS, WILLIAM ADAM, JR. 1961. *The Hawaiian Republic (1894-1898) and Its Struggle to Win Annexation* (Selinsgrove, Pa., Susquehanna University Press).

SALOUTOS, THEODORE. 1960. *Farmer Movements in the South, 1865-1933* (Berkeley and Los Angeles, University of California Press).

SELLERS, JAMES BENSON. 1950. *Slavery in Alabama* (University, Alabama, University of Alabama Press).

—— 1953. *History of the University of Alabama* (1 v., Tuscaloosa, University of Alabama Press).

SIEVERS, HARRY J. 1968. *Benjamin Harrison, Hoosier President: White House and After* (Indianapolis, Bobbs-Merrill Company).

SMELSER, MARSHALL. 1959. *The Congress Founds the Navy, 1787-1798* (Notre Dame, University of Notre Dame Press).

SMITH, G. WAYNE. 1959. *Nathan Goff, Jr.: A Biography* (Charleston, W. Va., Education Foundation).

SMITH, THEODORE CLARKE. 1925. *The Life and Letters of James Abram Garfield* (2 v., New Haven, Yale University Press).

SPERO, STERLING D., and HARRIS, ABRAM L. 1931. *The Black Worker: The Negro and the Labor Movement* (New York, Columbia University Press).

SPROUT, HAROLD and MARGARET. 1939. *The Rise of American Naval Power, 1776-1918* (Princeton, Princeton University Press).

STAMPP, KENNETH M. 1956. *The Peculiar Institution: Slavery in the Ante-Bellum South* (New York, Alfred A. Knopf).

STEALEY, O. O. 1906. *Twenty Years in the Press Gallery: A Concise History of Important Legislation from the 48th to the 58th Congress* (New York, published by the author).

STEGNER, WALLACE. 1954. *Beyond the Hundredth Meridian: John Wesley Powell and the Second Opening of the West* (Boston, Houghton Mifflin Company).

STEPHENSON, GEORGE M. 1939. *American History Since 1865* (New York and London, Harper & Brothers).

SUMMERS, FESTUS P., ed. 1957. *The Cabinet Diary of William L. Wilson, 1896-1897* (Chapel Hill, University of North Carolina Press).

SWANN, LEONARD ALEXANDER, JR. 1965. *John Roach, Maritime Entrepreneur:*

The Years as Naval Contractor, 1862-1886 (Annapolis, United States Naval Institute).

TAYLOR, CHARLES CARLISLE. 1920. *The Life of Admiral Mahan: Naval Philosopher* (New York, George H. Doran Company).

THOMPSON, CHARLES WILLIS. 1906. *Party Leaders of the Time* (New York, G. W. Dillingham Company).

THOMPSON, HOLLAND. 1921. *The New South: A Chronicle of Social and Industrial Evolution* (New Haven, Yale University Press).

TUGWELL, REXFORD G. 1968. *Grover Cleveland* (New York, Macmillan Company).

TYLER, ALICE FELT. 1927. *The Foreign Policy of James G. Blaine* (Minneapolis, University of Minnesota Press).

WARREN, ALDICE G., ed. 1910. *Catalogue of the Delta Kappa Epsilon Fraternity* (New York, John C. Winston Company).

WEST, RICHARD S., JR. 1948. *Admirals of American Empire: The Combined Story of George Dewey, Alfred Thayer Mahan, Winfield Scott Schley, and William Thomas Sampson* (Indianapolis and New York, Bobbs-Merrill Company).

WHITE, LEONARD D. 1958. *The Republican Era: A Study in Administrative History, 1869-1901* (New York, Macmillan Company).

WILSON, JOHN LYDE. 1858. *The Code of Honor; or Rules for the Government of Principals and Seconds in Duelling* (Charleston, S.C., James Phynney).

WOODWARD, C. VANN. 1951. *Origins of the New South, 1877-1913* (Baton Rouge, Louisiana State University Press).

———— 1951. *Reunion and Reaction: The Compromise of 1877 and the End of Reconstruction* (Garden City, N.Y., Doubleday & Company).

———— 1966. *The Strange Career of Jim Crow* (2d rev. ed., New York, Oxford University Press; originally published 1955).

YOUNGER, EDWARD. 1955. *John A. Kasson: Politics and Diplomacy from Lincoln to McKinley* (Iowa City, State Historical Society of Iowa).

Index

DATE DUE

~~OCT 20 1999~~	